ANTIQUITIES

OF THE

CONTAINING

A CONCISE DESCRIPTION OF THE RUINS OF KING SOLOMON'S CITIES, TOGETHER WITH THOSE OF FORTY OF THE MOST ANCIENT AND RENOWNED CITIES OF THE EAST, INCLUDING BABYLON, NINEVEH, DAMASCUS, AND SHUSHAN.

EMBELLISHED

With three beautiful lithographs, and seventy full-page engravings.

BY

M. WOLCOTT REDDING.

NEW YORK:
REDDING & CO.,
544 BROADWAY.
1873.

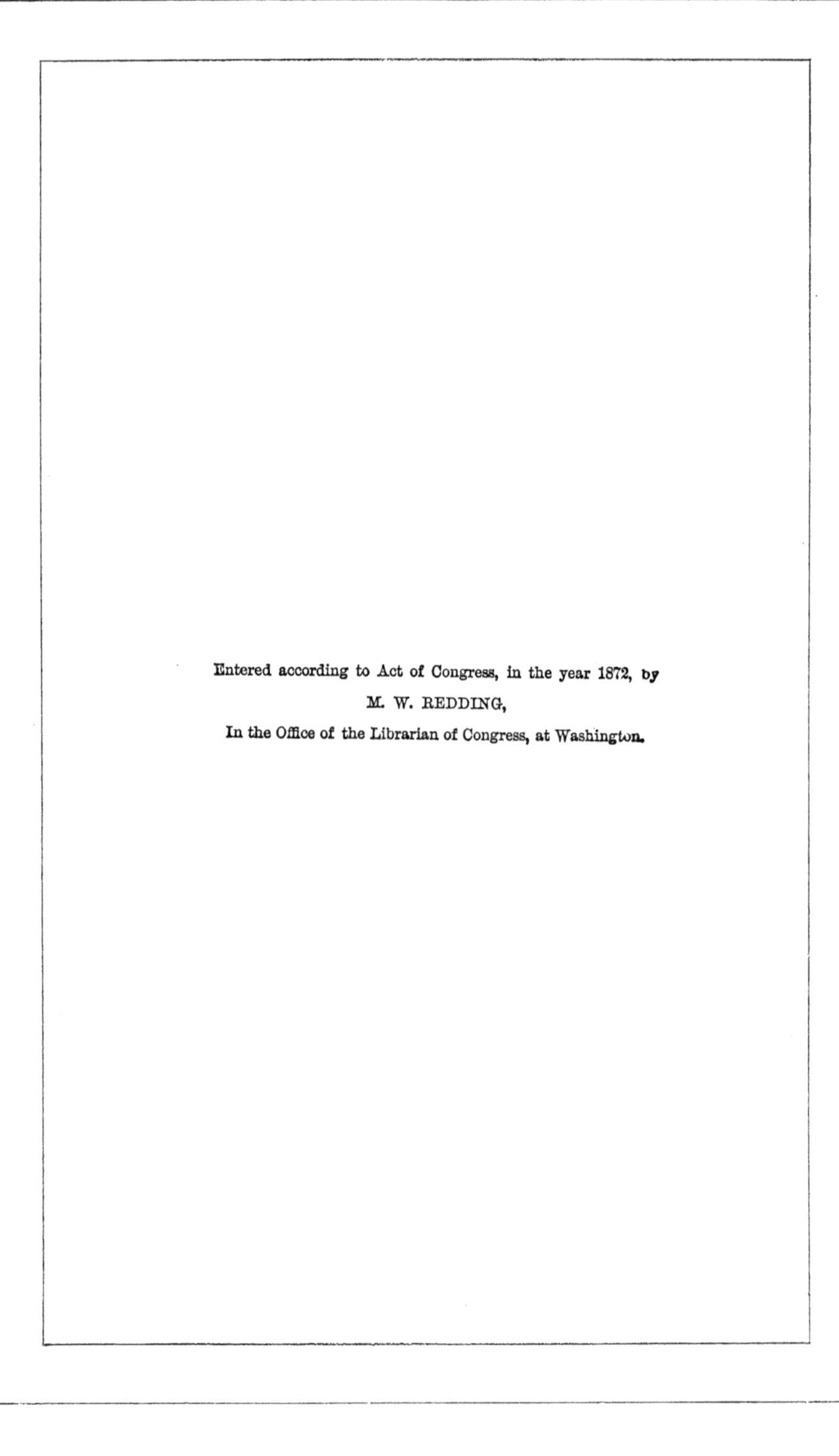

PREFACE.

WITHIN a few years past, extensive explorations have been carried on throughout the East, which have resulted in remarkable discoveries in nearly all of the ancient and renowned cities known to sacred history.

Among the most important of these discoveries are those made in Jerusalem, in the excavations around and under the Temple site—among the ruins of King Solomon's store cities, Baalbek, Tadmor and Hamath—at Babylon, Nineveh, and Shushan.

These discoveries have awakened an interest that will not be satisfied with anything less than a description of the ruins of all the important cities of the East.

In the ordinary works of Eastern travelers and writers, so much space is given to incidents of travel, and the speculations of travelers, that but little room is left for a description of antiquities or relics.

The aim of this work is to comprise in a convenient compass the results of *all* the important explorations and excavations made in the East,—especially among the ruins of King Solomon's cities. To this end, this work has been made strictly descriptive and historical; yet containing only enough of history to render the subject intelligible. By this plan a description of the ruins, as *now seen*, of forty of the most famous cities of antiquity is given in the space of this volume.

THE AUTHOR.

CONTENTS.

CHAPTER I.

JERUSALEM.

ITS ORIGIN AND A SKETCH OF ITS HISTORY—ORIGIN—ASSAULT AND CAPTURE OF THE CITY BY DAVID—DAVID'S DEATH—HE IS SUCCEEDED BY SOLOMON, WHO BUILDS THE MAGNIFICENT TEMPLE, AND THE STORE CITIES—SIEGE OF JERUSALEM BY TITUS, IT IS TAKEN AT MIDNIGHT—WANTON DESTRUCTION OF THE TEMPLE BY FIRE.................................PAGE 17

CHAPTER II.

A SKETCH OF THE TOPOGRAPHY OF THE CITY AND ADJOINING COUNTRY.

JERUSALEM—VALLEY OF JEHOSHAPHAT—VALLEY OF HINNOM — THE TYROPŒON — WALLS — VIA DOLOROSA — DAVID STREET.................................PAGE 41

CHAPTER III.

RELICS, OBJECTS AND PLACES OF INTEREST.

ANCIENT POTTERY—LAMPS—KNIVES AND OTHER RELICS—ZION BRIDGE—ANCIENT CASTLE OF DAVID—GATES OF THE CITY—POOLS—FOUNTAINS—VALLEY OF JEHOSHAPHAT—VILLAGE OF SILOAM—ANCIENT TOMBS AND VAULTS—VALLEY OF HINNOM—ACELDAMA, THE FIELD OF BLOOD.................................PAGE 47

CHAPTER IV.

PLACES OF INTEREST NEAR THE CITY.

THE VALLEY OF JEHOSHAPHAT—OF HINNOM—ACELDAMA —MOUNT OF OFFENCE—ANCIENT SEPULCHRES—SCOPUS RIDGE—MOUNT OF OLIVES—THE ROAD OVER WHICH CHRIST RODE INTO JERUSALEM................PAGE 69

CHAPTER V.

CONCERNING THE TEMPLE OF KING SOLOMON.

MOUNT MORIAH—THE TEMPLE AREA, OR ENCLOSURE—WILSON'S ARCH—ROBINSON'S ARCH—MASONIC HALL—FOUNDATION WALLS OF THE TEMPLE—SOUTH, WEST, AND EAST GATES—DOME OF THE ROCK—MOSQUE EL AKSA....................................PAGE 79

CHAPTER VI.

THE PRIVATE MARKS OF THE BUILDERS AND THE REMARKABLE ANCIENT QUARRY UNDER JERUSALEM.

MARKS FOUND ON STONES IN THE FOUNDATION WALLS OF THE TEMPLE AREA—MARKS FOUND IN SAMARIA AND HEBRON....................................PAGE 109

CHAPTER VII.

PLACES HISTORICALLY CONNECTED WITH SOLOMON'S TEMPLE AND THE BUILDERS.

ANCIENT TYRE, HIRAM'S TOMB—JOPPA—MT. LEBANON—PASS OF THE JORDAN—HEBRON, ITS IMPORTANT RELICS OF ANTIQUITY, AND SINGULAR MOSQUE—THE RUINS OF BEEROTH—KIRJATH JEARIM—SAMARIA, CHURCH OF ST. JOHN—KING SOLOMON'S STORE CITIES, BAALBEK—TADMOR—HAMATH AND GEBAL................PAGE 133

CHAPTER VIII.

THE CRADLE OF THE HUMAN RACE.

THE GARDEN OF EDEN—AMOUNT ARARAT—THE DISPERSION OF THE PEOPLE—THEIR LOCATION, OR THE PLACES OCCUPIED BY THEM—THE FIRST SETTLEMENTS OF THE HUMAN FAMILY................PAGE 194

CHAPTER IX.

THE FIRST CITIES BUILT, THEIR RISE, FALL, AND RUINS, AS NOW SEEN.

THE RUINS OF BABYLON—ERECH—ACCAD—CALNETH—NINEVEH—DAMASCUS—SHECHEM—GAZA—BEERSHEBA—BETHEL—BETHLEHEM—SIDON—JERICHO—SHUSHAN ....,....PAGE 199

CHAPTER X.

THE KNIGHTS TEMPLARS, ORIGIN OF THE ORDER—THE FATAL BATTLE OF HATTIN—MASSACRE OF THE KNIGHTS—DESCRIPTION OF THE REMARKABLE RUINS OF THE ANCIENT CITY OF GERASH—DESCRIPTION OF THE RUINS OF ATHLETE, AND THE WILD ARAB TRIBE THAT INHABITS THE PLACE—DESCRIPTION OF THE SPLENDID ANCIENT CITY OF PERGAMOS—DESCRIPTION OF THE HAURAN—ITS RUINS OF CITIES AND DESERTED VILLAGES—SHILOH—RABBAH—SARDIS—THE RUINS OF TARSUS — TIBERIUS — CÆSAREA — PANEAS—CAPERNAUM — ANTIOCH — EPHESUS — GADARA — LYDDA—NAZARETH.......................................PAGE 280

CHAPTER XI.

CONCERNING THE CRUCIFIXION.

DAVID'S TOMB—THE LAST SUPPER—THE GARDEN OF GETHSEMANE—CHRIST'S AGONY—HILL OF EVIL COUNCIL—CHURCH OF THE HOLY SEPULCHRE—PLACE OF CRUCIFIXION—HOLY SEPULCHRE—PLACE OF ASCENSION...PAGE 307

CHAPTER XII.

SCRIPTURE ACCOUNT OF THE BUILDING OF KING SOLOMON'S TEMPLE.

MT. MORIAH—DAVID'S PREPARATION FOR BUILDING THE TEMPLE AND CHARGE TO SOLOMON—SOLOMON BUILDS THE TEMPLE—ITS—DEDICATION—DESTRUCTION..PAGE 253

ILLUSTRATIONS.

FRONTISPIECE:—ANCIENT QUARRY UNDER JERUSALEM, WHERE THE STONES WERE QUARRIED FOR SOLOMON'S TEMPLE.

TOPOGRAPHICAL PLAN OF JERUSALEM, AND THE SITE OF KING SOLOMON'S TEMPLE.

JERUSALEM AS IT WAS, B.C. 1012.

JERUSALEM AS IT IS.

INTERIOR VIEW OF THE TEMPLE.

THE GOLDEN GATE.

INTERIOR VIEWS OF THE EAST AND SOUTH GATES OF THE TEMPLE ENCLOSURE.

REMARKABLE ARTIFICIAL CAVE UNDER THE TEMPLE SITE.

KING SOLOMON'S CISTERNS.

ROBINSON'S ARCH AND SECTION OF THE WALL OF THE TEMPLE ENCLOSURE.

INTERIOR VIEW OF WILSON'S ARCHES.

ECCE HOMO ARCH—A PART OF THE WALL OF THE PRESENTATION IN THE TEMPLE.

RUINS OF ANCIENT TOMBS AND TOWERS.

FIFTEEN GROUPS OF THE PRIVATE MARKS OF THE BUILDERS.

THREE COURSES OF STONES IN THE FOUNDATION WALLS OF THE TEMPLE ENCLOSURE, WITH THE PRIVATE MARKS ON THEM.

INTERIOR VIEW OF A GALLERY AT THE FOUNDATION OF THE WALL. EXPLORER EXAMINING MARKS.

INTERIOR VIEW OF THE ANCIENT QUARRY UNDER JERUSALEM IN WHICH THE STONES WERE QUARRIED FOR THE TEMPLE.

PILASTER IN MASONIC HALL.

ANCIENT FIGURED PAVEMENT.

MT. LEBANON AND THE BAY FROM WHICH THE TIMBER WAS FLOATED FOR THE TEMPLE.

THE CITY OF JOPPA, WHERE THE TIMBER WAS LANDED.

THE CITY OF TYRE AS IT NOW IS.

HIRAM'S TOMB NEAR THE CITY OF TYRE.

HIRAM'S WELL.

KING SOLOMON'S STORE CITIES—THEIR RUINS.

BAALBEK.

TADMOR.

KIRJATH JEARIM.

HEBRON.

SAMARIA.

SIDON.

GEBAL.

THE RUINS OF NINEVEH.

THE RUINS OF BABYLON.

THE RUINS OF SHUSHAN.

DAMASCUS.

THE RUINS OF RABBAH.

THE RUINS OF EPHESUS.

THE RUINS OF GADARA.

EXCAVATIONS AT SHUSHAN.

IMAGES.

VALLEY OF MURDER, JERICHO.

SUCCOTH.

ST. JOHN'S CHURCH.

THE PALACE AT SHUSHAN.

ABDEL KADER.

AN ACACIA TREE.

ANCIENT POTTERY—LAMP—AND INK BOTTLE SUCH AS WAS USED BY THE SCRIBES.

THE CASTLE OF DAVID.

GETHSEMANE.

ANCIENT COFFIN.

GOLGOTHA.

PLAN OF THE CHURCH OF THE HOLY SEPULCHRE.

BETHANY.

SHECHEM.

EPHRAIM.

DAVID'S MOSQUE AND TOMB.

MOUNT ARARAT.

A GROUP OF CAPTIVES.

KING SOLOMON, FROM AN ANCIENT SCULPTURE.

COLLECTING CONTRIBUTIONS FOR REBUILDING THE TEMPLE.

BATTLE-FIELD OF HATTIN.

WAR HORSES AFTER THE BATTLE.

THE REMARKABLE RUINS OF THE ANCIENT CITY OF GERASH.

THE RUINS OF ATHLETE.

RUINS OF PERGAMOS.

ANCIENT CITY IN THE HAURAN.

ANCIENT KITCHEN AND UTENSILS.

ANCIENT DRINKING CUPS.

ANCIENT MUSICAL INSTRUMENTS.

INDEX

TO THE PLAN OF JERUSALEM AND ITS RUINS.

No. **1.** Armenian Convent on Mt. Zion.
2. Episcopal Church, and Consulate of St. James.
3. David Tower.
4. Hezekiah Pool, built by Herod; now used.
5. Castle of David.
6. Greek Convent.
7. Coptic Convent.
8. Latin Convent.
9. Church of the Holy Sepulchre.
10. Pilate's house (ancient citadel), now the Pasha's residence.
11. Bethesda Pool.
12. St. Ann Church.
13. Prussian Consulate—near the site of Herod's palace.
14. Ruins of an ancient temple.
15. Valley Gate, near the Jaffa Gate.
16. Ancient gate, now closed (Bethezo was near it), on Zion.
17. Essenes' Gate, on Zion South.
18. Tower of Siloam.
19. East or Sun Gate.
20. The Stairs of David—now in use.
21. Intermediate Gate, between the two walls at the Junction of the Tyropœon and Kidron Valleys.
22. The House of David—it spanned the Tyropœon Valley here.
23. The Tower that lieth out over the Virgin Fountain.
24. Water Gate; on Ophel.
25. The Great Tower—Tower of Ophel.

No. **26.** Horse Gate, near the S. E. corner of the Temple.

27. Tower of the Flock (Micah iv., 8).

28. Sheep Gate—near the present St. Stephen's Gate.

29. Tower of Hananeel; N. E. corner of the Temple Area.

30. Fish Gate—near the present St. Stephen's Gate.

31. Gate of Benjamin—North and East.

32. Cemetery.

33. Throne of the Governor.

34. Damascus Gate; facing North.

35. Broad wall between Ephraim and the corner Gate.

36. Corner Gate—near the N. W. corner on the West.

37. Tower of Furnaces; in the West end of the East and West wall.

38. First Gate; in the first wall, near Jaffa Gate.

39. The Armory, or House of the Forest of Lebanon, in the N. E. corner of Zion.

40. Prison Gate; Shallecketh, in the Temple.

41. Miphkad Gate; the Stocks for detaining and punishing criminals were near this Gate, at the West end of the Tyropœon bridge.

42. Second Gate in the Tyropœon.

43. Tower of Hippicus; the ruins are in the N. W. corner of the city wall, called the Giant's Tower.

44. Phasaelus—a Tower named after Herod's brother, near the Gennath Gate.

45. Mariamne—named by Herod after his Queen; on Zion.

46. Gennath (gardens) Gate—near the Jaffa Gate, in the third wall.

47. Psephinos; an octagon tower, North of Hippicus.

There were 90 towers in the third wall; no other names have been recorded. In other walls there were other gates, of which no ruins exist.

48. Fort of Zion; the Great Acropolis, so famed during the Syrian Wars.

49. Castle of Zion; taken by David from the Jebusites.

50. Zion Bridge.

51. Citadel; was high and overlooked the city.

52. Millo; at the Junction of the Zion and Tyropœon Valleys.

No. **53.** Road over which Christ rode into Jerusalem.
54. Golgotha.
55. Castle of Antonia; containing the Judgment Hall.
56. Baris; the Acropolis of Akra.
57. Strabo's Tower, near Antonia.
58. Illustration showing the form of the original hill Mount Moriah.
59. Upper Pool of Gihon.
60. Jews' Wailing-Place; here are to be seen some of the foundation-stones of the Temple.
61. Garden of Gethsemane.
62. Church of the Ascension.
63. Entrance to the great underground quarry, where the stones were quarried and prepared for King Solomon's Temple.
64. Village of Siloam.

Besides these there are records of a great many palaces, market-places, and synagogues for instruction in the Scriptures and traditions, of which there remains no vestige by which they can with certainty be identified.

MOUNT MORIAH—SITE OF SOLOMON'S TEMPLE.

A, A, A, A, Temple Area.

No. **1.** Dome of the Rock; Ancient Christian Church: now a mosk.
2. Mosk el Aksa; the Ancient Knight Templar's Church.
3. Mogrebins Mosk.
4. The Sea of Solomon, underground.
5. Vaults under the platform.
6. Ancient South Gate of the Temple; now Double Gate.
7. Ancient West Gate, now Prophet's Gate.
8. Gate of the Chain.
9. Gate of the Bath.
10. Iron Gate.
11. Gate of the Inspector.
12. East or Golden Gate.

CHAPTER I.

JERUSALEM.

ITS ORIGIN, AND A SKETCH OF ITS HISTORY.

Origin—Assault and Capture of the City by David —David's Death—He is succeeded by Solomon, who builds the Magnificent Temple, and the Store Cities—Siege of Jerusalem by Titus, it is taken at Midnight—Wanton Destruction of the Temple by Fire.

THE city of Jerusalem, with its ruins of temples, towers, walls, and tombs, is one of the most profoundly impressive localities in all the world. While reflecting on the history of this city, wave on wave of thought rush in on the mind from out the limitless ocean of the past, and while contemplating its ruins the mind is carried far back through the dim vista of ages, to the time when Mt. Zion was the Jebusite's stronghold, and when the site of the magnificent Temple of Solomon was a threshing-floor.

In all other holy places there were worshiped beasts and birds (Apis and Ibis, Egypt), the human form (Greece), and hideous images of things found neither in the heavens nor the earth (India). But here the shepherds of Canaan, who watched the flocks among the hills, bowed to Him who is still called the God of Abraham, Isaac, and Jacob. In Genesis we read that in the beginning God created the heaven and the earth, and, as the great Architect of the Universe, he claims the exclusive worship of man. Since the day when the tent of the wilderness (the Tabernacle) was enlarged into the Temple, what various and thrilling events have made the temple site famous! There swiftly passes in review the foundation of that sacred and stately edifice, with its spacious courts and white marble walls, resplendent with fine gold; the magnificent rites and ceremonies, the solemn prayers and costly sacrifices, and the mysterious Holy of Holies, the Shekinah.

Then follows the destruction of this sacred place by the idolaters from Babylon, and its restoration by Zerubbabel and Ezra, when some who had seen the first house wept, while others shouted for joy. And finally, Herod's Temple, larger and more magnificent than the others, which had been forty-six years in progress when Jesus spake in it of its final destruction, which came with Titus and the Romans; and of all its precious and beautiful furniture and sacred vessels, there remains only a time-worn sculpture of the Candlestick and the crumbling Triumphal Arch of Titus at Rome.

Besides these material things there is a long procession of good men and women, kings, prophets, and priests, who frequented this place to worship, and held the same faith with us; whose lives are our example, and whose songs are our psalms and hymns of praise. The dark side of the picture is stained with frightful idolatries, devilish wickedness, falsehoods, blasphemies, hypocrisies, and murders, even in the midst of the most awful denunciations against sin in every form.

The view is also darkened by accounts of sieges, famines, destructions, captivities and dispersions, desolations and wars unnumbered, with but a few rays of blessings in restorations. Uncounted millions for nearly two thousand years have directed towards this shrine their hopes and prayers. This eventful history and its present condition lead to the inquiry, Will the Temple ever be rebuilt? Will Jerusalem ever be restored? Will the twelve tribes ever be regathered?—questions that can only be answered by the Great Director of human events.

From Abraham to the present time a knowledge of the one true God has been the chief source of inspiration, and there have been many great teachers who have instructed, counseled, warned, and threatened the people; always magnifying the service and the rewards of the true faith. Will there ever be another great teacher there?

ORIGIN.

The name of this famous and sacred city suggests inquiry into its origin and history.

The name, Jerusalem, is first found in Joshua x. 1, 3, 5, 23. It is next called Jebus or Ha Jebusi, and its inhabitants Jebusites. The Greeks called it Hiero Solyma (Holy City of Solomon); but Jerusalem has been the common name since Solomon's time.

The second son of Noah was Ham, who begat Canaan, whose descendents were the Jebusites, who dwelt in the hill country in which Jerusalem is situated, and had their stronghold on Mount Zion, and, as there is no *reliable* record or tradition of its occupation by any other people previous to its occupation by the Jebusites, the conclusion is very evident that the city was founded by them, but there exists no data for determining the precise time.

"And the Lord spake unto Moses, saying,

"Send thou men that they may search the land of Canaan, which I give unto the children of Israel—

And Moses sent them to spy out the land of Canaan, and said unto them, "Get you up this *way* southward, and go up into the mountain.

"So they went up, and searched the land from the wilderness of Zin unto Rehob, as men come to Hamath.

And they returned from searching of the land after forty days.

And they went and came to Moses, and to Aaron, and to all the congregation of the children of Israel, unto the wilderness of Paran, to Kadesh; and brought back word unto them, and unto all the congregation, and shewed them the fruit of the land.

And they told him, and said, We came unto the land whither thou sentest us, and surely it floweth with milk and honey; and this *is* the fruit of it.

The Amalekites dwell in the land of the south: and the Hittites, and the *Jebusites*, and the Amorites, dwell in the mountains: and the Canaanites dwell by the sea, and by the coast of Jordan." (Numbers xiii. 1, 17, 21, 25, 26, 27, 29.)

"And the border went up by the valley of the son of Hinnom unto the south side of the *Jebusite;* the same *is Jerusalem:* and the border went up to the top of the mountain that *lieth* before the valley of Hinnom westward, which *is* at the end of the valley of the giants northward:

And the border came down to the end of the mountain that *lieth* before the valley of the son of Hinnom, *and* which *is* in the valley of the giants on the north, and descended to the valley of Hinnom, to the side of *Jebusi* on the south, and descended to En-rogel,

And Zelah, Eleph, and *Jebusi*, which *is Jerusalem*, Gibeath, *and* Kirjath; fourteen cities with their villages. This *is* the inheritance of the children of Benjamin according to their families." (Joshua, xv. 8—xviii. 16, 28.)

HISTORY.

The first recorded siege was by Judah and Simeon (about 1400 B.C.).

Now after the death of Joshua it came to pass, that the children of Israel asked the Lord, saying, Who shall go up for us against the Canaanites first, to fight against them?

And the Lord said, Judah shall go up: behold, I have delivered the land into his hand.

And Judah said unto Simeon his brother, Come up with me into my lot, that we may fight against the Canaanites; and I likewise will go with thee into thy lot. So Simeon went with him.

And Judah went up; and the Lord delivered the Canaanites and the Perizzites into their hand: and they slew of them in Bezek ten thousand men.

Now the children of Judah had fought against

Jerusalem, and had taken it, and smitten it with the edge of the sword, and set the city on fire. (Judges, i. 1, 2, 3, 4, 8.)

But they only took the lower city—the fortress of Zion and upper city being too strong for them.

Following this was an attack by the Benjamites, but with no better success.

These sieges and attacks were continued through the time when Israel was ruled by the judges, and the reign of Saul, and the reign of David at Hebron. But the Jebusites successfully resisted every attempt on the fortress of Zion, and thus remained practically masters of the city until about 1049 B.C., when David with an army of 280,000 men, choice warriors, the flower of Israel (1 Chron., xii. 23, 39), advanced to the siege, and with little trouble took the lower city, but, as before, the citadel on Zion held out until the Jebusites tauntingly said to him: "Except thou take away the lame and the blind thou shalt not come up thither" (2 Samuel, v. 6, 7, 8). Which roused David's anger, and he proclaimed to his host, that the first who would climb the rocky side of the fortress and kill a Jebusite should be made chief captain of the host; upon which a crowd of warriors rushed forward to the attempt, but Joab's superior agility gained him the day, and the citadel—the fortress of Zion—was at last taken. The fall of this hitherto impregnable stronghold created a great sensation throughout the length and breadth of the land.

David at once proceeded to fortify and secure him self in his important acquisition by enclosing the city and citadel with a strong wall. The ark was brought from the house of Obed-Edom, (near Kirjath-Jearim,) and deposited here with the most impressive ceremonies, and the city then became the religious centre and political capital of the country.

Previous to this the seat of government had been wherever the judges or rulers had their residence; their place of residence and the ark constituting the capital and religious centre for the time being. These transient capitals were successively Gilgal, Shiloh, Shechem, Nob, and Gibeon. (Joshua, iv. 18, 19).

David was succeeded by his son Solomon 1016 B. C., whose great works were the Temple with its east wall and cloister, the house of the forest of Lebanon, the walls of Jerusalem, with large towers thereon, the great cisterns or sea under the temple area, the throne, a palace for his Egyptian wife, 40,000 stalls for his horses, the garden, Baalath, Beth-horon, Gezer, Hazor, Megiddo, and Tadmor. The crowning glory of his reign and adornment of the holy city was the Temple or House of Jehovah. The magnificence and marvelous beauty of this edifice did not arise so much from its size as from the whiteness of its walls, the style and finish of its many columns and pillars, and lavish use within and without of the gold of Ophir and Parvaim. (See page 341) Through the whole time that this Temple was in building the tranquillity of the city was not broken by the sound of the workman's ax or hammer, and the only dark shade to the picture is the fact of the practical reduction to bondage of the strangers in the land, the remnant of the Canaanite races; one hundred and fifty-three thousand of whom were sent off to the forests of Lebanon and the quarries. Even the Israelites were compelled to take place by rotation at the same labor.

The addition of the splendid Temple, Palaces, Walls, and Towers, together with other great improvements made in the City by King Solomon, rendered it at the close of his reign the most beautiful capital of the age. Its population at this time was about 130,000.

Rehoboam, son and successor of King Solomon, ascended the throne 976 B.C., and reigned 17 years. Under his reign the ten tribes revolted and formed the Kingdom of Israel, under Jeroboam, with their capital at Shechem, Jerusalem remaining the capital of the Kingdom of Judah.

Rehoboam was succeeded by his son Abijam, who reigned 3 years, and was succeeded by Asa his son, who ascended the throne 951 B.C., and reigned 41 years. In the eleventh year of his reign God gave him the victory over the vast army of the Cushite King Zerah.

Asa was succeeded by his son Jehoshaphat 914 B.C. His reign was distinguished by the cleansing of the land from idolatry, the restoration of the divine ordinances, and provision for the religious instruction of the people. The great error of his life was an entangling alliance with Ahab, whose infamous daughter Athalia early began to afflict the kingdom of Judah, of which she was afterwards queen. Jehoshaphat united with Ahaziah in a commercial enterprise which, proving to be a failure, he declined a second trial: he, however, united with Joram in a war with Moab, in which he was assailed by a vast army of

SOLOMON, KING OF ISRAEL.

Moabites, Ammonites, Edomites, and Syrians, but through his faith in God he was victorious. After a highly prosperous reign of 25 years, he died at the age of 60.

Joram succeeded his father, after reigning with him four years, then reigned four years alone; in all 8 years. Unfortunately he was married to Athalia, daughter of Ahab and Jezebel, whose evil influence did much to render his reign a curse to the kingdom. He slew his brothers, five in number, and seized their possessions. He also introduced Phœnician idols and idolatry into Judea, by which he incurred the divine displeasure, which was shown by leaving him unaided under a revolt of the Edomites, which was successful. His kingdom was invaded by the Philistines and Arabians, who ravaged the country, the city, and even his own house. His reign ended 885 B.C., when he was succeeded by Ahaziah his son, who reigned but a short time—meeting his death at the hand of Jehu while in company with Joram, son of Ahab. After the premature death of Ahaziah, his mother Athalia ascended the throne and sought to secure herself on it by the murder of all the seed royal. Joash, her grandson, then an infant one year old, was the only one who escaped—being concealed by his Aunt Jehosheba. Six years afterwards the faithful and fearless high-priest Jehoiada caused the blood-stained Athalia to be put to death, and crowned Joash king. The reign of Joash began 877 B.C. Through the faithful care of Jehoiada, Joash served God and prospered; but after the death of his venerable friend and adviser he followed less wholesome counsels, idolatry revived, and Zachariah the high-priest rebuked the guilty people, upon which the ungrateful king caused this servant of God to be stoned to death. Misfortunes soon multiplied on his head; he was repeatedly humbled by the Syrians, and had to buy them off with the treasures of the Temple. A conspiracy among his servants cut short his life, and thus ended his reign.

Joash was succeeded by his son Amaziah, who began to reign 838 B.C., and reigned 29 years. Having established himself on his throne and punished the murderers of his father with death, he mustered an army of 300,000 men of Judah, and hired 100,000 men of Israel for a war on Edom. At the command of God, he reluctantly dismissed the hired forces, after which the victory was given him without their assistance. Notwithstanding the divine aid in his behalf, he carried home with him the idols of Edom, and set them up to be his gods. For this defiance of Jehovah, he was threatened with destruction by a Prophet of the Lord—which came in a war in which he was defeated and humiliated. Fifteen years after this, a conspiracy was formed against him, upon which he fled to Lachish, where he was overtaken and slain.

Amaziah was succeeded by Azariah—elsewhere Uzziah—who began to reign B.C. 808. At first his reign was prosperous; but afterwards, presuming to offer incense in the Temple, he was smitten with leprosy, from which he suffered till his death.

Jotham, son of Azariah, succeeded to the throne 756 B.C. No event of importance transpired during his reign—which was wise and prosperous. He was suc ceeded by his son Ahaz, who ascended the throne 742 B.C., and reigned 16 years. He was noted for his idolatry and contempt of God. He made his children pass through the fire to idols; he altered the Temple to the Syrian model, and afterwards closed it altogether. In punishment for this defiance of Jehovah, he was defeated in battle with Pekah and Rezin; the Edomites revolted, and his borders were harassed by the Philistines. Turning still more away from God, in his distress he sought aid from Pul, king of Assyria, which fatal step made him tributary to Pul and his successor Tiglath-Pileser. Ahaz died at the age of 36, and was refused burial with his ancestors the Kings.

Hezekiah, son of Ahaz, succeeded to the throne and began his reign about 726 B.C. His reign is memorable for his efforts to restore the worship of the true God. In the fourteenth year of his reign, the king of Assyria marched against Jerusalem, and sent an insulting and blasphemous message, demanding the surrender of the city, which being communicated to Hezekiah, he repaired to the Temple and there implored divine aid against the presumptuous invader, in response to which the Lord sent an angel that night who smote and destroyed the Assyrians—185,000 men—who were found corpses in the morning.

"Now in the fourteenth year of king Hezekiah did Sennacherib king of Assyria come up against all the fenced cities of Judah, and took them.

And the king of Assyria sent Tartan and Rabsaris and Rab-shakeh from Lachish to king Hezekiah with a great host against Jerusalem: and they went up and came to Jerusalem. And when they were come up, they came and stood by the conduit of the upper pool, which *is* in the highway of the fuller's field.

And when they had called to the king, there came out to them Eliakim the son of Hilkiah, which *was* over the household, and Shebna the scribe, and Joah the son of Asaph the recorder.

And Rab-shakeh said unto them, Speak ye now to Hezekiah, Thus saith the great king, the king of Assyria, What confidence *is* this wherein thou trustest?

"And it came to pass that night, that the angel of the Lord went out, and smote in the camp of the Assyrians a hundred fourscore and five thousand: and when they arose early in the morning, behold, they *were* all dead corpses." (2 Kings, 17, 18, 19—xix. 35.)

Hezekiah died 697 B.C. and was succeeded by Manasseh, who began to reign when he was twelve years old, and reigned 55 years. The commencement of his reign was noted for his shocking idolatries, cruelty, and tyranny, for which God suffered him to be carried a prisoner to Babylon in the twenty-second year of his reign, by Esar-Haddon, king of Assyria. Here, however, he so humbled himself, that God moved the Assyrians to restore him to his throne as a tributary; and thenceforth, he set himself to undo the great evil he had done. He abolished the worship of idols and repaired the defences of the city, enclosing with a wall more space at the west, and Ophel on the south-east, and after a long reign he died in peace, and was buried in Jerusalem. Manasseh was succeeded by Amon, who began to reign at the age of 22, 642 B.C. His servants conspired against him and slew him in his own house; but the people killed the conspirators and established his son Josiah on the throne, who commenced to reign 640 B.C. He set himself at once to work to destroy every vestige of idolatry out of the land. He defiled the altars of the idols at Bethel by burning upon them the bones of their deceased priests; as had been foretold more than three centuries before (1 Kings, xiii. 2). The Temple was cleansed and repaired at his command, and it was while doing this that the priest found the Temple copy of the law; perhaps the original copy from Moses' own hand. Pharao-Necho, marching to attack the king of Assyria, passed across the territory of Josiah, who, in an attempt to stop him, gave him battle, in which he lost his life, 609 B.C. Josiah was succeeded by Jehoahaz, who reigned only about three months, when he was deposed by the king of Egypt.

Jehoiakim, second son of Josiah, succeeded Jehoahaz on the throne, and began to reign about 609 B.C. In the third year of his reign Nebuchadnezzar took the city and carried to Babylon a part of his princes and treasures. A year after this his allies the Egyptians were defeated on the Euphrates, yet he despised the warnings of Jeremiah and cast his book into the fire. At length he rebelled against Nebuchadnezzar, and was defeated and slain. Jehoiachin, son of Jehoiakim, succeeded to the throne 599 B.C. After reigning three months, he was carried captive to

Babylon, where he remained imprisoned 36 years, but was then released and treated with favor by Evil Merodach.

Zedekiah.—When Nebuchadnezzar took Jerusalem and carried Jehoiachin away captive, he put in his place Mattaniah, whose name he changed to Zedekiah, and made him swear that he would maintain fidelity to him. Yet in the ninth year of his reign he revolted and applied to Pharaoh-hophra for assistance. Upon this Nebuchadnezzar marched to Jerusalem, and after a siege of a year and a half took the city 588 B. C. Entrance was gained at midnight when the city was wrapped in the pitchy darkness characteristic of an eastern town, and nothing was known by the Jews of what had happened till the generals of the invading army entered the Temple and took seats in the middle court. Then the alarm was given, when Zedekiah hastily collected his remaining warriors and stole out of the city by a gate at the south side—near the present Bab-el-Mugharibeh, crossed the Kidron above the royal gardens, and made his way over Mount Olivet to the Jordan valley; but the Chaldeans pursued and overtook them on the plains of Jericho, Zedekiah was taken and carried to Nebuchadnezzar, then at Riblah in Syria, who reproached him with his perfidy, ordered his children to be slain before his face, and his eyes to be put out; and then loading him with chains of brass, ordered him to be sent to Babylon.—(See Babylonish captivity, page 393.)

Meantime the wretched inhabitants suffered all the horrors of assault and sack; the men were slaughtered, old and young, prince and peasant; and the women violated in Mt. Zion itself. On the 7th day of the following month Nebuzaradan arrived, collected the captives and booty, and on the tenth the temple, the royal palace, and all the more important buildings of the city were set on fire, and the walls thrown down and left as heaps of rubbish. This destruction of the city and deportation left the land nearly deserted.

The subsequent history of Jerusalem may be epitomized as follows:—About 332 B.C. it was taken by Alexander of Macedon. Shortly after his death Ptolemy Lagus, of Egypt, took it by assault on the Sabbath, when it is said the Jews scrupled to fight. 199 B. C., Scopus, an Egyptian general, recovered Judea to the King of Egypt. 170 B. C., it was taken by Antiochus Epiphanes, who razed its walls, set up an image of Jupiter in the Temple, and used every means to force the people into idolatry. Under the Maccabees the Jews again recovered their independence 165 B. C. About 100 years later it was conquered by the Romans, and Herod the Great expended vast sums in its embellishment.

A. D. 63, the Jews renounced their allegiance to Vespasian, upon which hostilities at once began. The insurgents held the Temple and lower city. In the Castle of Antonia was a small Roman garrison. Fierce contests lasted for several days, each side endeavoring to gain possession of the part held by the other. At last the insurgents became masters of the city and Temple. Cestius Gallus, then encamped on Scopas, advanced on the city and for six days assaulted the walls, but without success. He then drew off to his camp. Thither the insurgents followed him, and in three days gave him one of the most complete defeats ever undergone by a Roman army.

The Jews then repaired the walls of the city and made great preparations for its defense against another expected attempt by the Romans—which was soon made by Titus, who arrived and encamped on Scopas and Mount Olivet, and commenced the siege. April the 15th the first breach was made in the walls. June the 11th the Tower of Antonia was taken. July the 15th a soldier wantonly and without orders set fire to the Temple, which was destroyed except the edifice of the Sanctuary. September the 11th the city was taken, and its destruction completed, except the three great towers—Hippicus, Phasaelus, and Mariamne, which were left standing as memorials of the massive nature of the fortifications.

A.D. 135, Adrian banished the Jews and planted a Roman colony there. He also consecrated the city to heathen deities, so as to defile it as much as possible, and did what he could to obliterate all traces both of Judaism and Christianity.

About A.D. 326, Helena, the mother of Constantine, built two churches in Bethlehem and on Mount Olivet. Julian endeavored to rebuild the Temple, A. D. 363, but his design was frustrated, as contemporaneous writers relate, by an earthquake and by balls of fire bursting among the workmen.

A.D. 613 Jerusalem was taken by Chosroes, king of Persia, who slew 90,000 men, and demolished the buildings and objects venerated by the Christians. In 627 Heraclius defeated Chosroes, and Jerusalem was

RECEIVING CONTRIBUTIONS FOR REBUILDING THE TEMPLE.

recovered by the Greeks. 637 it was taken by Omar, the second of the Kalifs, and thus passed under Mohammedan rule. The Mosque of Omar on the Temple site was built by this Mohammedan Kalif. From this time Jerusalem continued under the Kalifs of Bagdad, till 868, when it was taken by Ahmed, a Turkish sovereign of Egypt. From this till 1099 it was ruled alternately by Turk and Saracen. At this latter period it was taken by the crusaders under Godfrey Bouillon, who was elected king. He was succeeded by his brother Baldwin, who died in 1118. In 1187 Saladin, Sultan of the East, took the city. In 1242 it was restored to the Latin princes by Saleh Ismail, Emir of Damascus. In 1291 it was taken by the Sultans of Egypt, who held it until 1382. Selim, Sultan of Turkey, made conquest of Egypt, Syria and Jerusalem in 1517, and his son Solyman reconstructed the walls of the city, as now seen, in 1534. Since this time, with the exception of the 2 years it was held by Ibrahim Pasha of Egypt, and two years by the Fellahin, it has remained subject to Turkey. It is now included in the pashalic of Damascus, but with a resident Turkish governor.

Altogether, Jerusalem presents a history unexampled in the number of its sieges and other tragical events. It has greatly declined from its former size and splendor, and has now a population of only 20,000.

Jerusalem as it was in the time of Solomon—Population 150,000.

Jerusalem as it is—Population 20,000.

CHAPTER II.

A SKETCH OF THE TOPOGRAPHY OF THE CITY AND ADJOINING COUNTRY.

Jerusalem—Valley of Jehoshaphat—Hinnom—Tyropœon—Walls—Gates—David Street—Via Dolorosa—Mount Zion.

To render the situation and description of the points of interest intelligible to those who are not familiar with the subject, a slight sketch of the topography of the city and adjoining country will be necessary.

Jerusalem is situated on the summit of the ridge which extends through Palestine from north to south; the only approach to the city being by wild mountain roads. The spur or plateau on which the city is built has a general slant to the south-east, and its average height above the Mediterranean is 2,475 feet.

This plateau is of tertiary limestone, the upper beds of which are a hard, compact stone called by the Arabs "Mezzeh," while the lower consists of a soft white stone called "Melekeh." It was in this latter that most of the ancient tombs and cisterns were cut.

The city is nearly surrounded by two ravines or valleys: Jehoshaphat on the east, and Hinnom on the west and south.

THE VALLEY OF JEHOSHAPHAT

commences well around to the north of the city, and at first its course is nearly east for a mile and a half; it then makes a sharp bend to the south, which course it follows to En Rogel, a deep well a short distance below the city. From this point it winds its way through the wild hilly country of Judea, twelve miles to the Dead Sea. Through this valley runs the brook Kedron.

THE VALLEY OF HINNOM

commences west of the city, and its course is at first south-east to nearly opposite Jaffa gate, where it bends to the south, which course it follows to a short distance below the lower pool of Gihon; at this point it makes a sharp bend to the east, and, passing the south end of the city, joins the valley of Jehoshaphat at En Rogel. Both of these valleys are at first very shallow, mere depressions in the ground, but after changing their courses, the Hinnom to the east, and Jehoshaphat to the south, they fall and deepen more rapidly, so that at En Rogel they are six hundred and seventy feet lower than at their starting points. Between the valley of Hinnom and Jehoshaphat there is another ravine.

THE TYROPŒON, VALLEY OF THE CHEESE-MONGERS, commences near the Damascus gate, and running nearly south, joins the Jehoshaphat at Siloam. This ravine divides the plateau on which the city stands into two unequal halves, the western spur being one hundred and twenty feet higher than the eastern; on the latter—Mount Moriah—once stood the temples of Solomon, Zerubbabel, and Herod. On the western was the upper city of Josephus, and here also stood the three great towers—Hippicus, Phasælus, and Mariamne. The sides of these valleys are now encumbered with much rubbish, still they are sufficiently steep to be difficult of access, so that in ancient times they must have afforded a strong natural defence for the south, west, and east sides of the city, and this it was which gave the Jebusites such assurance when they said to David, "Thou wilt not come up hither; the blind and the lame shall drive thee back." *

The original city was built on Zion, and was surrounded by a strong wall, and as the city was enlarged a second wall was built; afterwards a third. The city is not near as large now as at the time of Christ, being only about two and a half miles in circumference. The present wall is very strongly built, its thickness being from twelve to fifteen feet, and its height varying from thirty to seventy feet, according to the inequalities of the surface of the ground.

* Rendering in the German version.

GATES.

There are five gates now in use: the Damascus gate on the north, St. Stephen gate on the east, the Sun and Dung gates on the south, and the Jaffa* gate on the west.

There are also five ancient gates, now closed, viz.: the Bab Azzahire on the north, the Golden gate on the east side of the Temple area, and the Single, Double,† and Triple gates on the south side.

DAVID STREET

runs from Jaffa gate on the west to the Temple area on the east; *Dolorosa* runs from St. Stephen gate on the east to the Church of the Holy Sepulchre. North and west of David street is the Christian quarter of the city; near the centre of this quarter, at the west end of Dolorosa, is the church of the Holy Sepulchre; south of this is Zion, Zion gate, and the lepers' huts. South of this is David's resting-place, or tomb of David. North of the Temple area is a hill which is doubtless the Bezetha of Josephus. It is now occupied by Moslem houses, a convent built by the Cœurs de Sion, and the British, Prussian, and Austrian consulates.

MOUNT ZION.

Mount Zion is in the south-western part of the city. It is bounded on the west and south by the valley of

* Ancient Joppa, now Jaffa gate.

† The ancient South gate of the Temple.

Hinnom, and on the east by the Tyropœon. From the valley of Hinnom the sides anciently rose up in steep rocky precipices, but the ruins from the many destructions of the city have been tumbled into these valleys so as to cover up, in many places, the precipices, and entirely obliterate all traces of the original brow of the hill. This is especially the case with the Tyropœon valley, which is now so filled with the accumulations of ruins, that opposite to Mount Zion it has hardly the appearance of a valley; even on the top of the hill, where a few years since the English church was built, nearly fifty feet of rubbish was dug through before the original soil was reached.

The southern brow of Zion is bold and prominent, and at the southwest corner of the city it is one hundred and fifty feet above the valley, and on the south three hundred.

Upon this mount the original city was built. Here was the stronghold of the Jebusites, which was captured by David, and here was the palace of the kings of Israel. But now how changed! On ground once thickly covered with public edifices and dwellings, among mounds of ruins, large patches of barley and wheat may be seen growing. "Therefore shall Zion, for your sake, be ploughed as a field, and Jerusalem become heaps, and the mountain of the house as the high places of the forests." (Micah iii. 12.)

Several valleys begin north and west of the city, and wind south and west to the sea, the largest of which is Wady Beit Hanina, continued in Wady Surar. The mountains round about Jerusalem are higher than the city on every side ; so it is necessary to go *up* to the city from any direction.

The names and localities of the several hills are plainly given on the engraving.* The walls of the modern city are indicated by the heavy black line. The more ancient walls are shown by dots and marks arranged and named on the engraving.

In the Bible and Josephus there are given the names of the gates, towers, and notable edifices, the sites of which are laid down on the plan in accordance with the reports of the latest ordnance surveys and explorations.

* **Jerusalem and its ruins—See first part of the Book.**

CHAPTER III.

RELICS, OBJECTS, AND PLACES OF INTEREST.

Ancient Pottery—Lamps—Knives and other Relics—Zion Bridge—Ancient Castle of David—Gates of the City—Pools—Fountains—Valley of Jehoshaphat—Village of Siloam—Ancient Tombs and Vaults—Valley of Hinnom—Aceldama the Field of Blood.

In the description of the Subterranean Quarry a cut of a lamp is given showing how the quarry was lighted while the men were at work. It will be interesting to notice some of the many forms of lamps, with their singular marks and inscriptions, that have been found among the rubbish in the various excavations under Jerusalem, in cisterns or sewers, where they have been accidentally dropped, or in chambers where they were left when the rooms were abandoned. Nearly all of those found are broken, a few only being whole, which had been lost, perhaps. Many of the objects found in the rubbish were the work of Greeks or Romans, and may have been imported from Europe. But there are also specimens of Phœnician or Hebrew workmanship, especially the most ancient articles which were found in the deepest places, apparently where they had lain undisturbed since the time of Solomon.

Of the earthenware and terra-cotta there are five classes of objects among those discovered.

1. Ancient Hebrew and Phœnician.
2. Greek or made by Greek colonies.
3. Roman or their colonies.
4. Christian, of the early ages.
5. Arabic, middle age and modern.

Of the first there are a large number of fragments, the most interesting of which are vase handles with curious devices stamped on the clay before it was burned in the kiln. Some of these were found at a depth of sixty-three feet below the present surface. There is on nearly every one a figure of Baal with letters above and below it, signifying that the maker had the royal license of manufacture. Some of these have a cross, as the potter's mark. There was a royal guild of potters in Jerusalem, as mentioned in Chron. iv. 23.

Two of the Greek specimens are of the most ancient and curious make; they are round lamps with four lips or places for wicks. These lamps were found in a cave on Mount Olivet. Others of this pattern have been found on the Island of Cyprus, and in Malta and other Greek localities. The caves of Olivet have furnished many specimens of vases, dishes, and lamps of various patterns and of different workmanship, Greek, Roman, and later. One of these is saucer-shaped, ten inches across, and has three legs, each perforated, forming rings by which the article was hung up when not in use. Some of

Ancient Knives, Lamps, and Ink-bottle.

the Greek articles were of yellow ware ornamented with red patterns in the true Greek style. Similar jugs and vases may now be seen in use among the Arab Kabyles in Algeria. One piece of the upper part of a jug was ornamented in imitation of a girl with a shawl thrown over her shoulders figured in a Grecian pattern and very skilfully executed.

Six different vases were found whole or broken, of precisely similar patterns and ornaments to some that were found in Egypt. They are of a very hard black substance and coated with a crimson glaze. Five are shaped like a cedar cone, but ribbed in sections besides the seed markings.

Third.—Fragments of several kinds of pottery of Roman work were found in different places, some of which were very beautiful, and bore inscriptions. The Romans used pottery to a great extent, and always left fragments of broken ware wherever they camped, and some interesting specimens have been found in Jericho and other places in Palestine.

Fourth.—Among the articles of the Christian period there are a great number of lamps, nearly all of which are rendered interesting by the inscriptions inscribed on them, or from the locality where they were discovered. Judging from the material and style of lamps the early Christians were very poor and also very devout. The devices stamped on them are various, and include the cross in many styles—the seven-branched-candlestick, formed after that which lighted the Holy Place in Solomon's Temple, and emblematical of Christ the light of the World; the palm branch suggested by the passage in Psalms xcii., and St. John's Gospel, xii. 13, and in Revelation ii. 9. Nearly all of these lamps are pear-shaped, and ornamented around the edge of the top only. (See No. 8.) The round lamp (see No. 7) is of Greek workmanship, and is ornamented. Inscriptions are found on some of them, one of which reads P H Ō S' φως Christus (xs), phenipacin *ΦΕΝΙΠΑΚΙΝ*, and may be translated "Christ the light of all," or "the light of Christ shines out." Another has the legend *ΙΧΘ*. Jesus Christ God, or it may be the Symbol of the fish ICTHUS meaning Christ—in Greek also Jesus Christ Saviour.

Fifth.—The Arabic pottery is interesting from its material and designs. One pattern has a design painted on it, in blue and black lines, and is similar to specimens found in Egypt. Some of them have inscriptions in the peculiar Coptic letter, and probably date as far back as the age of Haroun al Raschid. The wall tiles of the Mosque of the Sakkara at Jerusalem are of similar materials, and also those of the Great Mosque at Damascus, where they are ornamented with a pattern in blue lines on a pale green ground.

The articles of glass that have been found are highly interesting as antiquities, as they prove the use of the material in ancient times. One of the glass vessels found is double, and was doubtless an ink-holder. It had three handles, one on each side, and one on the top, the last having been broken (see No. 6); the color is a pale green, ornamented with circular and zigzag lines of a dark blue tint, relieved by a darker blue. The large glass lamp, with

Ecce Homo Arch.

a wide open top, has three handles for suspending chains, and is of a pale green color. The old Coptic Convents in Egypt are lighted to this day by similar lamps, some of which have inscriptions in the Coptic language selected from the New Testament.

Objects in bronze, copper, and stone are quite numerous, and highly interesting as specimens of ancient workmanship, and as showing some of the tools and implements in use at the time of the two Hirams.

THE ECCE HOMO ARCH.

This arch is over the Via Dolorosa opposite the Governor's house, and is traditionally said to bear the very chamber and window from which Jesus was shown to the people by Pilate when he said "Behold the Man" (ecce homo).

This Arch spans the principal street of the city, being the one that leads from St. Stephen's Gate on the east to the Joppa Gate on the west, along which thousands of pilgrims from different countries pass in all sorts of garb and every variety of style, on foot, on donkeys, camels and horses. Some loaded with baggage, others with books or relics, and, mingling with these, the natives in equally varied costume and condition carrying fruit, water-jars, and children. No greater picture of confusion could be imagined than is seen in Jerusalem about the time of Easter every year, when nearly every nation under the sun is represented by pilgrims of every degree, from the wealthy nabob on horseback to the poor and lame hobbling on foot.

THE ACACIA-TREE.

The Acacia Seyal is one of the most beautiful evergreens of Palestine. It is often found growing in the dry bed of some extinct brook where all other trees have died out. The wood is fine-grained and hard, of a brown color. The leaves are small and pinnulate, and its blossoms are little tufts of yellow fiber-like hair; the seeds are in pods.

The largest acacias in Palestine are those growing near the fountains of Engedi, on the west shore of the Dead Sea; several of which are from six to eight feet in diameter. They are found growing all along the course of the Jordan south of the Sea of Galilee.

The gum-arabic of commerce and medicine is produced by this tree spontaneously and from incisions in the bark. The Arabs use it for food in time of scarcity. Camels eat its thorny foliage. Its use by the fraternity is well known, and refers to it as an evergreen, and therefore a very appropriate emblem of life beyond the grave.

Acacia Tree.

Sprig of Acacia.

ZION BRIDGE.—NO. 52.

This bridge crossed the Tyropœon Valley, connecting Mount Zion with Mount Moriah. There is but little remaining of this ancient structure except on the Moriah side, where it united with the Temple wall; here a portion of one of the arches still remains. This is doubtless the bridge mentioned by Josephus, the construction of which is ascribed to Solomon.

THE ANCIENT CASTLE OF DAVID.

The large space just inside of the Jaffa Gate, to the south, where are seen the numbers 3, 5, 44, 48, and 51, is the area once occupied by the ancient Castle of David, Fort and Castle of Zion, and other works of defence. But little now remains to be seen of them except the Tower of David, No. 3, and the Citadel, No. 5.

THE CITADEL, or Castle of David (No. 5), near the Jaffa gate, is remarkable for its great strength and venerable antiquity. The lower part of it is built of massive stones, from nine to thirteen feet in length, and from three to four feet thick. Their Jewish origin is indicated by the deep bevel round the edges. The height of the tower above the present level of the fosse is forty feet. It is built solid, and recent excavations show that for a considerable height above the foundation it is formed of the natural rock, hewn into shape and faced with stones. This is one of the towers saved by Titus as a memorial of the almost impregnable strength of the city he had captured.

No. 20.—The Stairs of David are a flight of steps cut in the native rock near the Siloam pool. (See Nehemiah xii. 37.)

THE JAFFA GATE.—(ANCIENT JOPPA GATE.)

This is the entrance to the city from the east. From this gate roads lead to Bethlehem, Hebron, Gaza, and Jaffa. A little to the right of this gate, on the outside, are heaps of ancient ruins; but what buildings once stood here none can now tell.

THE DAMASCUS GATE.

The entrance to the city from the north is through this gate. From this gate roads lead to Mt. Tabor, the Sea of Galilee, Damascus, and Palmyra, in the interior; and Tyre and Sidon on the coast.

ST. STEPHEN GATE.

This gate is on the east side of the city, a short distance north of the Temple area. From this gate roads lead to Bethany, Bethphage, Jericho, Gilgal, and the River Jordan.

THE LEPERS' HUTS.

Lepers are seen around Jerusalem now as in the ancient time. They are mostly found at the Zion

The Castle of David.

David Mosk, and Tomb.

Gate, where they have their huts or dwellings. These miserable creatures intermarry and have children, thus transmitting and perpetuating their loathsome and mysterious disease.

WATER SUPPLY.

Since the chief supply used in the Temple area is now derived from SOLOMON'S POOLS, as it was in his day and doubtless has been ever since, with very few intermissions, as at sieges, etc., it will be interesting to give a short account of these pools. They are situated at Etham, eight miles from the city, south-west of Bethlehem.

The SEALED FOUNTAIN (mentioned in Canticles iv. 12) is a few rods above the pools, and is 30 feet under ground, in a rock-hewn room, containing a fine copious fountain, and an entrance room arched over and roughly walled—the work of Solomon. This is the main source of supply for the pools.

The water first flows into the upper pool (380 by 236 feet, and 25 feet deep); and then from that 160 feet to the second (423 by 250 feet, and 39 deep); and then 248 feet farther to the third (582 by 207 feet, and 50 deep), and from the last pool the water is conveyed by an aqueduct to Jerusalem.

All of these pools are built of large hewed stones, and are well lined with cement, with a rocky bottom in terraces. Broad flights of steps lead down into them. There are rooms under the lower pool, at its lower end, having walls and arches similar to those at the Sealed Fountain. These arches are in a good state of preservation, key-stones and all, and are good evidences of the antiquity of the whole.

The aqueduct is made of cylinders of red pottery from 12 to 15 inches long by 8 to 10 inches in diameter, cemented and covered with earth over two feet. There are several places provided with stone open mouths, where the water can be dipped out. The valley of Hinnom is passed above the pool of Gihon on 10 arches (which are now almost covered with rubbish), and winding around Zion reaches the great pool at Jerusalem. (See Engv*) The water-supply of the city is not very abundant nor of a very good quality, but anciently, before Hezekiah stopped the great fountains in Gihon, and when even the present sources were better cared for, there must have been plenty of good water. Nearly every house has now one or more cisterns for holding rain or spring water.

THE POOL OF SILOAM.

This is one of the most noted fountains about Jerusalem. The Saviour, having anointed the eyes of the blind man with a mixture of dust and spittle, said: "Go wash in the pool of Siloam," and he went and washed, "and came seeing." Above this pool is the *fountain of Siloam* or *Virgin fountain*, from which the water flows to the pool of Siloam through a subterranean passage 1,750 feet in length, *chiselled by the hand of man through the solid rock of Ophel!* At the upper end of this pool is an old arched stairway, now tumbling into ruins, by which a descent

* Engraving in first part of the Book.

can be made to the mouth of the subterranean passage through which the water enters. Six ancient pillars of Jerusalem marble are embedded in a portion of the eastern wall of the pool, which, in connection with others that have now disappeared, once supported a roof over the pool.

THE UPPER POOL OF GIHON.

This pool is in the centre of the basin which constitutes the head of the valley of Hinnom, and is about 127 rods from the Jaffa Gate. It is 315 feet long, 208 feet wide, and 20 feet deep. This pool supplies the Hezekiah pool, just inside of the Jaffa Gate.

THE LOWER POOL OF GIHON

Is in the valley, nearly opposite the southwest angle of the city, and about 23 rods below the Jaffa Gate. It is 600 feet long, 260 feet broad, and 40 feet deep. These two pools are capable of holding water for many thousands of people. There are several notices of them in the Bible. The Prophet Isaiah was commanded by God to go forth and meet Ahaz "at the end of the conduit of the upper pool in the highway in the Fullers' Field."

At the same place Rabshakeh stood when he delivered the royal message of his imperious master, the king of Assyria, to the messengers of Hezekiah. (See Isa. vii. 36 and 37.)

EN ROGEL.

This is a large well, south of the Pool of Siloam, at the junction of the two valleys, Jehoshaphat and Hinnom. It is 125 feet deep, and strongly walled with large stones. This wall terminates in an arch at the top, the whole bearing evidence of great antiquity. This well is still a place of great resort, as the water is better than most of the water about the city. A large flat stone with a circular hole in the centre constitutes the mouth of the well. The water is still drawn, as in ancient times, in leathern buckets and earthen jars attached to ropes; deep creases are worn into the edge of the aperture through the cap-stone, where these ropes have for many centuries been drawn up.

THE VIRGIN FOUNTAIN.

This fountain is a large, deep, artificial cavity in the hill-side, cut entirely in the solid rock. It is reached by a broad stone stairway of 26 steps. The water is about 25 feet below the entrance on the hill-side, and some 10 or 15 feet below the bottom of the valley. The water is contained in a basin 15 feet long by from 5 to 6 broad, and 7 feet deep. The usual depth of the water is about 3 feet, the bottom of the basin being covered with pebbles, an accumulation of dirt, and rubbish. It is said by some to get the name, "Fountain of the Virgin," from the fact that these waters were considered a grand test for women accused of incontinence. If innocent, they drank it without injury; if guilty, they immediately fell down dead! When the Virgin Mary was accused she submitted to the ordeal, and thus established her innocence.

NO. 4.—THE HEZEKIAH POOL

Is in the city, near the Jaffa Gate, and is 240 feet long by 144 feet wide. Its bottom is formed of the natural rock, levelled and cemented. This pool supplies several large baths with water.

Near the Cotton Bazar is the WELL OF HEALING, 85 feet deep, through rock. There are several chambers and passages connected with this well, whose uses are unknown.

The POOL OF BETHESDA (Moat of Antonia) is 365 feet long, 131 wide, with a branch at the south-west corner 142 feet long and 45 wide. The north half of it is walled over by foundations for houses, and built upon. The MEKHEMEH POOL is under ground near the Wailing Place, and is 84 feet by 42, built against the Temple area wall, arched over but not now used. The BATH OF BATHSHEBA was near the Jaffa Gate, north, is 120 feet long by 50 wide, and 20 deep;—now filled up with rubbish. HELENA'S CISTERN, near the Coptic Convent, is 60 feet long by 30 wide. and is supplied with good water the year round.

CHAPTER IV.

PLACES OF INTEREST NEAR THE CITY.

The Valley of Jehoshaphat—of Hinnom—Aceldama —Mount of Offence—Ancient Sepulchres—Scopas, Ridge—Mount of Olives—The Road over which Christ rode into Jerusalem.

THE VALLEY OF JEHOSHAPHAT.

From the head of this valley, on the north of the city, to St. Stephen Gate, its fall is about one hundred feet, and its width at this point is nearly four hundred feet. Across the valley, a little below this, is the Garden of Gethsemane. A little lower down the valley begins to deepen rapidly, the hills rising in steep precipices on both sides. Passing the Fountain of Siloam the valley again widens; and here are found pleasant gardens and cultivated terraces. A short distance from, and in strange contrast to, these are "Tophet and Black Gehenna, called the Type of Hell." Jehoshaphat might properly be called the Valley of Sepulchres. On its west side, just under the wall of the Temple area, the Mohammedans have a cemetery, where thousands of their singular-looking tombs may be seen. On the opposite side of the valley is the Jewish cemetery, the great silent city of their dead. Here generation after generation, since the days of David and Solomon, have been gathered unto their fathers. For thousands of years the Jewish dead have been interred here; the dust of the children mingling with the ashes of their forefathers, until a large portion of the east bank of the valley and far up the side of the Mount of Olives is covered with the tombs of the countless descendants of Abraham,—the dying Jew still craving it as one of the greatest privileges to be interred here. For here they believe the coming Messiah will stand in the resurrection. In the bottom of this valley is the bed of the Brook Kedron, which is now dry for a considerable distance below the city, except in the rainy season.

NO. 64.—VILLAGE OF SILOAM.

The modern village of Siloam is nearly opposite the Fountain of the Virgin, on the eastern bank of the Valley of Jehoshaphat. The steep declivity on which it stands is covered with ancient tombs.

It is a wretched place, containing about seventy dwellings, formed by dispossessing the dead of their tombs, walling up the fronts, and transforming them into abodes for the living. Their interiors present a gloomy and filthy appearance; human bones still remaining in many of them. The appearance of the inhabitants is in keeping with their miserable dwellings; and their reputation for rudeness and lawless-

Ancient Tombs and Vaults.

Door of a Tomb.

ness is such that the prudent traveler gives the place a wide birth after nightfall.

ANCIENT TOMBS.

Just above this village in the side of the hill are many tombs and vaults.

Among them are those of Zacheas, Absalom, and the cave of St. James.

The tomb of Zacheas is cut in the rock, and there was in front of it four Doric columns supporting a cornice and a pyramidal roof (18 feet high over all). The cave of St. James is ornamented with a portico in front, having four columns cut from the native rock. Tradition says that James, the brother of Jesus, retired to this cave after the Crucifixion.

The tomb of Absalom is the most noted of these valley tombs, and is also cut from the solid rock. The dome on the roof is peculiar, terminating in a foliated tuft. The Mohammedans have idealized this into a monument of the hateful ingratitude of Absalom, whose example is held up as a fearful warning to all disobedient sons; therefore every passer-by is supposed to cast a stone at it with appropriate maledictions.

The whole vicinity is occupied by graves which are covered with flat stones inscribed in Hebrew or Arabic.

THE VALLEY OF HINNOM.

Opposite Jaffa Gate this valley is about one hundred yards wide, and forty-four feet deep. From this point its course is first south, then east around

Zion, past the south end of the city to its junction with the valley of Jehoshaphat. Above the lower pool of Gihon it falls gradually, but at a short distance below this pool it commences to deepen rapidly, and continues to fall until it reaches En Rogel. A short distance above this it is a deep, gloomy dell. In many places the bottom of this valley is covered with loose stones, yet it is cultivated, and portions of it abound with olive-trees. Along the south side of the valley is a steep, rocky ledge, nearly the whole surface of which is covered and penetrated by tombs. These tombs are of many shapes and different sizes, some small and plainly constructed, while others are very large, and penetrate far into the hillside. In the upper part of the valley there is a large rock, a part of which has been leveled and made as smooth as a house-floor. This was an ancient threshing-floor, such as Araunah the Jebusite had on Mount Moriah.

ACELDAMA.—THE FIELD OF BLOOD.

This place is just across the valley of Hinnom, near its junction with Jehoshaphat. It is a rocky cliff, full of tombs; portions of the front of Aceldama have been walled up, and behind this are deep excavations and gloomy sepulchral passages. In some places large quantities of human bones and skulls are seen scattered about in promiscuous confusion. This is the field which was purchased with the thirty pieces of silver received by Judas for the betrayal of Christ.

"Then Judas, which had betrayed him, when he saw that he was condemned, repented himself, and brought again the thirty pieces of silver to the chief priests and elders, saying, I have sinned, in that I have betrayed the innocent blood. And they said, What is that to us? See thou to that. And he cast down the pieces of silver in the temple, and went and hanged himself. And the chief priests took the silver pieces, and said, It is not lawful for to put them into the treasury, because it is the price of blood. And they took counsel, and bought with them the potter's field, to bury strangers in" (St. Matthew xxvii.).

MOUNT OF OFFENCE.

This mount or hill is across the valley of Jehoshaphat to the eastward of the pool of Siloam. "He built an high place to Chemosh, the abomination of Moab, in the hill that is before Jerusalem, and for Moloch, the abomination of the children of Ammon, and likewise did he for all his strange wives, which burned incense and sacrificed unto their gods" (1 Kings ii.). A short distance below this, in the valley, was Tophet. Under the apostate kings of Judah this portion of the valley became the seat of the most horrible idolatrous services. Here "Moloch, horrid king, besmeared with the blood of human sacrifices and parents' tears," had his groves and altars.

SCOPAS.

At a short distance north of the city is the high ridge of Scopas. As there are none of the ravines on this side which form the natural defences of the other sides of the city, this side was usually the point from which it was attacked by its enemies. The camp of Titus was on this ridge, and from this point he commenced the siege which ended in such destruction and ruin to the city.

THE MOUNT OF OLIVES—CALLED BY THE ARABS JEBEL ET TUR.

This mount lies east of the city, and is separated from it by the valley of Jehoshaphat. Its height above the valley varies from 500 to 680 feet. It is 250 feet above the Temple area on Mount Moriah, so that it commands a fine view of many points of interest; first, Jehoshaphat, Gethsemane, and the Kidron; then, beyond these, the ancient walls, domes, and minarets of the city. Far away to the south, from among a group of smaller hills, rises Bethhacerem, where Herod had his paradise, and where his bones are supposed to be interred. To the eastward is the hill country of Judea, with the wilderness, gloomy and sterile; a rough mountainous region, whose deep yawning chasms form secure hiding-places for Bedouin robbers and beasts of prey. Olivet was once very fertile, and was covered with beautiful gardens and olive orchards; but, with the exception of small portions of the eastern side, the soil has long since been exhausted, so that only a few olive and fig trees are to be seen, and no signs of cultivation except an occasional patch of barley inclosed by a tottering stone wall.

THE ROAD OVER WHICH CHRIST RODE INTO JERUSALEM.

On the Engv. will be seen the road to Bethany, winding around the southern base of the Mount of Olives. It was over this road that Christ rode into

Jerusalem. "And it came to pass that when he was come nigh to Bethphage and Bethany,* at the mount called the Mount of Olives, he sent two of his disciples, saying, Go ye into the village over against you, in the which at your entering ye shall find a colt tied, whereon yet never man sat; loose him, and bring him hither. And they brought him to Jesus, and they cast their garments upon the colt, and they set Jesus thereon, and as he went they spread their clothes in the way" (St. Luke xix. 29, 30, 35, 36).

* These villages are on the eastern side of the Mount of Olives.

CHAPTER V.

CONCERNING THE TEMPLE OF KING SOLOMON.

Mount Moriah—The Temple Area, or Enclosure—Wilson's Arch—Robinson's Arch—Masonic Hall—Foundation Walls of the Temple—South, West, and East Gates—Dome of the Rock—Mosque El Aksa—The great Subterranean Quarry.

MOUNT MORIAH.

THIS spur or plateau is between the valley of Jehoshaphat on the east, and the Tyropœon valley on the west, and is just within the walls of the city on the east. Its hight at the Dome of the Rock above the valley of Jehoshaphat is 140 feet, and above the Mediterranean, 2,436. By reference to No. 58 on the engv, an idea of its original appearance may be formed.

To the Christian world this is a spot of great interest, for here once stood the magnificent Temple of King Solomon, which was dedicated to the worship of the Most High, and was the favored house of God. In it was the Holy of Holies, and it was the repository of the Ark of the Covenant.

To Masons this is also a place of great importance and interest, as the Temple was erected by the ancient craftsmen, of whom King Solomon and the two Hirams were the first Grand Masters.

The foundation of King Solomon's Temple was laid 1012 B.C. (A. M. 2992), in the month of May (Zif).

The history of this great edifice introduces the three worthies, Solomon, King of Israel, Hiram, King of Tyre, and Hiram the builder (Abif), *who formed a society for mutual assistance in counsel, skill, and wisdom*, that they might the better contrive and execute the designs for the various grand structures proposed by Solomon, including of necessity the management of the large number of mechanics, artisans, overseers, and laborers required to carry on all those enterprises. The peculiar wisdom of these measures will be seen when it is stated that Solomon, at the time of his coronation as king, was but 19 years old.

The writings of Josephus confirm the Scripture account of the friendly relations between Solomon and Hiram, King of Tyre, and also between David and Hiram. They exchanged presents, and, according to oriental custom, propounded problems and difficult questions one to the other (see 2 Chron. ix.). The correspondence between the two kings on the building of the Temple was preserved among the Tyrian archives in the days of Josephus (Ant. viii. 2, 8), who gives copies of the letters. Eupolemon also mentions the letters and gives copies of those between Solomon and Hiram, also between Solomon and Apries (see Eusebius, Prae. Evang., ix. 30).

SUCCOTH.

The long peace between the two nations, the Jews and the Phœnicians, which was never really broken by either side, can be safely referred to the influence of the *secret and mysterious tie* which bound the principal persons of both people into a common brotherhood.

Moses was initiated into the mysteries of the Sacred Order of Priests in Egypt before he was permitted to marry a daughter of a priest. He afterwards transmitted those mysteries to the Jewish people. *Joshua continued them;* and Solomon, associated with the two Hirams, *adapted the whole system to the laws and customs of the people of Palestine.*

Phœnician historians give an account of a marriage between Solomon and a daughter of Hiram, King of Tyre. (See Tatian. Græc. § 37.)

Jewish writers pass lightly over the fact that Hiram the King was not circumcised, and have a tradition that because he was a God-fearing man, and assisted in building the Temple, he was translated alive into Paradise.

Of Hiram Abif it is recorded that he was of a mixed race, Jewish and Phœnician, of the tribe of Naphtali. His father was a Tyrian, skilled in the arts of working metals, wood, and cloth, for ornamentation in architecture, also articles for public and private luxury and display, from whom he inherited his eminent abilities, and learned the details of his calling. He was appointed the chief architect and engineer by Hiram, King of Tyre, and sent to Jerusalem to assist Solomon. His title of Abif (our father) was given as a recognition of his dignity and acquirements, and his exalted and useful position, which he adorned by faithful and excellent service. The title was given after an ancient oriental custom —many instances of its observance being familiar to readers of history, as that of Joseph in Egypt, who says, "God hath made me a *father* unto Pharaoh" (Gen. xlv. 8); and also in Maccabees (1 xi. 32), the term is used as a mark of respect and esteem, and nearly all Roman coins have among other titles that of "father," as given to the emperor.

We have preserved but few details of the life of Hiram, King of Tyre. That he was master and overseer of his people who were in the service of Solomon is recorded, and he was long remembered as such.

A complete description of the Temple of Solomon is given in Kings, Chronicles, Ezekiel, and Jeremiah. The two pillars, JACHIN and BOAZ, are minutely described in Kings and Jeremiah; Ezekiel also mentions two pillars—one on each side of the entrance.

Josephus writes about the great stones and of the foundation wall with understanding, because he saw them (as well as Herod's Temple, which was an enlargement of Zerubbabel's), and within a few years past the Palestine Exploration Society has verified many of his accounts.

The great stones which were sawed with saws (1 Kings 17; vii. 9) lie just where they were placed by the builders, still bearing their craft-marks or directions for placing them. The lower courses were protected from wear and the action of the elements by the dirt, mingled with stones, chips, etc., which was piled against them, and has never been disturbed until recently. The soil above this layer was full of pottery, glass, etc., the usual evidences of occupation and use. Some of these stones are 6 feet or more thick, and 15 to 30 long. Their peculiar faces are shown on the plan—No. 58.

TEMPLE AREA OR ENCLOSURE, MARKED A A A A ON THE PLAN.

The Temple area is 1,500 feet long, by an average width of 950; not regular, but as shown on the plan. The walls enclosing it are from 8 to 10 feet thick at the base, and 3 to 4 at the top, and 50 to 75 high above the present surface outside; and 10 or 12 feet above the floor. The ground is highest at the N.W. corner, and slopes south and east.

The original hill (see No. 58) was very uneven and sloping, nowhere having a level place large enough for the proposed temple; it was therefore necessary to build up a large platform, which was done by piers or columns arched over and filled in at the top with stone and earth. (Ant., XV., xi. 3.)

These substructures are still in their original position, and are very minutely described by Dr. Barclay (City of the Great King), who measured them carefully when employed as an assistant to the Chief Engineer of Repairs by the Pasha of Jerusalem. The extent from east to west is 319 feet (marked VAULTS on the engv); and from north to south from 247 to 186 feet. The piers vary in size from 3 to 8 feet square, and in hight from 30 down to 2 or 3 feet, as the rock slopes. The Triple Gate (51 feet wide and 25 feet high) once opened into these galleries which

Piers and Vaults.—Foundations of the Temple.

are called Solomon's stables; there are three passages leading from them up to the area above, one of which is 247 feet long, the others shorter. It is supposed that this is the passage for the animals for the sacrifices, because the ascent is gradual all the way.

There is a small doorway with a pointed arch 105 feet from the S.E. corner of the south wall, which was the stable-door leading into the splendid colonnade. These stables are mentioned by El. Alemi, in 1495.

THE ANCIENT GATES OF THE TEMPLE ENCLOSURE.

No. 6.—The ancient South Gate, now Double Gate, alluded to by Josephus (Ant., XV. xi. 5), has all the marks of Jewish architecture, with an addition of Roman work outside. Originally the doors were 18 feet wide and 20 high. In the inside there is an entrance hall 50 feet long and 40 wide, having in the centre a column 21 feet high and 6 feet in diameter, of a single block of limestone. Its capital is ornamented with large leaves, finely sculptured in stone, but not in any architectural order; and resting on this capital are the springs of four arches, which support four domes forming the ceiling of the room. It has been Romanized by four white marble columns which adorn the doorway. The sides of the hall are built of huge blocks of limestone, cut with the peculiar Jewish panel; the term bevelling is applied to the Jewish rebatement, which is a channel cut a half-inch, less or more, deep all around the edge of a block on the same level plane as the face, and never slanted or bevelled.

From this entrance hall a flight of nine stone-steps (in the midst of which stands a stone pillar oval, 6 feet high by 4 feet in diameter) leads up to a passage 259 feet long, which is divided by piers, pillars, and a wall; is vaulted over each half the entire length and bears every mark of Jewish make. Another flight of stone steps leads to the area above. This is the ancient South Gate of the Temple.

No. 7.—On the west side of the Temple area is an ancient doorway walled up, built against by modern houses and nearly all hidden; only half of the lintel being in view. It was 40 feet wide and 40 deep. The lintel is 6 feet 9 inches thick. A flight of steps inside formed an approach to the area above, as at Huldah Gate. On the inside may be seen a closed gateway, so covered up with modern rooms as to be almost hidden. Some of the stones are very large—15 to 25 feet long and 8 or 9 feet deep. This was the West Gate of the Temple.

No. 12.—The ancient entrance to the Temple Enclosure on the east is now walled up and kept closed by the Mohammedans, because of a superstitious fear that the Christians will enter by this gate and drive them out. The length is 70 feet and breadth 55, and it projects 6 feet beyond the wall; two columns divide it into a double arcade lighted at the west end by two domes. The columns are formed out of single blocks of marble, and the walls are eleven feet thick. The style is ancient, and its interior is ornamented with rich and elaborate carvings in the Grecian style. The effect of the whole is grand and imposing. A grand stairway of massive stone blocks leads from the gate up to the platform, which is 25 feet above.

This was the East Gate, called by the Crusaders the Golden Gate (Porta Aurea). Josephus is silent about gates on the north, but the Jewish Mid-

Interior view of South Gate.

Interior view of East Gate.

doth (Book of Measures) says the north wall was nearer to the Temple and had but one gate, called TEDI. The same authority says it was a small gate and for a special purpose.

There is a flight of stone steps in front of the Golden Gate, now buried under rubbish and soil, the deposit of centuries since the Crusades. The writers of that age speak of many steps "that lead down to the valley." The whole of the space outside of the wall in the Valley of Jehoshaphat, and especially on the east of the Temple site, is used as a cemetery, and every available foot of soil has been occupied over and over many times, and always guarded with superstitious fidelity against all "infidel" intrusion. It is therefore only possible to examine the locality by underground passages. A Mohammedan, in A.D. 1150, describes the chief buildings very much as they are now; and also that the Door of Mercy (Golden Gate) was closed, but passage was had through the small one, El Asbat (the tribes), a bow-shot from which was a large and beautiful church, dedicated to St. Mary and called Gethsemane.

NO. 1, TEMPLE AREA.
THE DOME OF THE ROCK—MOSQUE OF OMAR.

This splendid edifice stands nearly in the centre of the Temple area (see engv*) It is eight-sided and 170 feet in diameter, and about the same height, covered outside with beautifully colored porcelain tiles; the roof and dome are covered with copper; is very symmetrical and graceful, and is tipped with

* Engraving.

a lofty bronzed crescent. The lower part of the octagonal sides is covered with marble of various colors and patterns. On entering, the visitor is at once impressed with its exquisite proportions, the simplicity of the design, and admirable finish.

The 16 stained glass windows of the circular upper building are peculiar in richness, harmony of color, and elegance of design. The lower octagon has 56 windows, over each one of which are sculptured sentences from the Koran in letters which are measured by feet in height. There is a harmony of color everywhere,—in the windows of stained glass, the colored marble pillars and walls, porphyry columns, gilded capitals, and rosettes of the ceiling; the rich canopy of crimson and green silk over the rock in the centre, on every side masses, and groups, and points of blue, red, purple, yellow, gold, and crimson, intensified by the rays of the sun, or mellowed by the gloom, which carries the beholder in imagination back to the days of the Magnificent Caliphs, whose works have been the wonder and delight of ages, both in romance and reality. The central dome is 66 feet in diameter. Occupying the centre of this rotunda is the

SACRED ROCK.

This rock is about 60 feet long from north to south, and about 50 broad; it rises several feet above the floor of the Mosque, and is surrounded by a gilded iron fence, seven feet high and very strongly built, while over it is stretched a rich awning of particolored silk. What sacred and interesting associations cluster around this spot! for the Rabbins say that this is the identical rock on which Jacob pillowed his head during that eventful dream; on which Abraham offered Isaac, and where David saw the Angel, and where Jesus was laid after the crucifixion;—the rock that afterwards became the altar of burnt-offering for the great Temple of Solomon. It is hollowed into a handsome chamber, fifteen feet square by eight feet high, called the Noble Cave. An ornamented floor (tessellated) covers a passage into some unknown excavations below, but the superstitious fears of the Moslems prevents any examination, for they say that here is the well of souls, the real opening into Hades! The most ancient account of this structure is that it was built by Constantine the Great and his mother Helena. A pilgrim of the 12th century copies some inscriptions written by the Christians on the places where there are now Arabic sentences from the Koran, which were doubtless placed over the first by Saladin. The building stands on an artificial platform about 15 feet high, which is reached by eight gateways (with stone steps) in elegant Saracen style. The Mohammedan believes that in this dome, next to Mecca, prayers are most acceptable to Deity above all other places in the world.

NO. 2.—THE MOSQUE EL AKSA.

This Mosque stands near the south-west corner of the Temple area (see engv), and is a showy and elegant building, 280 feet long and 183 broad, with a dome nearly as large and high as the Dome of the

Rock. It was originally in the form of a cross, but from additions by the Crusaders it is now a parallelogram. It has been altered and remodelled so many times that it cannot now be said to belong to any particular style of architecture, unless it is the *Composite.*

Some interesting coincidences in the style, &c., to the Temple of Solomon, are found in an Egyptian Temple at Edfoo, in Egypt. There is a porch with an entrance between two pillars, leading to a court which is surrounded with pillars; and winding stairs (by square, not spiral, steps), leading to a middle chamber, from which the sanctuary was reached, and only by the initiated (see 1 Kings vi. 8). Near the Mosque El Aksa is the Mogrebins Mosque—No. 3.

Under the southwest corner of the Temple area, beneath a part of the Aksa Mosque, there are immense cisterns, one of which is, no doubt, the sea mentioned by the son of Sirach, and the Commissioner of Ptolemy. This body of water is 736 feet in circumference, and 42 feet deep.—No. 4.

The roof is supported by rude stone pillars, which were once cased with metal, but are now bare or plastered. Its capacity is about two million gallons. Eight openings for drawing up water were formerly in use, but now only one is open. It may be entered from above by a flight of 44 wide stone steps, cut in the rock. The aqueduct from Solomon's pool ended in this great subterranean reservoir.

Ancient Artificial Cave under the Temple Area—Noble Cave.

King Solomon's Cisterns.

WILSON'S ARCH.

THIS arch was discovered in 1866 by Capt. Wilson, R.E., when making explorations in the city for a better water supply. From the discovery of this arch originated the idea of a scientific exploration in and about the Temple area, which was developed in the Palestine Exploration Fund and Society, whose explorations have been carried on under the direction of Capt. Warren, R.E., who has discovered the foundation walls of the Temple enclosure in many places, together with arches, vaults, and secret passages connected therewith, outside and inside of the Temple area..

Wilson's Arch is just outside of the gate of the chain under the street called David, and 15 feet below the present surface of the ground. This arch has a span of 42 feet, and is 43 feet wide. Portions of it are in ruins, and the walls are much decayed. At 3½ feet below the springing of the arch, a bed of hard concrete is found formed of small cubical stones set in a dark cement. At 24 feet, voussoirs and drafted stones of a fallen arch, and well are found, the stones being similar to those in the Sanctuary Wall.* At 40 feet water is found, which appears to run in at the northern end of the shaft, and run out at the southern end. At 51 feet 9 inches, the bottom course of the foundation wall of the Temple enclosure is seen resting in a groove which was cut in the rock † for the better security of the wall.

* Wall of the Temple Enclosure.

† Nearly the whole surface of Moriah is a limestone rock.

The whole of the wall exposed here is evidently in its original position, and consists of 21 courses of drafted stones, averaging from 3 feet 8 inches to 4 feet in hight, the wall now being 75 feet above the rock. The corbels on the haunches of the north side of the arch appear to have supported a balcony—the continuation of a secret passage, which entered the Sanctuary Wall just south of Wilson's Arch. When this wall was first built, it was exposed to view from its foundation upwards. It is one of the oldest portions of the enclosure of the Sanctuary now remaining, and is held in great veneration by the Jews, as they claim this to be *the* Wall of the Sanctuary. Connected with Wilson's Arch there has recently been discovered by Capt. Warren a large number of vaults, arches, and secret passages leading in various directions, but, with the exception of Wilson's Arch, probably none of them have ever been exposed to view, as they were undoubtedly used as secret stores for provisions and water in the time of sieges.

MASONIC HALL.

In one of the passages from Wilson's Arch leading west is an opening which leads down into an ancient vault or chamber, which from tradition has acquired the name of Masonic Hall. The entrance opens down to it from the north, and the passage is steep and shelving, and at first the explorer could only gain access by being lowered into it by means of a rope, but the aperture has been enlarged so that a ladder is now used. This chamber is 30 feet 8 inches in length by 23 feet in width, rectangular and vaulted;

Interior view of Wilson's Arch.

the walls are built of square stones, well jointed, and laid without cement. There were pilasters at each corner, but only the one at the north-east angle remains in a moderate state of preservation (see cut). Nearly in the centre of the chamber is a part of a column or pedestal sticking up. At the south-east angle was a double entrance with lintels over it: these have ornaments on them and on the jambs, but they cannot now be accurately traced. This Hall has every appearance of being one of the most ancient pieces of masonry in Jerusalem. Through a small hole in the south wall of this chamber, a passage is found leading into one of the Saracenic vaults supporting the Hall of Justice. There is still another passage leading from this vault south into another which is now filled with debris and earth. A short distance from Masonic Hall is a secret passage leading under David Street; this passage is about 12 feet wide and is nearly filled with rubbish; it has been traced 250 feet in the direction of the Joppa Gate, which was doubtless its ancient termination.

Fragment of Pilaster in Masonic hall.

ROBINSON'S ARCH.

This arch is outside of the south-west corner of the Sanctuary Wall, opposite the Mogrebin's Mosque (see Temple Area), and is considered to have been the entrance to the royal cloisters of King Herod. Seventy-four feet below the springing of this arch is a rock-cut canal, 4 feet wide, and 12 feet deep, running south. Jammed in over this canal are two fallen voussoirs of an arch. One of these is much decayed, but the other is in a better state of preservation, and measures 7 feet in length, 5 feet thick at the extrados, 4 feet 4 inches at the intrados, and 4 feet high. In the middle of one side is a square joggle hole 14 inches by 11 and 4½ inches deep. Opening out of this canal to the south, is a chamber cut in rock with a segment arch. To the south a passage leads into a circular cistern cut in the rock, 16 feet in diameter, by 14 feet 4 inches in hight. In the centre of the roof is a manhole leading down from the roof of the pavement under Robinson's Arch. Near this are two curious rock-cut chambers, rectangular, and measuring 16 feet by 6 feet. In one of them is a flight of steps leading up above. Also, a base of a column which had fallen in through the roof. Several lamps, weights, jars, and an iron bar were found in this canal; also an ancient stone roller for rolling flat roofs on houses, precisely like the rollers now used for the same purpose.

Several excavations have been made in the vicinity of Robinson's Arch, in making one of which at a depth of 21 feet 6 inches a polished limestone slab 6 feet square was found covering the main sewer of the city. This sewer is 6 feet high by 3 feet wide, cut in the rock, nearly full of sewage, through which a current of water runs south. This is doubtless the sewer through which the fellahin entered the city in the time of Ibrahim Pacha, who appear to have penetrated up as far as David Street and found exit through some of the vaults there. In sinking a shaft near this the remains of a colonnade were found just below the surface, consisting of piers built on the rock 12 feet 6 inches apart, with fallen arches between. These piers were built of well-dressed ashlar of soft sand-stone, similar to the ruins of Suwaineh in the Jordan Valley.

In sinking another shaft the dèbris of a stone building, and part of a white marble column twelve inches in diameter, were found. Twenty-two feet below this is a chamber cut in the rock, ten feet square, and ten feet high, covered with plaster two inches thick and very hard. Entrance to this chamber was effected through two manholes through the roof, and it has the appearance of having been used as a secret store for grain.

Twenty feet to the south of the Gate of the Bath is a large cistern which runs east and west and pierces the Sanctuary Wall. Near the Effendi's house is another cistern or rather prolongation of the first, but narrower. At this place it is thirty-four feet six inches from the surface of the ground to the bottom, width twelve feet, and length from east to west fourteen feet nine inches. A surface of twenty eight feet in hight by twelve in length of the Sanctuary Wall is exposed at this place.

From an excavation made near the Sanctuary Wall on the east side of the Temple enclosure, a small passage was found which leads downwards, passing through the roof of, and into another passage, which runs east and west. This latter passage is three feet nine inches high by two feet wide, running nearly horizontal, and at its eastern end opens through the Wall of the Sanctuary, and is closed by a large stone having three cylindrical holes through it five and one-half inches in diameter each, through which water at some former period ran. It is probable that troops defending this part of the wall came down here for water.

THE TOWER OF ANTONIA.

This tower is at the north-east angle of the Temple enclosure, and is built up from the Sanctuary Wall, and is formed by the portion forming the wall continuing to recede from four to seven inches, while that forming the tower recedes only one and one-quarter inches, so that at twenty-two feet from where the tower begins the slant inwards is two feet, and at the surface, forty feet above, the slant amounts to seven feet.

DISCOVERY AT ST. STEPHEN'S GATE.

An excavation was made outside of this gate. When at a depth of six feet a flat stone was found which, sounding hollow, an aperture was made through it, when a circular cave was exposed to view which

Robinson's Arch.

was found to be nine feet in diameter and four feet high; it is divided into five loculi by plaster partitions about three inches thick and twelve inches high, and had been used as a tomb.

A shaft leads down from this into another chamber twenty-six feet long by six feet wide, which is divided latitudinally into ten loculi. Another passage leads into two other and similar chambers also divided into loculi. A shaft forty feet deep leads from this down into another range of these singular chambers, nine in number, one of which has the appearance of having been used as an ante-room, the rest were divided into loculi. These chambers were cut in a very soft kind of melekeh and are nearly on a plan with the Phœnician tombs at Saida, as they are systematically arranged tier upon tier with shafts leading down through them. In making these excavations ancient pottery and glass vases were found at various depths.

RUINS AT DAMASCUS GATE.

One of the most interesting relics of antiquity is found in an ancient tower at the Damascus gate. This structure is very massive, and bears the peculiar Jewish marks similar to the Temple area walls. The lower courses of the city wall, for some distance on each side of the gate, bear the same character of large blocks, beveled edge, with the whole surface hewn smooth, exhibiting an earlier and more careful style than most other walls here. In the tower on the east side of the gate there is a flight of winding stairs of square steps, with square turnings--not spiral—measuring 7 feet long by 3 wide. This was the kind of stairway leading to the middle chamber in the Temple porch (1 Kings vi. 8).

WAILING PLACE OF THE JEWS.—No. 60.

A short distance below David Street, in the foundation-wall of the Temple enclosure, are several courses of large stones, bearing the Jewish bevel, and other marks of great antiquity. They were doubtless placed here by Solomon's builders when the foundation of the Temple was laid.

These are the Stones of Wailing, and this is the nearest that the Jews are now permitted to come to their ancient place of worship and sacrifice. This place is resorted to at all times by the devout, but Friday afternoon is the set time for Jews to meet here to mourn and weep for their departed power, the glory of their ancient city, and the hallowed and glorious associations of the Temple. And thus they may be seen. Old men with white flowing beards, young men in the vigor of manhood, aged women, and rosy-cheeked girls ; some sitting, some standing, some leaning their heads affectionately against these ancient time-worn stones, frequently giving vent to their grief in loud weeping and wailing.

Second only in interest to the Temple Area are the ruins of the Hospital of St. John of Jerusalem. This building was erected by the Knight Templars, (Hospitallers) of Jerusalem, in the time of the Crusades, and its magnificence may be gathered from accounts of it by ancient writers, and from ruins of it still standing, with remains of quaint carvings, and traces of colors. The style seems to have been that of an

Oriental *Khan*, being a vast quadrangular structure around an interior court, the chambers opening on the galleries. There are marks found on the walls, and many curious ornaments sculptured in the cornice.

The Great Hospital of St. John is described as standing A.D. 1322, by Sir John Mandeville, as a palace supported and ornamented by 178 stone pillars. The order of Knights Templar was gathered from the nobles of all Europe, and was at first charitable for the relief of pilgrims, but afterwards became religious and military. They were recognized as an order as late as 1800, at which time Malta was restored to them by England and France, when Paul, the Emperor of Russia, was the Grand Master. But England now holds the island, and the knights have lost all dominion and power.

The gateway of the ruined hospital in Jerusalem is still standing, though very ruinous. It presents a flattened pointed arch, which is succeeded by a round arch behind, ornamented with rich historical and emblematical carvings in stone. Among many finely designed and chiselled figures may be seen the LAMB, which was the peculiar emblem of the order. There are broken stairs, a court surrounded by a cloister in ruins, with the remains of several rooms, also the remains of the chapel, large, and ornamented with a window, with stained or painted glass. This monastery was founded in honor of St. John the Baptist (Saewolf, A.D. 1102).

These mouldering ruins are memorials of the noble order of Knights, whose strong arms were for ages the bulwark against the aggressive Moslems, and whose deeds have made the names of Acre, Rhodes, and Malta, stir the heart of many readers of ancient history.

Every remnant of this remarkable edifice also indicates the handiwork of the same craftsmen who erected the Temple of Solomon, as its emblems, signs, and inscriptions are closely analogous to those found on the ruins about the Temple Area, other ruins in Palestine, and in the Cathedrals of Europe, especially, in the ancient Cathedral in Glasgow, where may be seen characters nearly identical with those found on the Sanctuary Walls at Jerusalem.

CHAPTER VI.

THE PRIVATE MARKS OF THE BUILDERS AND THE GREAT SUBTERRANEAN QUARRY.

Marks found on Stones in the Foundation Walls of the Temple Area.—Marks found in Samaria and in Hebron.—The Great Subterranean Quarry.

It is a matter of the highest interest, while carrying on antiquarian researches, to discover the evidences which preceded us in our particular calling.

Although Free Masonry is now speculative, still there was a time when the Master Mason was the real. director of the construction of Beautiful Edifices, of which the Magnificent Temple of Solomon, and latterly the wonderful Cathedrals dotted all over Europe, are specimens; the evidences of which work in the written record has long been familiar on the page of history, but the symbolic private marks of the builders, used by the master workman, for the guidance of the craft in laying the stones in their places, have escaped their proper notice. Many of these marks have been found on stones, in the foundation walls of the Temple enclosure, at Jerusalem. They are also found in other parts of Palestine, and in every country where the Craft have since left evidences of their skill and industry. These marks have been found on a large number of stones, in different courses in the Sanctuary Wall, and having been covered with earth, were protected from the action of the elements, and the busy hands of men.

The few of which sketches are given, give a complete idea of the whole, as they are almost repetitions of similar characters, found wherever edifices and other works have been constructed by the Craft, and were doubtless put on by the Master workmen to indicate the position of the stones in the walls or structures where found. These marks have been found on the east of Jordan, on the stones of Palmyra, Bozrah, and other cities that were built since the time of Solomon, and, wherever the characters are found, they are of the same style and color, being made with red paint. The base of this paint is red chalk, which is a natural production and nearly indestructible by time or the action of the elements. It is found on the Egyptian monuments, where it has stood fresh and bright for 35 centuries.

Several of the groups of these characters were recently discovered by Captain Warren, R. E., while carrying on explorations around the south-east corner of the Sanctuary Wall (wall of the Temple enclosure). A shaft was sunk at about twenty feet south-east of this corner of the wall, and at a depth of fifty-three feet a gallery was excavated westward, which reached the Wall about six feet north of the corner; from this point galleries and shafts were excavated which uncovered the wall at several places, and here were found most of the following groups of these marks:—

Group No. 1 was found cut in on stones in the third and fifth courses.

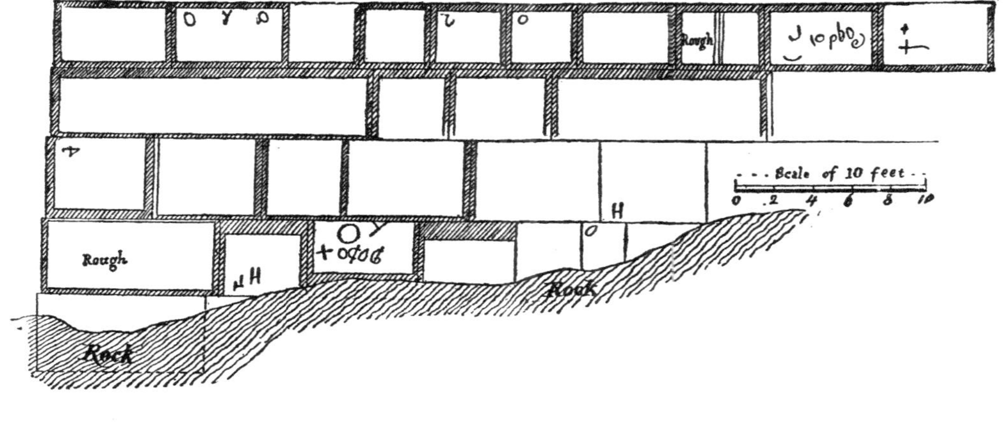

A section of the wall on which marks were found.

No. 2 was found on the second stone from the corner in the second course—made with red paint.

No. 3 was on the wall a short distance from Group No. 2.

No. 4 was on the corner-stone in the third course —red paint.

No. 5. This Group was found in that part of the gallery where the explorer is seen examining the marks on the wall. These marks resemble the letters **O Y Q**—red paint.

No. 6 was on the third stone north in the second course—red paint.

No. 7 was on the sixth stone in the third course, and on a stone in the tenth course a small cross was found cut in.

No. 8. This group was found on stones in the west wall of the Sanctuary, near the Jews' wailing-place; and at the base of the Tower of Antonia, north-east angle of the wall, was found another group of marks in red paint.

No. 9. Found in a cave near the Cœnaculum.

No. 10 is a group of marks gathered from the ancient structures of Kuryet el Enab, and also known as Abu Gosh village, the Emmaus of the time of Christ, and the more ancient Kirjath Jearim of Solomon's age. Here are several very neatly made and familiar figures, not unlike some in use at this day. They were very clearly drawn, in red color, as nearly all of such marks are, in every country where the craft have had use for them.

The group No. 11, from Samaria, claims equal attention for their peculiar design and evident antiquity. The structures at Samaria date from the time of Shemer, who was nearly contemporary with Solomon, and in style, design, and finish, as far as the remains have been examined, they carry the evidence of originality with them, and the work of the builders of the age of the three grand masters.

No. 12 is on a stone at Beeroth, and looks familiar with its letters so like our **K** and **R**, with a cross and arrow, and at first glance suggests some of the monograms of Constantine, or Charlemagne, but a closer inspection determines them to be separate and distinct signs, not connected, as if for a name.

No. 13. This cross was found on a stone among the rubbish at the foot of the wall near the Damascus Gate.

Nos. 14, 15, and 16 were discovered by A. L. Rawson, who, disguised as a Mohammedan student of law, (Katib or Scribe) visited the ancient mosque at Hebron, and made sketches of the interior of the tombs, also the inscriptions, marks, and devices, which were *cut* in the wall in the different parts of this building. There seems to have been originally a small structure, over and around which several additions have been made from age to age, until it has grown into a colossal mass of buildings, and finally thrown off its character as a church and became a mosque with lofty minarets at the corners.

The walls are very ancient and portions of them are like the Sanctuary Wall at Jerusalem, and walls at other places, where the distinctive mark is the Phœnician or Hebrew bevel—this is found on all the old parts of the wall.

Explorer examining the marks on the wall.

Beneath this structure is a chamber, having for its roof a part of the floor of the mosque; and in a recess not now in use were found the three groups of marks.

No. 17. This group was found on the walls of the ancient Cathedral at Glasgow. These later groups all being very similar to those found on the Sanctuary wall, tell the same story of the work of the ancient builders.

At first glance several of the characters seen in the different groups of marks appear very much like the letters **H M C R D K O W** and others, but an examination of the Phœnician and Hebrew alphabets will show that these forms are only accidentally similar. The other marks are well known to the Craft, and need no explanation here.

Besides the ancient marks there are characters written on the walls which were repaired or built by the fraternity during the crusades. These are distinctly Roman letters and numerals, with a very small proportion of signs, which are repetitions of those used by the ancient builders, and evidently used for the same purpose. That purpose, it is quite certain, was, besides the proper placing of the stones in the walls, the designation of that part of the work which was done by any particular company or lodge. Some used the five-pointed star, others a circle divided into four or six parts. A circle with a **T** occurs very often on different parts of the works, and indicates either a large lodge, or a very industrious one. The antiquity of these marks may be the more certainly determined from the fact that there are no distinctive Christian emblems nor Mohammedan signs among them, only one, the cross of the Knights Templar, being subject to a date more recent than the age of Christ, except those mentioned as being on parts that had been repaired or rebuilt.

The chief interest in these antiquities centres in the fact that they are evidences that a certain order of men worked together for a certain purpose, in those early times, and have left behind them, without design, these signs of their occupation and method of working.

That they had a uniform system of marks and signs appears from the similarity of these characters wherever found, both in Palestine and Europe, where there are ancient monuments or cathedrals erected by those skilled workmen.

An idea of the great extent of the *systematic* work done in Jerusalem alone, can be formed from a summary of the recent explorations and discoveries there.

The substructions of Solomon's Temple have been almost entirely examined, and those columns are found to be built of carefully cut stones, with the characteristic rebate or bevel at the corners, forming panels every few feet. These columns support arches turned in the most skilful manner, and as solid as when built.

A large part of the massive ancient walls of the city, has been traced out, and these, with the ruins of aqueducts, vaults, and chambers are nearly always of the beveled style or Phœnician—which was the style of the Masonic craftsmen.

PRIVATE MARKS OF THE BUILDERS.

THE GREAT SUBTERRANEAN QUARRY.—NO. 63.

It is only a few years since that Dr. Barclay, an American physician and missionary, resident of Jerusalem, discovered the entrance to the ancient subterranean quarry, from which the great stones were taken for the foundation walls of the Temple built by Solomon. Certain passages in Kings and Chronicles were somewhat obscure until light was thrown upon them by an examination of the place where the workmen "sawed with saws, stones," "great stones," and carefully chipped off the rough corners, and finished the "costly stones" for those magnificent edifices which were the admiration of the age in which they were built, and the wonder of all succeeding ages.

The quantity of stone required for these structures was truly immense; that of the Temple foundations alone requiring more than one million square yards of stone, which are now in position in the walls and may be examined. This quarry is underground, and under that part of the city just north and west of the Temple Area, now called Bezetha, and occupied by the Mohammedans.

The entrance is a few rods east of the Damascus Gate, outside of the city wall. The largest room in the cave is 750 feet long, about 100 wide, and 30 feet high. Large pillars of the rock were left at intervals for the support of the ponderous ceiling. Several smaller rooms open from the larger one; in all of them are found marks of the workmen's tools. The stone is a soft limestone nearly as white and soft as chalk, and may be sawed into blocks now as it was in Solomon's time. The harder variety is a buff color, streaked with orange, and takes a fine polish. The white stone grows harder by exposure to air and water. There are many little shelves cut in the walls, on which the lamps were set, and the smoke from the burning lamps can still be traced on the white walls almost as black and sooty as though the quarrymen had left them last week instead of ages ago. Water trickles down from the roof of the cave in many places from leaky reservoirs or drains above, and has thus formed stalactites, and the drippings from these have made their opposites from below, rising from the floor in some places several feet in a great variety of forms. In the most southern cave there is a spring of water, but in consequence of the limestone formation of the locality it is not sweet. There is no doubt but that the builders had an opening in the south end of the quarry through which the stone for the Temple were easily slid down to the Temple site, for the whole of the quarry is higher than the Temple area. This

ANCIENT LAMP.

opening has not yet been found, but doubtless will be as soon as the Mohammedans will permit a search to be made.

Josephus says that the Jews hid away from Titus in a cave, and there is room enough in this quarry for the population of the city to have gathered without crowding. The floor is very uneven, with a general descent south, and there are precipices formed by the workmen taking out large blocks below the level of the floor in different places.*

The ground is everywhere littered with chippings and blocks of stone, large and small.

There are great blocks of stone, partly quarried, still hanging to the native mass. One of these was a stone about 10 feet high and between 3 and 4 feet square. The workmen had commenced by cutting a crease upon two sides about four inches wide, and had proceeded until it was about two feet deep on each side of the block. This must have been done with a long pointed instrument having a chisel-shaped end. They had no gunpowder in those days, and seem not to have understood how to split them with wedges, but literally chiselled them out by persevering labor. The work of cutting out this block was nearly completed, for the two grooves, one from the front and the other from the side, at right angles with each other, had

* A few years since a human skeleton was found at the bottom of one of these precipices, showing that some unknown explorer had stumbled over there, and thus perished in a place which thousands of years before was thronged with the busy workmen of Solomon.

been carried nearly to the necessary depth to allow the upright mass to be pried from its bed. The marks of the tool are as perfect as if made yesterday; but the workmen left this, with much more unfinished work, and never returned. Who can tell why? Was it in consequence of an attack on the city from an invading army? or was it found just at this particular time that no more stone were needed?

In proof of this being the quarry from which the stone for the Temple were procured, we have the following facts:—First, the stone is the same in every respect as that of portions of the old wall still remaining; second, the immense piles of chippings found in this quarry show that the stone were not only quarried, but dressed and finished here,—corresponding with the account, that they were brought to the Temple ready to be laid without the aid of hammer or graving tool; *third, the extreme age of this quarry, which dates back in legends and traditions to the time of Jeremiah;* lastly, there are no other great quarries near the city, from which this kind of stone could have been taken. So then this is the place where nearly three thousand years ago the craftsmen of Solomon prepared the stone for the magnificent Temple of God. It is now a solemn and gloomy cavern; large numbers of bats hang to the ceiling, and, aroused by the approach of the explorer, flit about his head. Occasionally a pile of bones brought in by jackals arrest his attention, and the giving away of the earth under his feet indicates the places where they burrowed. Darkness impenetrable and silence profound pervade the place. The grandeur of its lofty

ANCIENT QUARRY UNDER JERUSALEM, IN WHICH THE STONES FOR SOLOMON'S TEMPLE WERE QUARRIED.

ceilings, its vast extent, its legends and associations, all combine to inspire the explorer with feelings of astonishment and awe. The Crusaders have left many marks on the walls, showing that this quarry was known in their day, also proving the antiquity of several of the signs now in use by the craft.*

To all who hold the common faith in the God of Abraham, the historical evidence derived from this quarry, and all the surrounding facts in proof of the truth of Scripture history is beyond price, and must be convincing to all reflecting minds. And to masons who believe in the antiquity of the origin of the order this must be a source of great satisfaction, as this evidence, in connection with recent discoveries made about the temple area, including the private marks of the builders, leaves but little room to doubt that the order originated at the building of Solomon's Temple.

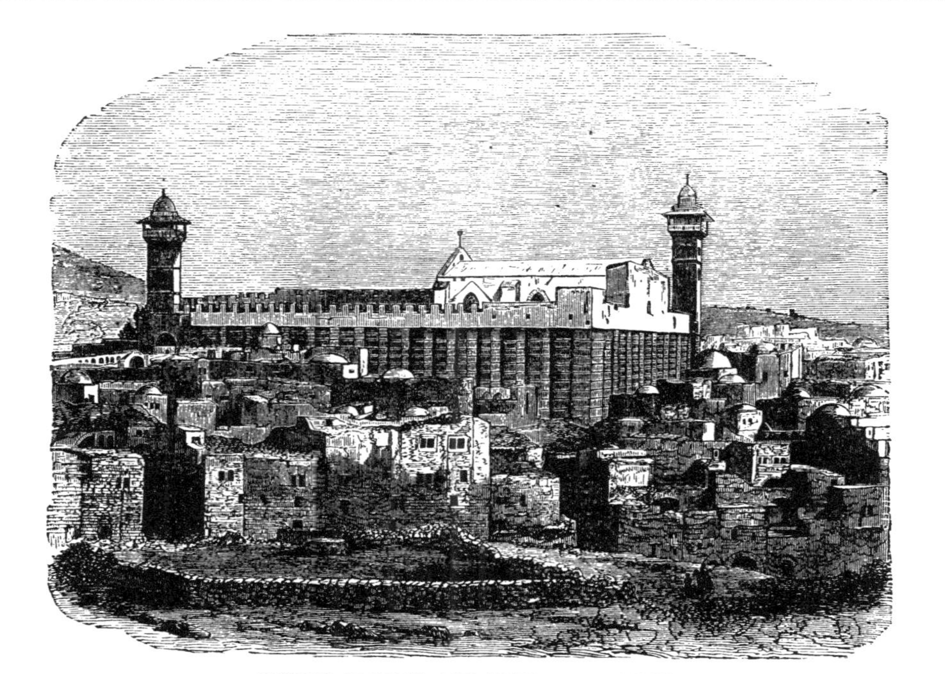

HEBRON—MOSQUE, AND TOMB OF ABRAHAM.

CHAPTER VII.

PLACES HISTORICALLY CONNECTED WITH KING SOLOMON'S TEMPLE, AND THE BUILDERS.

Ancient Tyre, Hiram's Tomb—Joppa—Mt. Lebanon—Pass of the Jordan—Hebron, its important Relics of Antiquity; its singular Mosque, and Fanatical Inhabitants—The ruins of Beeroth—Kirjath-Jearim—Samaria, Church of St. John—King Solomon's Store Cities, Baalbek—Tadmor, and Hamath.

TYRE

Is situated on a rocky peninsula which was an island until 350 B.C., when the city was besieged by Alexander the Great, who, after repeated failures to take it, built a causeway out to it from the mainland and thus reached the defences, and took the city.

The accumulation of sand around and over this causeway soon rendered it terra firma, thus forming the peninsula.

At the time of Solomon and the Hirams, Tyre was one of the richest cities in the world, its people being among the most skilful manufacturers and builders of that period, manufacturing many articles of luxury and use, and having for customers many nations and peoples.

Syria was thy merchant by reason of the multitude of the wares of thy making: they occupied in thy fairs with emeralds, purple, and broidered work, and fine linen, and coral, and agate.

Judah, and the land of Israel, they were thy merchants: they traded in thy market wheat of Minnith, and Pannag (Genseng), and honey, and oil, and balm.

Damascus was thy merchant in the multitude of the wares of thy making, for the multitude of all riches; in the wine of Helbon, and white wool. (Ezekiel, xxvii., 16, 17, 18.)

Among the principal articles of export were glass, sugar, and the famous Tyrian purple dye. This dye was extracted from a kind of shell-fish found on the coast. Sugar cane was cultivated to a considerable extent, and sugar made similar to that now made in the West Indies and other tropical regions.

Hiram, King of Tyre, sent cedar wood and workmen to build David a palace, (2. Sam. vii.), and he afterwards sent Hiram the widow's son, a Jew of the tribe of Naphtali, who cast the vessels of bronze for the Temple, King Hiram furnishing the metal, also the cedar and fir trees; and the Jews and Phœnicians worked together, the friendship between them continuing for over a century.

Afterwards, however, the Phœnicians sold Jewish children into captivity. (Joel iii. 6–8.)

Carthage was planted as a colony of Tyre 869 B.C.

There was a Temple at Tyre in honor of Hercules, in which he was worshiped as a god, under the name of Melkarth, and Arrian, the historian (B.C. 150), says that it was the most ancient Temple in the world.

Ashtoreth was also worshiped there, who is called Diana, and Queen of Heaven. Solomon built a shrine in honor of this goddess on the Mount of Olives, opposite Jerusalem, as a token of his friendship for Hiram of Tyre.

The most interesting relic of this ancient city now to be seen, is a large stone in the sea wall 17 feet long, 6½ feet high, and between 4 and 5 feet thick, lying in its original position, where it was placed 3,000 years ago. This stone has the rebate or bevel so noted in Phœnician and Jewish works. There are many columns and floors of marble buried under the rubbish all over the island and mainland city, and sunk in the sea along the shore for miles, and thousands of pieces of stone wrought into columns, capitals, and panels have been carried away to Joppa, Acre, Beirut and other cities, and built into modern houses or burnt into lime, and this work is still going on. Those that lie in the sea are fretted and perforated by ages of exposure to storms and tempests. Their number and style attest the grandeur of this once proud metropolis.

On the mainland there is a ruined Cathedral Church, which dates from the earliest ages, and has memories lingering around it of the pleasing old historian, William of Tyre, who was also a bishop of Tyre, and officiated within those walls.

It was one of the most beautiful churches which the Crusaders built in Palestine; its length was 205 feet, and nearly 140 wide, and has this peculiarity, that the transept projects 15 feet on each side. The other proportions and plans are similar to those of other churches at Samaria and Lydda. It has three naves and three apses, separated by a balustrade. This church was partly constructed from the spoils of ancient Temples. On the ground now lie prostrate magnificent columns carved in rose granite, monoliths which by their dimensions must have originally been parts of structures of the first order, and which were, undoubtedly the central pillars of the cathedral. The windows are curiously ornamented on the outside, having a scroll and fretwork, indented and rectangular.

The arch rests on an abacus with a very elaborate pattern.

The only part of this edifice now standing is the east end, the three apses enclosed in the wall of the modern city. The walls are built against by the mud-huts of the poor, like huge swallows' nests plastered into all the corners and transepts, and the ragged women and children fill the place with their noisy gabble, where had been heard in eloquent tones the voices of Paulinus its Bishop, and a brother of Eusebius, who wrote the consecration sermon, which we still have, and also wrote the early history of the church, and of William of Tyre, the bishop and historian, and greater than these, Origen, who may be said to have saved the Holy Scriptures from oblivion through his labors of a long lifetime, in collecting, translating, and arranging, from every country, the scattered fragments. This historic ruin now echoes to the gossip of poor Arabs who watched its slow decay ever since the last religious service was held in it—almost the last held by the Crusaders in Palestine.

At the time of Christ, Tyre contained a population of about 150,000 souls, but since it has been under Turkish rule (A.D. 1291), it has rapidly declined until it is now only a miserable Arab village of 3,000 inhabitants, many of the dwellings being constructed

Tyre as it now is

of stone, which had done service in the walls of splendid ancient public edifices and dwellings.

Throughout the old city heaps of débris and rubbish are found, in some of which piles of broken glass (doubtless the waste of the factories of ancient Tyre), and broken shells of the kind that furnished the famous purple dye,* have been discovered.

The traveler Sandys, writing in 1610, says of Tyre, "This once famous Tyre is now no other than an heap of ruins; yet have they a reverent respect; and do instruct the pensive beholder with their exemplary frailty."

In alluding to its fountains he says, "We passed certain cisterns some miles and better distant from the city; which are called Salmon's by the Christians of this country, I know not why, unless these are they which he mentions in the Canticles. Square they are and large; replenished with living water, which was in times past conveyed by aqueducts into the orchards."

The silence, desolation, and ruins of this once opulent city, all attest the complete fulfilment of the prophesies of its destruction.

"And they shall destroy the walls of Tyrus, and break down her towers: I will also scrape her dust from her, and make her like the top of a rock."

"It shall be a place for the spreading of nets in the midst of the sea: for I have spoken it, saith the Lord God: and it shall become a spoil to the nations."

* Robert Morris, in 1868, was so fortunate as to find a glass bottle among the rubbish, holding about three pints, and nearly perfect.

9

"And I will cause the noise of thy songs to cease; and the sound of thy harps shall be no more heard." (*Ezekiel*, xxvi. 4, 5, 13.)

HIRAM'S WELL.

There is a massive square structure over a fountain, which tradition claims is Hiram's well, where in the morning and evening may be seen long files of Arab women, with their ancient-looking water-jars, going and coming with the day's supply of the sweet water.

KING HIRAM.

Hiram, King of Tyre, was son of a former King of Tyre of the same name, and, like him, a friend of David. He congratulated Solomon at the commencement of his reign, and furnished essential aid in building the Temple. He provided timber and stones, together with gold, and received in return large supplies of corn, wine, and oil. And when the Temple and the King's palace were completed he was presented with twenty cities in the land of Cabul; but, not deeming them acceptable, he remonstrated with Solomon, saying, "What cities are these which thou hast given me, my brother?" (1 Kings ix. 13). He afterwards joined Solomon in his commercial enterprises (1 Kings ix. 26—28; x. 11—22). Josephus relates that he greatly improved his city and realm, and died, after a prosperous reign of thirty-four years, at the age of fifty-two.

HIRAM'S TOMB.

About six miles from the city of Tyre, among the

Hiram's Well.

hills which are dotted with many villages cosily bowered in groves of olive, orange, lemon, and pomegranate trees, there stands a grand and massive sarcophagus lifted high on a solid pedestal of limestone, with a deep arched well or large cistern near it. This sarcophagus is 12 ft. 11 in. long by 7 ft. 8 in. wide, and 3 ft. 6 in. high; the lid is roof-shaped and 3 ft. 6 in. high. The lid is apparently unfinished in the respect that there are none of the elevated corners so constant a feature in all other tombs in this vicinity, and as appears in the illustration; the shape of the stone favors the supposition that the corners may have been broken off. The base is formed of three tiers of stones each 13 feet long, by nearly 11 ft. wide.

The stones forming the third course project a little all around, and are 15 feet long, 10 wide, and 3 feet 4 inches thick. The next on which the coffin rests is 12 feet 3 inches long, and 8 feet thick.*

The view is from the west end, from which direction it is seen to the best advantage. There is no attempt at finish anywhere; the great blocks of stone were only squared and laid over one another, without any intentional architectural effect beyond the slightly decreasing size of the immense blocks. The capstone or lid is raised in the centre like a roof, in the manner of other lids of sarcophagi, which are found scattered about in many parts of Palestine.

The east end of this tomb has been broken open, but whether by robbers in search of plunder or by curiosity-seekers is not known. With the exception

* These dimensions were taken by Robert Morris in 1868, who made the most accurate measurement of them ever yet taken.

of the break this monument has not been injured, and only shows the touches of time during the many centuries it has been exposed to the severe winter storms of this coast.

The site was well selected for the sepulchre of the great Phœnician king, being high on the brow of a hill, or rather on the crest of a range of hills, where the eye may look over the plain to the sea and the city, which once boasted of its rule on that sea as a god.

The commanding location of this tomb, its massive proportions and neighboring ruins, are strongly corroborative of the tradition that this was the last resting place of King Solomon's friend. It is of great antiquity, and the surrounding ruins indicate that this was only the central body, around and over which was a structure adorned in a style befitting the purpose, the age, and the wealth of the nation, which boasted of its advanced position among the cultivated nations.

There are several other tombs scattered about in the fields in this vicinity, which are popularly said to have been those of various members of King Hiram's family.

These stone coffins are still quite numerous in this part of Palestine, although the Mohammedans have been breaking them up for building purposes, or burning them into lime for ages. Several hundred are still lying about the hill near Khan Khuldeh, twelve miles south of Beirut. Some of them are ornamented with carvings of flowers, wreaths of leaves, cherubs, Baal head figures of warriors, very well de-

signed, and nearly all have raised corners, somewhat like a horn.

But nowhere is there any instance of an inscription, mark, or character, except on the coffin of the King of Sidon, which was brought to light a few years since.

The whole vicinity of Hiram's tomb abounds in ruins of Phœnician character, the most important of which is a pavement in colored marble covering the whole inside area of a heathen temple, with figures of Greek and Phœnician deities, each with the name cut in ancient Greek or Phœnician letters on each side of the head and inside of a circle. There are altogether 40 gods and goddesses portrayed; besides on one side 48 circles containing fishes, animals, and fowls, and on the other 64 circles of the same character. Between the columns are animals chasing each other, such as leopards, lions, bears, chasing deer, boars, rabbits, etc. There is quite a natural history in this pavement. Some Greek words and names found here may help to fix the date of the structure, which has not yet been determined.

The number of important ruins in this part of Phœnicia is so great as to fill a large volume, with even a slight notice of each, proving that the Phœnicians were a highly-cultivated, skilful, and wealthy people, fond of the fine arts and full of public spirit. Their descendants who now occupy the country are simply barbarians in comparison, caring little for the arts, bent only on a fanatical display of veneration and devotion to God, and—his prophet Mohammed.

PASS OF THE JORDAN.

The difficulties in the way of determining the place where the army of Jephtha held the ford of the Jordan againt the Ephraimites, disappear on an examination of the topography of the country on each bank of the river.

Its tributaries on the east and west side, all run between ranges of rocky hills, the ravines all running south-east or south-west, towards the river. At the junction of the Wady Ferah with the Jordan, a sandbar has been formed,which constitutes this ford or pass.

The travel between two important cities—Shechem on the west side of the river, and Ramoth Gilead on the east, was over a main highway, which leads to the river at this ford. This is also the most reliable ford between the Sea of Galilee and the Dead Sea, especially after a rain, when the other fords are sure to be impassable, this one, from the great width of the river at this place, is practicable; this, with the historical and traditional evidence, leaves no room to doubt that this is the pass at which the guards were stationed to intercept the Ephraimites.

BATTLE WITH THE EPHRAIMITES.

And the men of Ephraim gathered themselves together, and went northward, and said unto Jephthah, Wherefore passedest thou over to fight against the children of Ammon, and didst not call us to go with thee? we will burn thine house upon thee with fire.

And Jephthah said unto them, I and my people were at great strife with the children of Ammon; and

Ancient Coffin.

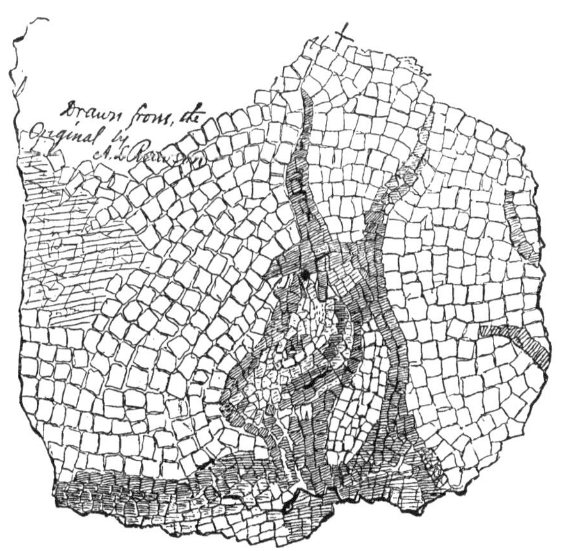

Pavement.

when I called you, ye delivered me not out of their hands.

And when I saw that ye delivered *me* not, I put my life in my hands, and passed over against the children of Ammon, and the Lord delivered them into my hand: wherefore then are ye come up unto me this day, to fight against me?

Then Jephthah gathered together all the men of Gilead, and fought with Ephraim: and the men of Gilead smote Ephraim, because they said, Ye Gileadites *are* fugitives of Ephraim among the Ephraimites, *and* among the Manassites.

And the Gileadites took the passages of Jordan before the Ephraimites: and it was *so*, that when those Ephraimites which were escaped said, Let me go over, that the men of Gilead said unto him, *Art* thou an Ephraimite? If he said, Nay;

Then said they unto him, Say now Shibboleth: and he said Sibboleth: for he could not frame to pronounce *it* right. Then they took him, and slew him at the passages of Jordan: and there fell at that time of the Ephraimites forty and two thousand.

And Jephthah judged Israel six years: Then died Jephthah the Gileadite, and was buried in *one of* the cities of Gilead. (Judges xii. 1 to 8.)

JEPHTHA'S DAUGHTER.

Then the Spirit of the Lord came upon Jephthah, and he passed over Gilead, and Manasseh, and passed over Mizpeh of Gilead, and from Mizpeh of Gilead he passed over *unto* the children of Ammon.

And Jephthah vowed a vow unto the Lord, and

said, If thou shalt without fail deliver the children of Ammon into mine hands,

Then it shall be, that whatsoever cometh forth of the doors of my house to meet me, when I return in peace from the children of Ammon, shall surely be the Lord's, and I will offer it up for a burnt offering.

So Jephthah passed over unto the children of Ammon to fight against them; and the Lord delivered them into his hands.

And he smote then from Aroer, even till thou come to Minnith, *even* twenty cities, and unto the plain of the vineyards, with a very great slaughter. Thus the children of Ammon were subdued before the children of Israel.

And Jephthah came to Mizpeh unto his house, and, behold his daughter came out to meet him with timbrels and with dances: and she *was his only* child; beside her he had neither son nor daughter.

And it came to pass, when he saw her, that he rent his clothes, and said, *Alas, my daughter!* thou has brought me very low, and thou art one of them that trouble me: for I have opened my mouth unto the Lord, and I cannot go back.

And she said unto him, My father, *if* thou hast opened thy mouth unto the Lord, do to me according to that which hath proceeded out of thy mouth; forasmuch as the Lord hath taken vengeance for thee of thine enemies, *even* of the children of Ammon.

And she said unto her father, Let this thing be done for me: let me alone two months, that I may go up and down upon the mountains, and bewail my virginity, I and my fellows.

Ephraim.

And he said, Go. And he sent her away *for* two months: and she went with her companions, and bewailed her virginity upon the mountains.

And it came to pass at the end of two months, that she returned unto her father, who did with her *according* to his vow which he had vowed: and she knew no man. And it was a custom in Israel,

That the daughters of Israel went yearly to lament the daughter of Jephthah the Gileadite four days in a year. (Judges xi. 29 to 40.)

MT. LEBANON, AND THE BAY FROM WHICH ITS CEDARS WERE FLOATED TO JOPPA FOR THE TEMPLE OF SOLOMON.

The mountain range known as Lebanon is in the northern part of Palestine, and runs parallel with the coast of the Mediterranean. Lebanon begins at the river Litany, two miles north of Tyre, and extends one hundred miles N. E., terminating at the river Nahr-el-Keber. Between the base of Lebanon and the sea is the long, narrow plain of Phenicia—the Phœnicia so famed in ancient history.

The region of the famous cedars of Lebanon is near the northern end of the range, and N. E. of the mouth of the river Nahr-el-Kelb (the ancient Lycus). From the small bay at the mouth of this river the cedar timber for Solomon's Temple was conveyed in floats to Joppa. By reference to the illustration, a correct idea of the situation of this historic locality may be had. In the foreground is the bay, and on the right are the points which jut out into it N. E. of

Beirut, whose every foot is cultivated or beautified with fruit or shade trees, with here and there a gray wall of some house—the residence of the wealthy merchants of Beirut. The mouth of the Nahr-el-Kelb is discovered just beyond the rocky promontory across the bay. On the promontory are inscriptions and sculptures engraved by the conquerors of Syria, from Egypt, Assyria, and Macedonia. Above, far away in the distant sky, the peaks of Lebanon are seen whitened with eternal snows.

The last relics of the primeval cedar forests are found on the highest ridges of the range, 6,300 feet above the level of the sea; and one group of cedars is close under the highest dome of the mountains, which is called Thor-el-Chodib, and is 10,200 feet high. There are only a few of the original patriarchs left in the midst of about 400 smaller trees. The largest measure 48, 40, 33½, and 20 feet in circumference.

There is another grove near Ain-Zehateh, on the road from Beirut to Damascus; and Professor Ehrenburg found the cedar growing quite abundantly on those parts of the mountain north of the road from Baalbek.

Hundreds of villages are scattered along the sides of Lebanon, some of them built amid labyrinths of rocks—and on the sides of steep cliffs. Every available spot is cultivated, producing figs, grapes, and olives in abundance.

The ruins of ancient temples have been discovered in various parts of Lebanon; some of them high up the mountain, where it must have been very difficult to build—all exhibiting a style of architecture similar

MT. LEBANON, AND BAY FROM WHICH THE CEDARS WERE FLOATED TO JOPPA.

to the remarkable structures of Baalbek. The ruins of one of these temples are visible from Beirut. It was built of immense hewn stone without cement, and with large columns in front. It is now little more than a heap of ruins.

Burkhardt found the ruins of four other similar temples on different parts of the mountain.

JOPPA

is on the coast, and 35 miles N.W. of Jerusalem. In the distribution of the land by Joshua it was given to Dan, and has been known to history ever since.* The city is situated on a promontory which rises to the hight of 150 feet, is crowned with a fortress, and presents views of historic interest in every direction. Towards the north Sharon and Carmel are seen. To the south the plains of Philistia. To the east the hills of Ephraim and Judea raise their towering heads, and to the west is extended the Mediterranean. The city is walled around on the south and east towards the land, and partially so on the north side, towards the sea. The site is very steep, so that, viewed from several points, the buildings have the appearance of standing on one another. The present population of the city is 15,000. With the exception of Cæsarea this was the only harbor possessed by the ancient Jews, and was then, as it is now, the seaport of Jerusalem. The harbor is formed by a low ledge of

* About 1443 B.C.

rocks which extend from the promontory into the sea, and is shoal and insecure.

The cedar timber from Lebanon and materials from Tyre for Solomon's Temple were landed here, and with the insecurity of the harbor, and the hight of the cliffs where they were landed, the undertaking must have been both hazardous and laborious.

HEBRON.

ITS SINGULAR MOSQUE — AND IMPORTANT RELICS OF ANTIQUITY—ITS FANATICAL PEOPLE.

Hebron is 16 miles S.S.E. of Jerusalem, and is beautifully situated among the mountains, in a valley running from north to south. Hebron is one of the very oldest cities in the world still existing—being a well-known town when Abraham entered Canaan, 3783 years ago. Its original name was Kirjath Arba, and was sometimes called Mamre. This city was the favorite residence of Abraham, Isaac, and Jacob, and the scene of some of the most striking events in their lives. Upon the death of his wife, Sarah, Abraham bought from Ephron the Hittite the field and cave of Machpelah, to serve as a family tomb.

Hebron was taken by Joshua from the Canaanites, and was afterwards assigned to the Levites and made a city of refuge. Here David dwelt during the seven and a half years of his reign over Judah. It was also here that Absalom raised the standard of revolt against his father.

A short time before the capture of Jerusalem, this

Joppa.

city was burned by an officer of Vespasian; and about the beginning of the 12th century it was taken by the crusaders. In 1187 it reverted to the Moslems, and has since remained in their hands.

At present Hebron is an unwalled city, containing nine mosks and two synagogues. The streets are narrow, and the houses are built of stone with flat roofs, surmounted by domes. The manufactories of glass are in the narrow, dark lanes near the north part of the city. The principal articles made are lamps, and rings of colored glass, the latter worn by women on their arms and fingers as ornaments. Large crates of these articles may be seen standing in the streets ready to be loaded on camels for transportation to Egypt and various parts of Palestine.

The environs of the city are very fertile, furnishing the finest vineyards in Palestine; also numerous plantations of olive-trees, and excellent pasturage.

The population is now about 5,000, and the inhabitants are the wildest, most lawless, and desperate people in the Holy Land; and it is a singular fact that they now sustain the same mutinous character as did the rebels of ancient times, who armed with David against Saul, and united with Absalom against David.

Among the remains of antiquity are those of two stone reservoirs; the largest being 133 feet square and 21 feet deep. They are still in daily use, and one of them tradition says was the "pool in Hebron" above which David hung the assassins of Ishbosheth. But by far the most ancient relic here is the cave of Machpelah—Abraham's family tomb, and the burial-place of the Patriarchs. It bears evidence of great antiquity; and both tradition and the best authorities concur in locating the cave of Machpelah here. It is covered by a Mosk—a large and singular structure, with lofty minarets at the corners. The exterior building is large and lofty, and is in the form of a parallelogram 200 feet in length by 115 feet in width. The walls are built of very large stones, beveled and finished similar in all respects to the most ancient parts of the temple enclosure at Jerusalem; indicating the high antiquity of the structure, and that it was built by the *same people, and the same class of builders* as the temple of Solomon.

No Christian is allowed to enter this building; but at the left of the principal entrance of the Haram is a small hole in the massive wall through which the Jews are permitted at certain times to look into the interior, and here they may be seen wailing and reading prayers.

The Mohammedans of Hebron are very bigoted, and jealous of strangers, especially Jews. A few years since a couple of travelers—a Jew and a Christian—stopped for a moment to look up at the marble stairs leading to the tomb of Abraham, when immediately a crowd came out of the bazars, and with threats and fierce gesticulations drove them away.

Another very interesting relic is found up the valley, about a mile from the town. It is an immense oak tree, one of the largest in Palestine, as its branches extend over a space of nearly a hundred feet in diameter. This is believed by some to be the veritable oak under which Abraham pitched his tent—it still bears his name.

PALMYRA.

ANCIENT TADMOR.

This city was founded by king Solomon about 995 B.C., and is 245 miles N.E. of Jerusalem, in lat. 34°18′, and 38°13′ E. lon. from Greenwich. It is situated on the borders of the Arabian desert, in the midst of a dreary wilderness, remote from human habitation. Tadmor was about 10 miles in circumference, and the ruins show that it once contained some of the most splendid edifices of antiquity.

To facilitate trade and commerce, king Solomon built store cities along the great trade routes through his dominions, in which provisions and other supplies for caravans and travelers were collected. Tadmor was one of those store cities.

"And Solomon went to Hamath Zobah, and prevailed against it.

"And he built Tadmor in the wilderness, and all the store cities, which he built in Hamath."—(2 Chron. viii.)

Its original name was preserved till the time of Alexander, who extended his conquest to this city, and changed its name to Palmyra.

In A.D. 211, it become a Roman colony under Caracalla. Subsequently, in the reign of Gallienus, the Roman Senate invested Oleanthus—a senator of Palmyra—with the regal dignity, on account of his services in defeating Sapor, king of Persia. On the assassination of Oleanthus, his celebrated wife, Zenobia, conceived the design of erecting Palmyra into an independent monarchy; and in the prosecution of this object, she for a while successfully resisted the Roman armies, but was at length defeated and taken captive by the Emperor Aurelian (A.D. 273), who left a Roman garrison in Palmyra. This garrison was massacred in a revolt, and Aurelian punished the city by the execution not only of those who were taken in arms, but likewise common peasants, old men, women, and children. From this blow the city never recovered.

The present appearance of Palmyra is indeed most striking. An awful stillness pervades the ruins; they stand as lonely and silent as when the last Palmyrenes left their city forever. The long lines of Corinthian columns, seen at a distance, are peculiarly imposing, and seem like sentinels guarding the tomb of the dead city.

The principal ruins are: the great Temple, the Temple of the Sun, the great Colonnade, supposed to have consisted of 1500 columns, and the Necropolis.

In the space around the ruins, sometimes a palace is found, of which nothing remains but the court and walls; sometimes a temple whose peristyle is half thrown down; then a portico, a gallery, and a triumphal arch. Lying around in every direction are vast stones, half buried, with broken entablatures, mutilated friezes, disfigured reliefs, violated tombs, and altars defiled by dust. The grand old ruins of the ancient city contrast strangely with the Tadmor of the present day—mud huts inhabited by Arabs.

The Necropolis of Palmyra lies a short distance N. W. of the Temple of the Sun, in the side of a rav-

RUINS OF PALMYRA—ANCIENT TADMOR.

ine. The tombs are very numerous and of singular form, being towers of from two to five stories high. One, the tomb of Jamblichus, built in A. D. 3, is still recognizable, but very much dilapidated, its stairs crumbled away, and the top story gone. An inscription in honor of the deceased is engraved on a tablet over the door-way. The tomb of Manaius is one of the most curious structures found here. It is a lofty tower, fifteen feet square, the principal apartment of which is ornamented with four Corinthian pilasters, one on each side, with recesses between them for mummies. Each recess is divided into five tiers by shelves, only one of which remains in position.

There was formerly a large number of mummies in these sepulchres, but the Arabs have carried them away and destroyed them in hopes of discovering treasure.

Some of the sculptures, now remaining in their original position in the palaces and tombs in Palmyra, are models of decorative art. These works indicate a period of high art culture, when architecture, sculpture, and painting were employed to a great extent in public buildings, for both ornamentation and religious purposes. The solidity of the walls, and the excellence of the workmanship, of columns, cornices, and sculptures, and the completeness of the designs of the several structures, are marks of great wealth and fine taste.

BAALBEK.

THE GRANDEUR AND BEAUTY OF ITS RUINS—KING SOLOMON'S SEAL.

Baalbek is 195 miles N. N. E. of Jerusalem, on the slopes of Anti-Lebanon, at the opening of a small valley into the plain El Buka.

In extent Baalbek was inferior to many Eastern cities; but in the size and magnificence of its public edifices, and the immense size of many of the stones with which they were built, this ancient city was without a rival.

The grand ruins of Baalbek stand at the western extremity of the town, and just within the modern wall. There are three orders of architecture, evidently belonging to as many distinct eras. First, the stupendous walls and platforms, built of hewn stones of enormous size, and traversed by vaulted passages in several directions; secondly, two very large temples, of a later date, surmounting the platforms; thirdly, the modern or Saracenic walls and towers, incorporated with the original structures when the place was converted into a fortress. The modern additions are oddly built up of cornices, architraves, and pillars, and incongruously contrast with the venerable relics which they encumber and obscure.

The site of the ruins is nearly a dead level, on which has been reared a platform 1000 feet long, 600 broad, and varying from 15 to 30 feet in hight. This platform is composed of huge cut stones, three of which are so large that it seems incredible that they could have been quarried, and brought from the quarry—a mile distant—and placed in position (25 feet above the foundation) by any human agency. One of these stones measures 64 ft. 8 inches in length, 19 feet in width, and 14 feet thick; the others do not vary much from it in size. In the quarry is another of these great stones finished, ready to be moved, which is 69 feet long, 17 wide, 14 thick, and estimated to weigh 1135 tons. Many other stones in the platform are from 25 to 30 feet long, or nearly half the size of the above. These stones are cut with the beveled edge exactly like the stones in the foundation walls of the Temple enclosure at Jerusalem, from which it would appear that both structures were the work of the same people, and the same class of builders. Among the cities mentioned in the 8th chapter of Chronicles, as being built by King Solomon, is Baalath, in Lebanon. The similarity of names and situation very clearly identifies it with Baalbek. Josephus also mentions Baalath as one of the places of pleasure built by Solomon in Syria, on account of its temperate climate and water, and the delicacy of its fruits.

The Arabs of the present day believe that the founder of Baalbek was a great magician, and reared these huge structures by the power of cabalistic words, and that if the famous Seal of Solomon could be found, the same power could now be used.

The principal ruins of Baalbek are the great Temple, and the Temple of the Sun. The main walls of the temples and the enclosures correspond to the four cardinal points of the compass. The main entrance fronts the east, and was formerly approached by a grand staircase, leading to a portico flanked by handsome pavilions on the right and left.

To the westward of this is a hexagonal court 180 feet in diameter, strewn with columns, mutilated capitals, and the remains of pilasters, entablatures, and cornices; around it is a row of ruined edifices which fifty years ago displayed all the ornaments of the richest architecture—but they are now very much weather-worn and broken. Further to the west is a quadrangular court 350 feet wide by 336 in length. At one end of this court are six enormous and majestic columns—the glory of Baalbek, and nearly all that is left of the temple dedicated to the "Great God of Heliopolis" (Baal). They are the principal objects in every view of the ruins. The shafts of these columns are 21 feet 8 inches in circumference, and 50 feet high, which with base and entablature gives the hight from the ground to the top of the pediment, 120 feet. The length of this edifice was 292 feet by 160 in width. In 1751 there were nine of the columns standing; but three have since fallen.

In the modern wall are found several bases, and other fragments of the fallen columns.

Flanking the court of the great temple are the ruins of several smaller structures, forming a sort of gallery with chambers, several of which are traced in each of the principal wings. These chambers were decorated with most beautifully sculptured niches and pediments, friezes, and cornices. The beauty of some of the friezes is beyond all praise. A bold cor-

THE GREAT TEMPLE AT BAALBEK.

TEMPLE OF THE SUN, AT BAALBER.

nice all along the wall gives a fine effect to the whole by forming alternately a semicircle and pointed pediment over each recess. Fragments of the columns that formed the front of these chambers are of beautiful granite.

Various are the conjectures as to the use of these apartments: Were they chapels or shrines for the worship of subordinate deities?—or recesses for the philosophers to sit and lecture in?—or was the great court a forum, and these places intended for the convenience of merchants or civil functionaries?

The Temple of the Sun stands south of the great temple, and the platform on which it stands adjoins the great one, but is considerably lower. The Temple of the Sun is one of the most perfect monuments of its kind in Baalbek, if not in the whole world. Its dimensions are 192 feet in length by 96 in width. It was formerly surrounded by a peristyle of Corinthian columns, the shafts alone of which were 45 feet high and 5 feet in diameter. They each consisted of three pieces of stone so admirably fitted together that not space enough can be found between them to admit the point of a penknife. The north and south sides were each ornamented by fourteen of these magnificent pillars—of which nine on the north and five on the south are still standing. At the west end were eight, of which the three most southerly are perfect—the others broken or prostrate.

The frieze and cornice are elegant and complete. The soffit of the peristyle is concave, and the panels are sculptured in imitation of network, a series of large busts and mythological designs running down the centre—each in the middle of a large diamond, and smaller busts occupying the angles formed by the interlacing compartments—a most intricate and indescribable design, but very beautiful.

The portico consisted of two rows of columns, of which only four remain perfect. The frieze and cornice above these four columns are in the same excellent style and finish. A battlemented tower has been built over them by the Saracens, who have barbarously raised a huge wall directly in front of the gate of the temple. The width of this portico is 22 feet; it is composed of nine stones, six forming the sides and three the top; the key-stone has slipped partly through, and hangs ominously overhead. The injuries the temple has sustained have most of them resulted from barbarian violence; the columns especially have been destroyed for the sake of the iron bars by which they were held together. But the tottering condition of the beautiful portal was produced by a concussion more destructive than even the mutilating hand of the Mohammedan—the great earthquake of 1750.

About 450 feet from the south-east angle of the Temple of the Sun is a beautiful little Corinthian temple—circular, and pierced externally with niches each flanked by two columns, so as to give the structure the appearance of an octagon. Earthquakes have sadly shaken this little edifice, so that now only four pillars are standing. Beneath the great platform on which the two temples stand are spacious vaulted passages of very massive architecture, and solidly constructed. Two of them run parallel with each other from east to west, and are connected by a third running at right angles to them from north to south. They are now used as storehouses and granaries. Beneath the Temple of the Sun there are subterranean chambers, with flights of steps leading down to them from the interior of the temple; they are lighted from above, and by openings in the side of the platform. What the original destination of these chambers was, it is now impossible to tell; but the Arabs, who ascribe the whole structure to the great magician King Solomon, and the Djins who wrought his behests, imagine them to be depositories for treasure. Indeed, it is the universal belief among the Turks and Arabs, that every great mass of ruins covers mighty heaps of treasure; nor can they be persuaded that travelers visit them for any other purpose than that of carrying away the spoils.

At a short distance west of the great ruins stand eight stumpy columns of Egyptian granite, highly polished, and for the most part without a scratch on them. One of these columns is distinguished from the rest by its green quartz. These columns are true Egyptian granite, and as no such rock is found anywhere in Syria, the query is suggested—how could pillars fifteen feet long and three feet in diameter be brought over Mt. Lebanon, which is difficult for travelers to cross, even unencumbered?

Baalbek is now a wretched Syrian village, with a population of less than 200; and the day is not far distant when the jackal and hyena will be undisputed masters of this once splendid city.

HAMATH.

ONE OF KING SOLOMON'S STORE CITIES.

Hamath is a very ancient city; and was the principal city of upper Syria at the time of the exodus (B.C. 1491). This city, like Jerusalem and Damascus, has retained considerable importance from the very earliest times to the present day.

It is 250 miles N. N. E. of Jerusalem, and is situated in the valley of the Orontes, about half way between its source, near *Baalbek* and the bend which it makes at Jisr Hadid. A part of the valley of the Orontes at one time constituted the kingdom of Hamath.

King Solomon took the kingdom of Hamath, and made the city a depot for stores and supplies. He also built other store cities in the district.

The government of Hamath includes about 120 inhabited villages, and 75 that have been abandoned, comprising most of the ancient kingdom of Hamath. The city now, as of old, stands on both sides of the river, which is spanned by four bridges. The upper part of the city is supplied with water from the river by means of immense water wheels, in the rim of which buckets are so arranged as to empty themselves into stone aqueducts, which conduct the water to the houses and gardens. There are about a dozen of these wheels, the largest being nearly 70 feet in diameter. Extensive ruins of the ancient parts of the city are found scattered about here, but so much decayed as to be scarcely recognizable. The chief

GEBAL.

trade of Hamath is with the Arabs, who buy here their tent furniture and clothes; there is also a considerable trade in cotton, woolen, and silk. The present population is 30,000.

GEBAL.

ITS STONE SQUARERS.

This was a very ancient seaport of Phenicia, 20 miles N. of Beirut, and 182 miles from Jerusalem, via Joppa and the Mediterranean.

Gebal was situated on a spur of Lebanon, close to the shore, and had a fine harbor, but which is now filled with sand, ruins of quays, and buildings.

The inhabitants were called Giblites—"stone-squarers." *Hewers of stone from Gebal were employed on Solomon's Temple.*

The ruins consist of the remains of a castle and extensive walls, and of beautiful columns. The ruins of the castle exhibit some of the best specimens of ancient masonry to be found in Palestine. The stones in its walls are beveled, and some of them are 20 feet in length. The style of the columns, and the extent of the walls, indicate the size and importance of the city.

BEEROTH.

PRIVATE MARKS OF THE BUILDERS.

Beeroth is ten miles from Jerusalem, on the great road to Shechem (Nabulus).

A delegation of the inhabitants of this city--Kirjath-jearim, Chephirah, and Gibeon—by resorting to the stratagem of wearing old tattered garments, and representing themselves as having traveled from a far country, deluded Joshua into a treaty of peace with them. Beeroth is again mentioned in connection with Kirjath-jearim and Chephirah, in the list of those who returned from Babylon. The murderers of Ishbosheth belonged to this city.

The modern town stands at the foot of a ridge, and contains about 700 inhabitants. Ruins of considerable extent are found here, the stones having the Jewish bevel—the same as those in the foundations of Solomon's Temple at Jerusalem; *and on one of the stones was found a group of the private marks of the builders.*

KIRJATH-JEARIM.

This city is first mentioned as one of the four cities of the Gibeonites, and is 9 miles N. W. of Jerusalem, on the road from Jerusalem to Jaffa. Near Kirjath-jearim the band of Danites pitched their camp before their expedition to Mount Ephraim and Laish, leaving their name attached to the spot long afterwards. One of the first names it bore was that of the Canaanite deity, Baal; and it was doubtless the sanctity implied by its bearing that name that induced the people of Beth Shemoth to appeal to its inhabitants to relieve them of the Ark of Jehovah,

KIRJATH—JEARIM.

EPHESUS.

SAMARIA.

which was bringing such calamities on their untutored experience. The Ark remained in the house of Abinadab, at Kirjath-jearim, 20 years; at the end of this time it was removed by David a short distance to the house of Obed-edom, where it remained until its removal to Jerusalem. There are but few of the ruins of this ancient city remaining, but those of the largest buildings indicate that they were built by the same class of men who erected the Temple of Solomon, as the stones have the same bevel and finish as those in the foundations of the Temple. On one of them was found a group of the private marks of the builders.

The site is now occupied by the village of Kuryet-el-Enab, usually known as Abu Gosh, from the noted robber chief whose headquarters it used to be.

SAMARIA,

ITS BEAUTIFUL SITUATION AND GREAT STRENGTH—THE TOMB AND CHURCH OF ST. JOHN.

Samaria is 40 miles N. by W. of Jerusalem, and 6 miles N.W. of Shechem. Its situation is strong by nature, and very beautiful. It stands on a large hill, surrounded by a broad deep valley, which is enclosed by four hills—one on each side; which are cultivated in terraces to the top, sown with grain and planted with fig and olive trees, as is also the valley.

The hill on which the ancient city was built, was chosen by Omri as the site of the capital of the kingdom of Israel. "He bought the hill of Samaria of Shemer for two talents of silver, and built on the hill, and called the name of the city which he built, after the name of the owner of the hill, Samaria."

This city was highly adorned with public buildings, and became the favorite residence of the kings of Israel instead of Shechem and Thirzah, the former capitals. Ahab built here a palace of ivory, and a temple to Baal—which Jehu destroyed. The natural strength of the position, and its strong fortifications, rendered it nearly impregnable against the then system of warfare. The Syrians twice invaded it; the first time B. C. 901, and again B. C. 892, but were both times repulsed. B. C. 724, it was attacked by the powerful Shalmaneser, king of Assyria; but he did not succeed in taking it until after a siege of three years—when he carried its people away captive. About 667 B. C. it was repeopled by Esar-Haddon with Cuthites from beyond the Tigris. The city was afterwards taken by Alexander the Great, who put a large part of the inhabitants to the sword, and permitted the remainder to settle in Shechem. He replaced them by a colony of Syro-Macedonians, and gave the adjacent territory to the Jews to inhabit. Afterwards the city came into the possession of Herod the Great, who colonized it with 6,000 veterans and others. He built a wall around it, and a magnificent temple in the centre. How long it maintained its splendor after Herod's improvements does not appear, and henceforth its history is uncertain. Septimius Severus planted a Roman colony there in the beginning of the third century. During the siege of Jerusalem it fell into the hands of the Moslems. The

RUINS OF ST. JOHN'S CHURCH—THE SITE.

present village is small and poor, and contains about 200 inhabitants.

The most conspicuous ruins are those of the church dedicated to *St. John the Baptist, erected over the spot which tradition claims to be the place of his burial.* The walls remain entire to a considerable hight, and enclose a large space, in which are now a mosk and the small building over the tomb. The tomb is a small chamber cut deep in the rock, to which the descent is by twenty-one steps. It is said that during the reign of Julian the Apostate, the heathen broke open this sepulchre, burnt the bones and scattered the ashes to the winds. Other ruins are found on three terraces, and consist of a number of columns, twelve of which stand in a row, the others are scattered about. These columns are said to have belonged to the Serai, or Palace. On the second terrace, heaps of stone, lime, and rubbish are found mixed with the soil in great profusion. On the third terrace but few traces of ruins are found.

Most of the public edifices at Samaria appear to have been the work of the same class of builders that built the Temple of Solomon at Jerusalem; the Jewish rebate and bevel being the prevailing style, and *the private marks of the builders found on the stones here are similar to those on the stones in the Temple substructions.*

CHAPTER VIII.

THE CRADLE OF THE HUMAN RACE.

The Garden of Eden.—Mount Ararat.—The dispersion of the people.—Their location, or the places occupied by them.—First settlements of the human family.

THE region embraced between the Black and Caspian Seas on the north, and the Mediterranean Sea and Persian Gulf on the south, may well be regarded as the cradle of the human race, as it comprises the Garden of Eden, where man made his advent on earth; and Mount Ararat, where the Ark rested after the flood subsided, and from whence the remnant of the human family went forth to repeople the earth. In this region their first settlements were made, and here the ruins of the first cities they built are found; particularly on the banks of the Euphrates and Tigris, and on the east coast of the Mediterranean.

THE GARDEN OF EDEN.

The only data for determining the location of this important spot is found in Gen. ii. 8, 11, 13, 14. As to the true interpretation of this account, the best authorities are about equally divided; some claiming that it was in the district at the head waters of the rivers

MT. ARARAT.

Euphrates and Tigris, and the Araxes and Phosis; while others believe that it was between the Euphrates and Tigris, near their junction—about 130 miles N. of the Persian Gulf. That one of these localities contained the Garden of Eden there can be but little doubt, as there is no other place which so nearly meets the requirements of the Scripture account.

MOUNT ARARAT

is in Armenia, 775 miles N.E. of Jerusalem, about 300 E. of the Caspian Sea, and is in 39° 30′ N. lat. and 43° 40′ E. lon. from Greenwich. It rises directly out of the plain of the Araxes, and is the loftiest and most imposing mountain in this region, being 17,560 feet above the level of the sea. About 1,200 feet below the highest summit is a secondary summit, and between the two there is a gentle depression, in which it is believed the ark rested.

Arguri is the only village known to have been built on the slopes of this mountain, and according to tradition it was the place where Noah planted his vineyard. At the foot of the mountain is Nachdjevan, where the patriarch is reported to have been buried.

THE IMMEDIATE DESCENDANTS OF NOAH, AND THEIR LOCATION, OR THE PLACES OCCUPIED BY THEM.

"And the sons of Noah that went forth of the ark were Shem, Ham, and Japhet —— —— these are the sons of Noah; and of them was the whole earth overspread."—(Gen. ix.)

Of the descendants of Ham, were Nimrod and Canaan. Nimrod settled in the land of Shinar, a district above the junction of the rivers Euphrates and Tigris. "And the beginning of his kingdom was Babel, and Erech, and Accad, and Calneh, in the land of Shinar."—(Gen. x.)

Canaan occupied the east coast of the Mediterranean, from Sidon to Gaza, including the hill country in which Jerusalem was built.

The descendants of Shem were distributed from Mesha on the Persian Gulf, and towards Sephar, a mount of the east. "By these were the isles of the Gentiles divided in their lands; every one after his tongue, after their families, in their nations."

CHAPTER IX.

THE FIRST CITIES BUILT—THEIR RISE, FALL, AND RUINS AS NOW SEEN.*

Babylon, its vast extent—its fall—its remarkable ruins—Erech—Accad—Calneh—Nineveh, a sketch of its history—Its wonderful ruins and inscriptions—Damascus—Bethel—Shechem—Bethlehem—Jericho—Rabbah—Gaza.

BABYLON.

ITS VAST EXTENT—ITS FALL—ITS REMARKABLE RUINS.

BABEL, or Babylon, is the first in order of the four cities built or occupied by Nimrod. It is 300 miles N. W. of the Persian Gulf, 200 above the junction of the river Euphrates with the Tigris, and 530 miles E. N. E. of Jerusalem. Herodotus, who visited Babylon after its conquest by Cyrus, is considered the best authority as to a description of the city, as his account is corroborated by the testimony and researches of all subsequent writers, and by the explorations and excavations of the present age.

He describes the city as a quadrangle of 15 miles on each side, surrounded, first, by a deep, wide moat, filled with water; and next by a wall 87 feet wide and 60 feet high. The 30 lower courses of brick in

* Hebron, Beeroth, Hamath, Jerusalem, Tyre, and Sidon, are also reckoned among the first cities.

the wall were wattled with reeds, and the whole cemented by hot asphalt. On each side of the top of the wall was a row of dwellings facing each other, the passage between being of sufficient width to admit of turning a chariot with four horses.

In the great wall there were 100 gates of brass, 25 on each side of the city; and between every two gates a tower 10 feet high. Although the outer wall was the chief defense, there was a second wall within, not much inferior in strength, but narrower.

The city was divided into two nearly equal parts, by the river Euphrates running from north to south; and the wall, with wide quays outside, was carried along each bank, the sides of the river being lined with brick. In the middle of each division of the city were fortified buildings; in one the royal palace, with a spacious and strong enclosure; and in the other the precinct of Jupiter Belus—a square building of 2 furlongs on each side. There were 50 streets in all, running from gate to gate; each street was 150 feet wide and 15 miles long.

The houses were three and four stories high. A bridge, admirably constructed of stones, bound together with plates of lead and iron, was built across the river about the middle of the city. At each end of the bridge was a palace, the old palace being on the eastern, and the new on the western, side of the river. The Temple of Belus occupied an entire square of the city. In the middle of this precinct was built a solid tower of one stade, both in length and breath, and on this tower rose another, and so on to the number of eight. An ascent to these was by spiral stairs, winding around the outside of the tower. About the middle of the ascent was a landing-place, with seats, where those ascending could rest themselves; and in the top tower stood a spacious temple, and in the temple a beautiful couch, and by its side a table of gold. No statue was erected in it; nor was any mortal allowed to pass the night there except only a native woman chosen by the god out of the whole nation. The Chaldeans, who were priests of this deity, say the Temple did not attain its full splendor until the time of Nebuchadnezzar, who greatly enlarged and beautified it. The summit of the temple was devoted to astronomical purposes. Herodotus states that the Greeks learned from the Babylonians the pole star, the sun-dial, and the division of the day into twelve parts; and Calisthenes the philosopher obtained for Aristotle Chaldean observations for 1903 years—from the origin of the Babylonian monarchy to the time of Alexander.

Berosus, a priest of Belus, appears to have sketched a history of the earlier times, from the delineations upon the walls of the Temple.

From Strabo we learn that Alexander attempted to repair the tower, and employed 10,000 men two months in clearing away the rubbish, but he did not live to accomplish the undertaking. With the exception of the stone bridge across the Euphrates, all the great works of Babylon were constructed of sun-dried and kiln-dried bricks, generally stamped with figures or letters. Straw or reeds were laid between the courses, and the whole cemented with bitumen, mortar, or slime.

The country around Babylon was intersected by numerous canals; the largest of these, the royal canal, connected the Euphrates with the Tigris, and was navigable for merchant vessels. Strabo tells that Alexander inspected the canals and ordered them to be cleared out, and that in clearing one in the marshes near Arabia, he discovered and examined the sepulchres of the kings, most of which were situated among the lakes.

Later writers—Diodorus and Strabo—describe yet more wonderful monuments in Babylon than are mentioned by Herodotus. Among these are a tunnel under the Euphrates, subterranean banqueting rooms of brass, and the famous hanging-gardens.

The palace connected with the hanging-gardens was unequaled in size and splendor. Its outer wall had a circuit of six miles, while within it were two other embattled walls and a large tower. All the gates were of brass. The interior of the palace was splendidly decorated with statues of men and animals, and furnished with vessels of gold and silver, and with every species of luxury, accumulated by Nebuchadnezzar in his conquests.

The population was estimated by Pliny to be 1,200,000, but others placed it at a much lower figure, as a considerable portion of the squares within the walls of the city was used for agricultural purposes, so as to render the city self-sustaining in the time of sieges; consequently the population would not be in proportion to the area of the city. Under the reign of Nebuchadnezzar, Babylon was the Mistress of the East. Pharaoh Necho was the first to take up arms against her, and marched as far as Carchemish, on the Euphrates, where he was defeated by the Babylonian army. It was immediately after this great battle that the Chaldeans marched upon Jerusalem, and carried captive to Babylon the Jewish nobles, among whom were Daniel and his three friends, Hananiah, Michael, and Azariah, while Judea remained a province of the Babylonian monarchy.

ITS DECLINE.

B. C. 556, Babylon was taken by Cyrus. Alexander the Great made it his capital, B. C. 324, and died there B. C. 323. On the division of his conquests, Babylon became the kingdom of Seleucus and his successors. Seleucus Nicator transferred the seat of empire to Seleucia, 300 stadia distant, on the Tigris, after which Babylon rapidly declined, so that in the early days of Arab power it had dwindled to a mere name, and A. D. 1101 the present town of Hillah was founded on a part of its site.

RUINS.

The ruins of Babylon are vast in extent, indescribably grand and desolate, the extensive plain for miles around being covered with large mounds of earth and brick. Among the rubbish are found fragments of pottery, glass, marble, and vitrified bricks, many of the bricks bearing inscriptions, while the soil itself is so impregnated with nitre as to destroy all vegetation.

The most extensive ruins are five miles above Hillah, on the left bank of the Euphrates. Here are found a series of artificial mounds of enormous size, consisting chiefly of three great masses of buildings —the high pile of unbaked brick-work, called by the Arabs Babil, the building denominated the Kasr, or palace, and a lofty mound, upon which stands a modern tomb.

The principal ruins are surrounded by lines of ramparts, and an embankment along the river-side. Scattered over a large area, on both sides of the Euphrates, are a number of notable mounds, nearly all standing single. The most remarkable of these is the vast ruin called Birs Nimroud—the Temple of Belus. This mound is 198 feet high, and has on its summit a compact mass of brick-work, 37 feet high by 27 broad—the whole being 235 feet in hight. It is rent into two parts nearly the whole way down, and the base is surrounded by immense piles of bricks bearing unmistakable evidence of fire.

It is laid out in the form of seven terraces, arranged in the order in which the Chaldeans supposed the planetary spheres to exist, each terrace being painted in a different color, representing its respective planet.

The lowest stage was black, and consists of bricks covered with bitumen.

The second stage represented the earth, and is of brownish bricks.

The third stage, Mars, and is of red bricks.

The fourth stage, the Sun—yellow bricks.

The fifth, Mercury—green bricks.

The sixth stage, Venus—blue, and the ruined tower on the summit, gray bricks.

A passage has been discovered in the second stage, leading within the brick-work; at the northern and eastern corners of the third stage were found two *terra-cotta* cylinders inscribed with the history of the building—stating that having fallen into decay in the course of 504 years since it was erected, it had been repaired by Nebuchadnezzar; this would fix the date of the original structure at 1100 B. C.

The next ruin of importance is the mound of the Kasr,—the site of the great palace of Nebuchadnezzar. This is an irregular square of about 700 yards each way, apparently the old palace platform, on which are still standing portions of the ancient palace or Kasr. The walls are of pale yellow burnt bricks of excellent quality, laid in lime cement. No plan of the palace can be made, as the ruins lie in great confusion on the highest part of the mound.

The sculptures, inscribed bricks, and glazed and colored tiles found at the Kasr, have caused it to be generally regarded as the site of the large palace celebrated for its hanging-gardens.

From the portions of wall standing, and from the surrounding detached masses, it would appear that all the bricks used in this structure were baked, and that the face of each was invariably placed downwards. In this mound there was found a rudely executed elephant, crushing a man beneath his ponderous weight. On the north side of the Kasr stands the solitary tree called by the Arabs Atheleh, and which, notwithstanding its great antiquity, still bears spreading green branches. According to tradition, it sheltered the Caliph Ali when sinking with fatigue after the battle of Hillah.

In the time of Alexander, antique monuments abounded in the Lamlum marshes, 76 miles south of Babylon; these monuments were said to be the tombs of the Assyrian kings. In confirmation of this, there have recently been discovered in some of them glazed earthen coffins.

In the excavation of these mounds of ruins tens of thousands of bricks have been found, all stamped with the combination of characters which reads Nebuchadnezzar.

Stamped bricks are not only found in the ruins of Babylon, but among ruins of towns and cities within an area of 100 miles in length by 40 in width, bearing the legend: Nebuchadnezzar, son of Nabopolassar, King of Babylon.

The composition of these bricks is such as to render them nearly imperishable, and the inscriptions on them, and on the cylinders found here, furnish many chapters of the long-lost history of those remote times—names of kings, and events in their order.

Since Darius destroyed the walls of Babylon, over 2300 years ago, its ruins have furnished a never-failing supply of bricks. City after city has been built from its materials. Celeucia, Ctesiphon, Al Median, Kufa, Kerbela, Bagdad, Hillah, besides many other towns and villages, have risen in succession from the ruins of the once vast and proud Babylon.

The modern town of Hillah, on the right bank of the Euphrates, stands nearly in the centre of the site

THE KASR—BABYLON.

BABYLON—ITS MOUNDS OF RUINS.

of Babylon. It is surrounded by wide walls, and a deep ditch, and has four gates.

The city being built from the Babylonian bricks, there is not a room where may not be seen bricks stamped with the name of Nebuchadnezzar.

The Euphrates at Hillah, in its medium state, is 450 feet wide and 7½ feet deep, with a velocity of 2½ miles an hour. It annually overflows its banks; inundating the country for many miles around. The soil is very fertile, and the air salubrious.

ERECH*

is about 100 miles S. E. of Babylon. It is now called Irak. The most noted ruins found here are the immense mounds, El Assayah, and the remains of coffins and bricks, scattered over a large district—indicating that it was a city of considerable size and importance.

ACCAD

is about 70 miles N. W. of Babylon, and is now known as Akari, Babel, and a primitive monument found here is still called Tel Nimrud, which signifies the hill of Nimrod. The most remarkable ruin consists of a mound or platform on which stands a mass of building, having the appearance of a tower. It is 400 feet in circumference at its base, and 125 feet in hight above the mound. It was built of bricks ce-

* Some authorities believe that Erech, Accad, and Calneh were suburbs of Nineveh.

mented by bitumen, and was divided into layers of from 12 to 20 feet thick, by reeds. There are also remains of reservoirs, canals, and other works, that show the importance of this very ancient city.

CALNEH

was the last in order of the four cities that were the beginning of Nimrod's kingdom. *Its site cannot* be determined, but it is believed to be at what was afterwards Ctesiphon, on the banks of the Tigris, about 20 miles below Bagdad. Among the ruins found here are those of a remarkable ancient palace, now called Tauk Kesra, which struck the Arab conquerors with amazement and delight.

NINEVEH.

A SKETCH OF ITS HISTORY—ITS WONDERFUL RUINS AND INSCRIPTIONS.

Far away in the East is a country now inhabited principally by tribes of Nestorians, and roving bands of Arabs, that was once an empire whose power and magnificence were both the terror and marvel of the ancient world. The capital of this empire lay buried in the sands of the earth, with no certain marks of its sepulchre. The extent of our knowledge of the location of this city was no more than vague tradition—which said that it was hidden somewhere on the river Tigris; but for many centuries it had existed only in name, a name that suggested the idea of an ancient capital of fabulous size and splendor, a walled city containing many fortifications, palaces, and temples; a city which had witnessed the tears of many princes and peoples, brought hither captive by its warlike kings.

After over two thousand years the grave of this dead city was found, and its shroud of sand and ruin thrown off—revealing to an astonished world its temples, palaces, and idols—its tablets, covered with records of its conquests and power. The Nineveh in which the captive tribes of Israel had labored and wept, and against which the prophecies had gone forth, was, after a sleep of over twenty centuries, again brought to light; and the proofs of its ancient splendor beheld by mortal eyes.

The site and ruins of this ancient city are on the river Tigris, 510 miles from its mouth, and 550 miles N. E. of Jerusalem. Nineveh was one of the oldest, largest, most powerful, and splendid cities in the world; and contained at one time a population of 600,000. Traditions of its unrivaled size and magnificence were equally familiar to the Greeks and Romans, and to the Arabian geographers.

The Assyrian Empire at one time included Media and Persia, and was then bounded on the north by the Caspian Sea and Armenia, on the east by Media, on the south by Arabia, on the S. W. and W. by the river Euphrates and Syria.

The Assyrians were one of the greatest commercial and manufacturing nations of the East. Assyria, from its proximity to the Persian Gulf, with which it was connected by the rivers Tigris and Euphrates, naturally became the great highway of trade between the sea-faring nations of the Indian seas and Central Asia. Consequently, Nineveh was a great centre of trade and manufactures, and here the merchants of nearly all the nations of the earth assembled.

Assyria was mentioned by Ezekiel as trading in "blue cloth and embroidered work." In these stuffs gold thread was introduced into the woof of many colors, and were the "dyed attire and embroidered work" so frequently mentioned in Scripture as the most costly and splendid garments of kings and princes. The cotton manufactures were equally celebrated and remarkable, and were mentioned by Pliny as the invention of Semiramis, *who is stated by many writers of antiquity as having founded large weaving establishments along the banks of the Tigris and Euphrates.* They also acquired the art of manufacturing glass; several bottles, and vases of elegant shape, were found among the ruins of the city.

The result of its immense trade, and the number of nations paying tribute to the kings of Assyria, was the accumulation of a vast amount of treasure in Nineveh, and the most extraordinary traditions were observed in antiquity, of the enormous amount of gold collected in that city.

As the recent discoveries of Botta and Layard, among the ruins of Nineveh, are exciting great interest and attention, a brief sketch of its history will help to render the subject intelligible. This city

NINEVEH—THE BURIED CITY.

was first known to history only as Nineveh; but it afterwards became the capital—first of the kingdom of Assyria, then of the Assyrian empire. According to Scripture, it was founded by Asshur about 2230 B.C., but according to Diodorus Siculus (quoting Ctesias), it was founded by Ninus 2183 B.C. This agrees with other good authorities, according to whom Asshur was the founder of the monarchy of Assyria, while Ninus founded the Assyrian empire and city of Nineveh. Justin, the Roman historian who abridged the history of Trogus Pompeius in the second century, gives the following account of Ninus. He says, "By his lust for empire he first brought wars against the people, as yet unused to resistance, to the very borders of Libya—which name was anciently applied to all Africa. . . . . . "His neighbors therefore being subdued, when by accession of strength he was stronger, he passed to others, and every new victory being the instrument of the next one, he subdued the whole East.

"His last war was with Oxyartes, king of the Bactrians. Here he met with a more powerful resistance than he had yet experienced, but after several fruitless attempts upon the chief city, he at last conquered it by the contrivance and conduct of Semiramis, wife of Menon, president of the king's council, and chief of Assyria." . . . . "The ability, courage, and beauty of Semiramis so captivated Ninus, that he used every imaginable persuasion and threat to induce her husband to bestow his wife upon him. Menon, however, would not consent, but in a fit of distraction he destroyed himself, and Semiramis was advanced to the regal state and dignity. Ninus had a son by Semiramis, named Ninyas, and died after a reign of fifty-two years, leaving her the government of his kingdom. In honor of his memory, she erected in the royal palace a monument, which remained till long after the ruin of Nineveh."

Of the size of this monument, Diodorus speaks in extraordinary terms. Following Ninus, Assyrian records give the names of thirty-four kings who reigned in Nineveh before the reign of Sardanapalus—whose throne was overturned by an invasion of the Medes, a people who dwelt on the shores of the Caspian Sea.

Arbaces, king of the Medes, led his army across the mountains, and made himself king of Assyria, about 804 B.C.

After the death of Arbaces the Mede, the Assyrians regained their independence. The first of the new line of kings was Pul. In his reign Menahem, king of Israel, invaded Assyria, and gained some temporary successes. In retaliation for which, Pul marched in the following year into Samaria. The frightened Israelites could make no stand against him, and purchased a peace at the price of 1,000 talents of silver.

Pul was succeeded by Tiglath Pileser, who also invaded Samaria B.C. 753.

Tiglath Pileser was succeeded by Shalmaneser (called by the prophet Hosea, Shalmo). In the ninth year of his reign, he invaded and conquered the kingdom of Israel, and carried the people away captive, 725 B.C.

Shalmaneser was succeeded by Sennacherib (B.C.

720). He invaded Judea in the fourteenth year of the reign of Hezekiah. In his old age Sennacherib, while worshiping in the temple of the Assyrian god Nisroch, was murdered by two of his sons, and was succeeded by his third son, Esarhaddon (about 683 B.C.), who was succeeded by Sardochæus (B.C. 667), who reigned over Nineveh, Babylon, and Israel twenty years. During his reign, Media revolted and gained its independence. The bright days of Nineveh's glory were now past; disaster followed disaster in quick succession.

(B.C. 647) Chyniladan succeeded Sardochæus, and reigned twenty years—Babylon was taken by the Chaldees, and in the year 625 B.C. their leader, Nabopolassar, ruled that city and the lower half of the valley of the Euphrates and Tigris. Two years later he marched northward against Nineveh, which he stormed and sacked. The city was then laid waste, its monuments destroyed, and a large portion of its inhabitants carried away into captivity or scattered. It never rose again from its ruins. (B.C. 401) Xenophon, with 10,000 Greeks, encamped during his retreat on or very near its site, but does not mention its name. The great victory by Alexander over Darius (B.C. 331) was won almost over the ruins of Nineveh. During the Roman period a small castle or fortified town stood on a part of the site. The Roman settlement was in its turn abandoned, for there is no mention of it when Heraclius gained the great victory over the Persians in the battle of Nineveh, fought on the very site of the ancient city, A.D. 627.

Frequent allusion is made to Nineveh in the Old

Testament. The first is in Genesis x. 11, and has reference to its origin. Jonah was sent to this city about 800 B.C. to warn it of its destruction (Jonah i. 1, 2; iii. 1 to 10). The Book of Nahum is devoted to "the burden of Nineveh." Isaiah speaks of the destruction of the Assyrian army by the angel of the Lord—of Sennacherib's return to Nineveh, and his murder by his two sons (Isaiah xxxvii. 36, 37, 38). The last mention of it is by Zephaniah, 630 B.C., "And he will stretch out his hand against the north, and destroy Assyria; and will make Nineveh a desolation, and dry like a wilderness" (Zeph. ii. 13).

The ruins of Nineveh are mostly on the east bank of the Tigris, opposite the city of Mosul, which also stands on a part of the site of the ancient city. Nineveh covered an area of nearly 16 miles, being the longest on the river, or from north to south. The ruins consist of shapeless heaps, and mounds of earth and rubbish, some of which are of enormous dimensions, and appear in the distance more like natural hills than like the work of men's hands. Upon and around them were found scattered many fragments of pottery, sculpture, and building materials. Some of these mounds had been selected by the natives as sites for their villages and small mud-built forts. The summits of others were sown with barley and corn. These mounds differ greatly in size and form; some are mere conical heaps, while others have a broad, flat summit, very steep sides, and are from 50 to 150 feet high. There are several groups of enclosures and mounds, the principal of which are called Khorsabad, Kouyunjik, Nebbi Yunus, Keramles and Nimrud. They take their names from the villages in their vicinity. Mosul is on the west bank of the Tigris, and at the north-west corner of the site of Nineveh.

From *Mosul*, by the aid of a good glass, a view of most of the ruins of Nineveh may be had. Directly opposite, on the other side of the Tigris, are the mounds of ruins called Kouyunjik, and Nebbi Yunus ; to the N. E. are the mounds of Khorsabad; to the S. E. are those of Keramles; and 17 miles S.S.E. is the important mound, Nimrud.

The ruins opposite Mosul consist of an enclosure, formed by a continuous line of mounds, resembling a vast embankment of earth, but marking the remains of a wall, the western face of which is interrupted by the two great mounds of Kouyunjik and Nebbi Yunus. East of this enclosure is an extensive line of defense, consisting of moats and ramparts. Here and there a mound more lofty than the rest covers the ruins of a tower or gateway. A part of the mound' Kouyunjik is very steep, and is 96 feet high ; the top of it is flat, and a small Arab village, now abandoned, stands upon it.

Nebbi Yunus is smaller in area than Kouyunjik, but about the same hight; upon it is a Turkoman village, containing the apocryphal tomb of Jonah, and a burial-ground held in great sanctity by the Mohammedans. Remains of gateways have been discovered in the north and east walls. In addition to the inner wall, there is an enormous outer rampart of earth,—in some places 80 feet high; a few mounds outside of the ramparts were probably detached towers.

That part of the ruins known as Khorsabad, cover an area of 975 feet by about 800. Near the middle of the south-west side is a cone, which is the most elevated point, being 50 feet higher than the rest of the mound, and presents quite an imposing and singular appearance. Near the northern angle of the mound is an ancient well, the bottom of which is covered with a stone with seven holes, through which pure fresh water gushes forth in great abundance. When first discovered by Botta, a village covered most of the top of this mound. As the country is infested with roving bands of freebooters, who do not hesitate to use the scimeter or rifle to obtain plunder, those disposed to make a permanent settlement chose elevated positions; hence all of the largest of these mounds, when first discovered by Europeans, were covered with villages and scattered habitations.

The fortified enclosure of Khorsabad forms a large and very regular rectangle; the wall surrounding it, and which looks like a long tumulus of a rounded shape, is surmounted at irregular intervals by elevations which indicate the existence of towers. From the northern angle the wall stretches very regularly to the south-east, becoming more elevated and distinct until it assumes the aspect of a large causeway; a great number of fragments of bricks and gypsum being observable on the surface of the soil. Outside of the outer wall a part of a ditch was found; and in one place a brick wall, containing twelve layers of bricks, similar to those comprising the mass of the mound.

The ruins in this mound consist of parts of halls,

EXCAVATIONS AT NINEVEH.

chambers, and passages, for the most part wainscoted with slabs of gray alabaster, sculptured with figures in relief. The calcined limestone, and the great accumulation of charred wood and charcoal, showed that the building, or at least its roof, had been destroyed by fire.

The mounds of Nimrud, notwithstanding their distance from the northern ruins, are believed by many to be a part of Nineveh. These mounds are about 4 miles in circumference and terminate at the northwest angle by a great mound 777 feet in circumference, and 144 feet in hight, once coated with bricks. Some of these have been found, and are about the same size as those of Babylon, and are inscribed with the arrowhead characters. At the southeast angle of this enclosure is a group of fifty mounds, called by the Arabs the mounds of Arthur. The mound of Nimrud is as clearly defined as that of Khorsabad, which it resembles in the quadrangular form of its line of consecutive mounds.

The great interest in these discoveries centres in the inscriptions, illustrations, and sculptures found in the courts, halls, and historical chambers of palaces and temples, the most important of which were found in the mounds at Khorsabad, Kouyunjik, and Nimrud. The inscriptions were found on slabs of stone and marble, arranged against the walls; on cylinders of pottery, images, and on obelisks. These inscriptions are nearly all in cuneatic characters, which are neither simple nor numerical figures, but alphabetical; and the inscriptions, like English writing, read from left to right. The character employed was the arrow-head, or cuneiform, so called from each letter being formed by marks or elements resembling an arrow-head, or wedge. This mode of writing prevailed throughout the Assyrian, Babylonian, and Persian Empires. The Assyrian or Babylonian alphabet contained over 200 signs or characters, of a very complicated and imperfect nature, some characters being phonetic, others syllabic, and others ideographic. The inscriptions were all systematically arranged, so that in many instances they gave a very full and connected account of public events—principally chronicles of the king who built the edifice where they were found, including a record of his wars and expeditions into distant countries—of the amount of spoil taken, and tribute exacted from the conquered peoples; of the building of temples and palaces, and of invocations to the gods of Assyria—altogether furnishing a complete key to the long-lost history of the Assyrian Empire and the city of Nineveh. Many remarkable events are represented by figures and illustrations, so ingeniously contrived and arranged that, by the aid of a short inscription, the story is as plainly told as it could have been by any written account. Among the first discoveries made in the mound' Khorsabad was a hall or entrance chamber between two courts. This chamber was 46 feet long by 10 wide, and its entrance was guarded by six colossal bulls, with human heads and eagles' wings—three of the bulls on each side of the entrance.* At the front end of the chamber was

* The entrance to all of the palaces and temples in the ruins of Nineveh were found similarly guarded.

formerly a strong gate, of one leaf, which was fastened by a huge wooden lock, like those still in use in the East,—the key to which is as much as a man can well carry,—and by a bar which moved into a square hole in the wall. It was doubtless to a key of this description that the prophet alluded: "And the key of the house of David will I lay upon his shoulder;" and it is remarkable that the word for key in this passage of Scripture — מפתח (Muftah) — is the same in use all over the East at the present day. The pavement of this chamber was of slabs of gypsum; and in the floor, at the entrance between the bulls, was a slab engraved with a long cuneiform inscription: there were likewise inscriptions between the fore and hind legs of the bulls. Farther on there were holes in the pavement, in which metal bars had been inserted to keep the door open at certain angles. Arranged against each side of this chamber were two rows of marble slabs, each row having two lines of illustrations, which were divided by a band of cuneatic writing, the whole so nearly entire that it afforded a very complete record of the annual tribute brought by two different peoples to the Assyrian King who occupied the palace within. This chamber, with its colossal bulls, and rows of illustrations and inscriptions, is a fair sample of many other chambers and passages found in palaces and temples in the mounds—Kouyunjik, Khorsabad, and Nimrud; —and may properly be called historical chambers. In one of these, in the mound Khorsabad, a procession is represented moving down a narrow hall, in two lines, headed by an officer who was conducting it into the presence of the King. The title of the officer is indicated by the word תרתן (Tartan). The first eight persons who follow Tartan wear the close turban, and are dressed in long tunics, with short over-garments. The first carries the model of a city, indicative of his office of governor of a province. At the head of the procession is an officer, who is followed by three persons, the first two each bearing two cups, the produce of the manufacture of the province; and the third bears a sealed bag upon his shoulders, containing the amount of tribute in gold-dust or precious stones furnished by the prince, ruled by the governor at the head of the procession. The arrangement of the procession appears to have been one chief to four men bearing tribute, and contained in all thirty persons.

The second line of illustrations in this chamber represents another procession, and which, like the first, is headed by a chief officer of tribute. These are evidently a different people from the first; their hair is arranged in cork-screw curls, their tunics are scanty, and confined at the waist by a sash formed of a collection of cords. Over the tunic is a covering made of sheep and leopard skins. The first person is a chief of this people, as signified by his long beard, and his bearing the model of a city; he is followed by a groom carrying two spears, and leading two horses richly caparisoned, having elegant crested ornaments upon their heads, and tasseled bands across their chests. Following this is a chief, attended by a groom with two spears and two horses, one of which the groom is forcing back into the line of march. After this comes another chief wearing a leopard-skin robe, but not bearing any insignia of office—his hands are held up in the attitude of astonishment and awe. In the last slab on this side of the chamber is an arch-shaped cavity which received the wooden lock when the valve was completely open.

In another line of these illustrations are seen eight chiefs, ten grooms, and fourteen horses. All of the chiefs are in an attitude of surprise. The sculptures on the last slab on this wall are entirely obliterated, having been destroyed by the burning of the door, which was of wood, and probably stood open against the wall when the building was destroyed.

In a part of the ruins of the royal palace was found the court of reception where the offerings were presented, and where justice was administered; the King's Gate—the gate of Judgment, the "porch for the throne where he might judge, even the porch of judgment." It was in a court of this kind, called תרא, teragn, gate in the royal abode of Babylon, that in after-times the prophet Daniel sat when Nebuchadnezzar had made him חשלטן, "the Sultan or ruler over the whole province," מדינת, medinet of Babylon. . . . . . . Most of the words are even now current in the country, so that if they were written in Arabic characters an Arab could read and comprehend them.

Many of the illustrations found represent sieges of cities by the Assyrians—who are always represented as being successful. One of these represents the siege of a strongly fortified place belonging to the people who wear the sheep-skin garments. Their castle is fortified by a double wall, and built upon an irregular hill, up the sides of which are urged two battering-rams, at which the besieged are throwing lighted torches to set them on fire. In a part of this illustration are seen tents, and various implements hung to the poles of the tents, as is still the practice here among the natives—the descendants of those ancient people.

Another series of illustrations and figures represents the siege of a city situated in a plain, and protected on one side by a shallow river. On one side a satrap, attended by his shield-bearer, is vigorously pressing the attack. He is habited in a long fringed and embroidered robe, sandals, bracelets, and circlet on his head, and long sword, and is discharging arrows under cover of the shield held by his attendant, who wears a helmet, and is partially clothed in mail. From the top of the battlements the besieged are seen pouring some inflammable liquid upon the war-engines of the enemy, who in turn are discharging water from a movable tower to extinguish the fire. On a lofty tower of the gate the women are seen tearing their hair in the agony of despair, while the men are still making strenuous efforts to defend the city. Beneath the towers of the gate are two men disputing the possession of a treasure which they have discovered while undermining the wall. Notwithstanding the resolute defense, the outer works appear to be fatally bombarded, and the people are falling from the walls in every direction. Further on, a number of women and a boy are being led into captivity by a soldier. The women are barefooted, and wear long robes peculiarly ornamented; around their necks are scarfs, and their hair hangs over their shoulders in long tresses, which they are tearing in despair. "I will cast thee out and the mother that bare thee into another country. For lo! our fathers have fallen by the sword, and our sons, and our daughters, and our wives are in captivity." This piece of history doubtless represents the realization of the prophecy of Amos—" and the people of Syria* shall go into captivity unto Kir, saith the Lord." "For the king of Assyria went up against Damascus and took it, and carried the people of it captive to Kir, and slew Rezin." The situation of Damascus resembles that here represented; and the liquid fire used by the besieged was doubtless the petroleum with which that country abounds.

In another representation is seen the fate which befell Zedekiah, king of Judah, as recorded in the second book of Kings. In the centre of the group stands the king; before him are three persons, the foremost of whom is on his knees imploring mercy, and the two others standing in a humble position. The king is represented thrusting the point of a spear into one of the eyes of the suppliant, while he holds in his left hand the end of a cord attached to rings in the under lips of all the captives, who are likewise both manacled and fettered; and above their heads a cuneatic inscription—perhaps the very words of their supplication for mercy.

In another historical chamber is represented a for-

* Syria should not be confounded with Assyria, as they are different countries.

tified city, built upon a considerable elevation, opposite to which is a still higher hill, surmounted by a castellated tower, from the base of which a narrow stream flows down into the valley that separates the two hills. It is especially to be observed that olive-trees are growing on the hill on which is the tower; and on the hill in the city is a walk or road, about half-way up, below which, and at the side of the stream, is a row of tombs. The relative situation of these objects exactly resembles the position of similar objects visible in approaching Jerusalem from the east. On the left is Mount Moriah and the high wall of the Temple; at the foot, the brook Kedron and the tombs of the Valley of Jehoshaphat; and on the right, the Mount of Olives.

In a hall occupied by representations of divinities, is one which appears to be connected with the worship of the Assyrian Venus, or Astarte. Lucian believes it to be identical with the Moon, or queen of heaven. From the situation of this frieze in the deepest recess of the chamber, and from its having a square slab of gypsum in the pavement before it, with a hole communicating with a drain, there can be but little doubt that some mysterious rites were enacted before it.

In another place is a representation of cavalry in pursuit of an enemy; another scene of pursuit and flight, two horsemen armed with spears, and wearing the conical cap, are pursuing one whose horse is fallen. Behind is a falling figure; overhead is a vulture, bearing evidence of having preyed upon the slain.

In all the sculptures and representations, the swiftness of the horses, and the ferocity of their riders, is particularly portrayed. "Their horses also are swifter than the leopards, and more fierce than the evening wolves: and their horsemen shall spread themselves, and their horsemen shall come from far; they shall fly as the eagle that hasteth to eat." The Chal dean cavalry were proverbial for swiftness, courage, and cruelty.

Among the most important discoveries in the ruins of Nineveh, is the black obelisk found in the northwest palace at Nimrud. This obelisk furnishes a chapter of the long-lost history of the Assyrian empire, and a specimen of the style of writing of that period.

The inscription on it gives nearly a complete history of the reign of Shalmaneser, son of Sardanapalus, comprising a period of thirty-one years, dating from 891 B. C. It is given in the language of the king himself, and commences with the following declaration: "This is the palace of Sardanapalus, the humble worshiper of Assarac and Beltis." Then follows an invocation to several deities, with Assarac at their head, as the supreme god of Heaven. The king gives his titles and then says:—"At the commencement of my reign, after that I was established on the throne, I assembled the chiefs of my people and came down into the plains of Esmes, where I took the city of Haridu, the chief city belonging to Nakharini. In the first year of my reign, I crossed the upper Euphrates, and ascended to the tribes who worshiped the god Husi; my servants erected altars in that land to my gods. Then I went on to the land of Khamana, where I founded palaces, cities, and temples. I went on to the land of Malar, and there I established the worship of my kingdom.

"In the second year, I went up to the city of Tel Barasba, and occupied the cities of Ahuni, son of Hateni. I shut him up in his city. I then crossed the Euphrates, and occupied the cities of Dabagu and Aburta, belonging to the Sheta, together with the cities which were dependent on them.

"In the third year Ahuni, son of Hateni, rebelled against me, and having become independent, established his seat of government in the city of Tel Barasba. . . . . Then I went out from the city of Nineveh, and crossed the Euphrates. I attacked and defeated Ahuni in the city of Sitrat, which was situated up the Euphrates, and which Ahuni the son of Hateni had made one of his capitals. The rest of the country I brought under subjection, and Ahuni, son of Hateni, with his gods, and his chief priests, his horses, his sons, and his daughters, and all his men of war, I brought away to my country of Assyria.

"In the fifth year I went up to the country of Abyari; I took eleven great cities; I besieged Akitta of Erri, in his city, and received his tribute.

"In the sixth year I went out from the city of Nineveh, and proceeded to the country situated on the river Belek. The ruler of this country having resisted my authority, I displaced him, and appointed Tisimba to be lord of the district; and I there established the Assyrian sway. . . . . From the city of Umen I went out and came to the city of Barbara. Then Hem-ithra of the country of Atesh, and Arhulena, of Hamath, and the kings of Sheta, and the tribes that were in alliance with them, arose; setting their forces in battle array, they came against me. By the grace of Assarac, the great and powerful god, I fought with them, and defeated them; 25,000 of their men I slew in battle, or carried away into slavery. Their leaders, their captains, and their men of war I put in chains.

"In the seventh year I proceeded to the country belonging to Khabni of Tel-ati, the chief city of Tel-ati, which was his chief place, and the towns which were dependent on it I captured and gave up to pillage. I went out from the city of Tel-ati, and came to the land watered by the head streams which form the Tigris. The priests of Assarac in that land raised altars to the immortal gods. I appointed priests to reside in the land to pay adoration to Assarac, the great and powerful god, and to preside over the national worship. . . . . .

"In the eighth year, against Sut Baba, king of Taha-Dunis, appeared Sut-Bel Herat, and his followers. . . . . .

"In the ninth year a second time I went up to Armenia, and took the city of Lunanta. By the assistance of the gods Assarac and Sut, I obtained possession of Sut Bel-herat, in the city of Umen—I put him in chains. Afterwards Sut Bel-herat, together with his followers, I condemned to slavery. Then I went down to Shinar, and in the city of

Shinar, of Borsippa, and of Ketika I erected altars, and founded temples to the great gods. . . . . .

"In the tenth year, for the eighth time, I crossed the Euphrates. I took the cities belonging to Ara-lura of the town of Shalumas, and gave them up to pillage. . . . . . I took the city of Arnia, which was the capital of the country, and I gave up to pillage 100 of the dependent towns. I slew the wicked, and carried off the treasures. At this time Hem-ithra, king of Atesh, Arhulena, king of Hamath, and the twelve kings of the tribes who were in alliance with them, came forth, arraying their forces against me. They met me, and we fought a battle, in which I defeated them, making prisoners of their leaders, and their captains, and their men of war, and putting them in chains. . . . . .

"In the thirteenth year I descended to the plains dependent on the city of Assar-animet. I went to the district of Yata. I took the forts, slaying the evil-disposed, and carrying off all the wealth of the country. . . . . .

"In the sixteenth year I crossed the river Zab, and went against the country of the Arians. Set Mesitek, king of the Arians, I put in chains, and brought his wives, and warriors, and his gods, captives to my country of Assyria; and I appointed Yanvu, the son of Khanab, to be king over the country in his place. . . . .

"In the twenty-first year, for the twentieth time, I crossed the Euphrates, and again went up to the country of Khazakan of Atesh. I occupied his territory, and while there received tribute from the countries of *Tyre*, of *Sidon*, and of *Gubal*.

"In the twenty-second year, for the twenty-first time, I crossed the Euphrates, and marched to the country of *Tubal*. Then I received the submission of the twenty-four kings of *Tubal*. . . . . .

"In the twenty-third year I again crossed the Euphrates, and captured the city of Huidara, the stronghold of Ellal of Meluda; and the kings of Tubal again came in to me, and I received their tribute.

"In the twenty-fourth year I crossed the river Zab, and passing away from the land of Kharkhar, went up to the country of the Arians. Yanvu, whom I had made king of the Arians, had thrown off his allegiance, so I put him in chains.

"I then went out from the land of the Arians and received the tribute of the twenty-seven kings of the Persians. Afterwards I removed from the Persians and entered the territory of the Medes, going on to Ratsir and Kharkhar. . . . . I established the authority of my empire in the city of Kharkhar. Yanvu, the son of Khaban, with his wives and his gods, and his sons and his daughters, his servants, and all his property, I carried away captive into my country of Assyria. . . . . .

"In the thirtieth year, whilst I was still residing in the city of Calath, I summoned Detarassar, the general of my army, and sent him forth to war in command of my cohorts and forces.

"Huelka, of Minni, had thrown off his allegiance, and declared himself independent, establishing his seat of government in the city of Tsiharta. My general therefore put him in chains, and carried off his flocks and herds, and all his property, and gave his cities over to pillage.

"In the thirty-first year, a second time whilst I abode in the city of Calah, occupied in the worship of the gods Assarac, Hein, and Nebo, I summoned the general of my army, Detarassar of Ittana, and I sent him forth to war, in command of my troops and cohorts. He went out accordingly, in the first place to the territories of Daten of Hubiska, and received his tribute; then he proceeded to Enseri, the capital city of the country of the Bazatsera, and he occupied the city of Enseri and the thirty-six other towns of the country of Bazatsera. And he afterwards moved to the country of the Arians, where, by the help of the gods Assarac and Sut, he captured their cities, and continued his march to the country of Kharets, taking and despoiling 250 towns, until at length he descended into the plain of Esmes, above the city of Umen."

RELICS.

Many curious relics have been discovered among the ruins of Nineveh. At Nimrud fragments of bronze furniture were found belonging to the palace —terra-cotta vases, some of which were glazed with a blue vitrified substance; three engraved cylinders or rolling seals, one of which is of transparent glass; a silver ring; fragments of ivory, delicately carved, some being gilt. Many painted bricks were found, some of them cylindrical in form. On the sides of these bricks were stamped cuneiform writings, showing that a very near approach to the art of printing was made by the Assyrians over 3000 years ago. Besides the letters on the bricks, there was discovered on one of them the footprints of a weasel, which must have sported over the brick before it had been baked. Thus the little animal and the mighty king had stamped the record of their existence on the same piece of clay.

In excavating in the mound Khorsabad a large gate was discovered, which appears to have been one of the entrances to the city; two long rows of columns, also the cellar of the palace, containing regular rows of jars, which had the appearance of having been filled with wine, for at the bottom of the jars there was a deposit of a violet color. In another place copper nails, of various shapes and sizes, were found, which doubtless belonged to the roof, as some of them had undergone the action of fire when the roof was burned, and were partially melted. A ring was found fixed in the wall above a bronzed lion. A fragment of a circle was also found, which was doubtless a part of a wheel, as on its inside the ends of spokes are still to be seen. One of the courts was paved with square kiln-baked bricks, on which was stamped a cuneatic inscription containing the name of the king who built the palace. Before the three doors of the façade forming the porch are holes the size of one of the bricks, and about 14 inches in depth. These holes are lined with tiles, and have a ledge round the inside, so that they might be covered by one of the bricks without betraying the existence of the cavity. In these cavities were found small images of baked clay of frightful aspect, some with a human head and a lion's body, others with a lynx's head and human body.

At the entrances of temples and palaces were found —first, either symbolic bulls or winged divinities, on which were long inscriptions, always the same—probably incantations or prayers, followed by the aforementioned secret cavities, in which images of a compound character were hidden. Thus the sacred and the royal precincts were trebly guarded by divinities, inscriptions, and hidden gods, from the approach of any subtle spirit, or more palpable enemy that might have escaped the vigilance of the guard.

In a floor beneath a mystic basso-relievo was found a slab 10 feet by 8, and two feet thick, which was ascended by steps, the sides being inscribed, and appeared to have been used in connection with some sacrifice. Around the slab was a conduit, to carry off the blood of the victim, and under the stone there were found some bones, and some fragments of gold leaf. Besides this there were two other hollowed square stones, in the north-eastern corner of the chamber.

The ground on which the city of Mosul stands is also a part of the site of Nineveh; and here too are several mounds of ruins—the sculptures and inscribed slabs from which have been used as building material by the natives; but the authorities have not yet permitted an examination to be made here.

Beker Effendi, while digging in the mound Kouyunjik for stone to build the bridge at Mosul, found a

IMAGES.

DIVINATION CUP.

15

sepulchral chamber in which was an inscription, and among the rubbish the following articles: A woman's (khal khal) ankle bracelet, of silver cord with turquoise, colored with rust; a bracelet of gold beads, quite perfect; and some pieces of engraved agate.

Among the latest discoveries made at Nineveh are those by Layard in the mound' Nimrud. He effected an entrance into the old Nimrud palace, where he found an extraordinary collection of relics —swords, shields, bowls, crowns, caldrons, ornaments in ivory and mother-of-pearl. The vessels were formed of a kind of bronze, some of them perfectly preserved, and as bright as gold when the rust was removed. The engraving and embossing on them comprise mystic subjects, and are very elaborate and beautiful. In excavating in another part of this mound, he penetrated a mass of masonry, within which he discovered the tomb and statue of Sardanapalus, accompanied by full annals of that monarch's reign engraved on the walls. He also found tablets of all sorts—all of them being historical. But the crowning discovery made by Layard was in the mound, Kouyunjik. The great palace there had evidently been destroyed by fire, but one portion of this edifice seemed to have escaped its influence; and in excavating in that part, he found a large room filled with what appeared to be the archives of the empire, ranged in successive tablets of terra cotta, the writings being as perfect as when the tablets were first stamped. They were piled in huge heaps from the floor to the ceiling. From the progress already made in reading the inscriptions, the contents of these tablets will doubtless be made out. *There is a passage in the book of Ezra, where the Jews, having been disturbed in building the temple, prayed that search might be made in the house of records for the edict of Cyrus, permitting them to return to Jerusalem. The chamber above mentioned might be presumed to be the house of records of the Assyrian kings, where copies of the royal edicts were duly deposited.*

The condition of the ruins of Nineveh is highly corroborative of the sudden destruction that came upon that city by fire and sword, and the representations and inscriptions found on the walls of the many chambers and courts afford a strong confirmation of the prophecies. "Then shall the fire devour thee, the sword shall cut thee off." It is evident from the ruins that the city was first sacked and then set on fire. "She is empty and void, and waste." "For the stone shall cry out of the wall, and the beam out of the timber shall answer it. Woe to him that buildeth a town with blood and establisheth a city by iniquity" —the latter prophecy unmistakably indicating the rapacity and cruelty of the Assyrian nation.

The veritable descendants of the ancient inhabitants of Assyria and Nineveh are found in the Chaldean or Nestorian tribes, inhabiting the mountains of Kurdistan, and villages in the neighborhood of the ruins of Nineveh. Most of the so-called Arabs here are also descendants of the ancient inhabitants of the provinces of the Assyrian empire. These people still speak a Shemitic dialect, almost identical with the Chaldee of Daniel and Ezra. Their physical character also marks them as the same race.

Although the soil is rich and fertile, and capable of sustaining a vast population, still a curse appears to hang over the land, and the number of its inhabitants is yearly diminishing, so that there seems to be no prospect that for generations to come this once favored country will be other than a wilderness.

DAMASCUS.

ITS GREAT ANTIQUITY—A SKETCH OF ITS HISTORY—ITS SINGULAR ANCIENT RUINS.

This is the oldest city in the world still standing, and was an *ancient* city in the time of Christ. For over four thousand years Damascus has been a spectator of the events of the world. She takes note of time not by months or years, but by the kingdoms and empires she has seen rise, flourish, and pass away. From villages she saw Baalbek, Thebes, and Ephesus grow into cities that amazed the world with their size and grandeur—then witnessed their decay and desolation, and saw their ruins inhabited by owls and bats. She saw the kingdom of Israel rise, establish its capital at Jerusalem, become mighty, build the wonderful Temple of Solomon, and she saw it annihilated. She witnessed the advent of Greece among the nations of the earth—witnessed her career of two thousand years; then saw her perish. In her old age Damascus saw Rome built, the Roman Empire rise and overshadow the world with its power, then saw it perish. She has noted the rise and fall of a thousand of empires, and will doubtless see the tombs of a thousand more.

According to Josephus, Damascus was founded by Uz, son of Aram, grandson of Shem, and although it dates so far back in the history of the world, still but little is known of this city until the time of David, 1041 B. C.

Damascus was formerly the capital of the kingdom of Syria, and in the reign of David the Syrians of Damascus came to assist Hadadezer, with whom David was at war, but were completely defeated, and their territory garrisoned with Israelites by David. In Solomon's time, however, the Syrians threw off the foreign yoke, and in a few generations became a formidable rival of Israel.

The two Benhadads—father and son—waged long and bloody wars with the kings of Israel, and when Hazael killed his master and seized the throne of Damascus, it fared still worse with the Israelitish territories. He defeated the united forces of Israel and Judah, seized the country east of the Jordan, made the king of Israel his tributary, and even levied a contribution on Jerusalem.

In New Testament history, Damascus is chiefly celebrated as having been the scene, not precisely of St. Paul's conversion, but of his residence for a short time after his conversion, and his first labors in the cause of Christ. At that time the city contained a large Jewish population. Afterwards it became the seat of a Christian bishop, who ranked next in that

ANCIENT WALLS OF DAMASCUS.

DAMASCUS, FROM SALAHIYEH.

quarter to the patriarch of Antioch, and among the bishops who took part in the Council of Nice (A. D. 325) was Magnus of Damascus. But in process of time the Christian influence in Damascus was overshadowed by the Mohammedan. A. D. 635, the city fell into the hands of Khalif Omar—the Khalifs of the house of Ommyah even fixed their residence in it—so that Damascus again became the capital of a powerful empire. For nearly a century it sent forth armies that spread terror from the plains of Languedoc to those of Hindustan. But the dynasty of the Ommyades at length gave way to that of the Abassides, which fixed its seat at Bagdad and governed Damascus by a prefect. Subsequently, the city shared in the manifold vicissitudes which passed over the provinces of Western Asia, till A. D. 1516, when it fell into the hands of Sultan Selim I.; from which time it has remained under the sway of Turkey—the head of a large pashalic, and the most populous and flourishing city in Asiatic Turkey.

In tenacity of existence, and the power of retaining a certain measure of prosperity under all dynasties, and through the most varied successions of fortune, this city stands unrivaled in the world's history.

Damascus is 150 miles N. E. of Jerusalem, and is situated in a plain at the foot of the most eastern range of Anti-Libanus—2300 feet above the level of the sea, which gives it a temperate climate and cool breezes. The plain in which the city stands is 50 miles in circumference—open to the desert of Arabia on the south and east, and bounded on the north and west by the mountains.

The river Barada (ancient Abana) and its branches run through the city—which, with the river Pharpar, water and render very fertile a tract of country 30 miles in extent. The traveler, approaching Damascus from any direction, is fascinated by the view. In the midst of a vast plain is seen an island of deep verdure, walnuts and apricots waving above,—corn and grass below, and in the midst of this mass of foliage Damascus, with its white streets and lofty minarets. It is the most purely Oriental city remaining of all that are named in the Bible. Its public buildings and bazars are fine; and many private dwellings, though outwardly mean, are decorated within in a style of the most costly luxury. Its position has made it from the first a commercial city. The cloth called damask originated here; the Damask rose is a native; and Damascus steel has never been equaled. It still carries on an extensive traffic in woven stuffs of silk and cotton, in fine inlaid cabinet-work, in leather, fruits, sweet-meats, and every branch of Eastern commerce. For this purpose, huge caravans assemble here at intervals, and traverse as of old the desert routes to remote cities. Here, too, is a chief gathering-place of pilgrims from the north to Mecca.

The principal street is the one which tradition claims is the street called Straight in the Bible, and in which Saul took up his abode after his conversion. This street runs through the city nearly east and west, and is about a mile in length. It is not now by any means what it was in ancient times. In the Roman age, and up to the time of the Mohammedan conquest, it was a noble street, extending through the city much longer and wider than at present. It was divided by Corinthian colonnades into three avenues, opposite and corresponding to the three portals. The remains of these colonnades have been traced over a third of the length of the street. Wherever excavations are made in the line of the street, bases of columns are found, and fragments of shafts lying prostrate under accumulated rubbish. This street was like those seen in Palmyra and Jerash; but the devastations of war, and the vandalism of Turkish rulers, have destroyed most of its ancient grandeur.

Saul of Tarsus was particularly bitter against the then new sect called Christians, and started on a crusade against them. He went forth "breathing threatenings and slaughter against the disciples of the Lord."

"And as he journeyed he came near Damascus, and suddenly there shined round about him a light from heaven. And he fell to the earth and heard a voice saying unto him, 'Saul, Saul, why persecutest thou me?' And when he knew that it was Jesus that spoke to him he trembled, and was astonished, and said, 'Lord, what wilt thou have me to do?'" He was told to enter the city, and one would tell him what to do. Saul rose up and found that he was blind, so "they led him by the hand and brought him to Damascus, where he lay three days blind in the house of Judas * (which was in the street called Straight), during which time he neither ate nor drank. Then there came a voice to Ananias, saying, 'Arise and go into the street called Straight, and inquire at the house of Judas for one

* Not the Judas who betrayed his Master.

called Saul of Tarsus; for behold he prayeth. " Ananias went as ordered, found Paul, and ordained him to preach. At a short distance from the street called Straight is the reputed house of Ananias, and in a part of it is a room some 14 feet under ground, the masonry of which bears evidence of great antiquity, and is doubtless a part of the house of Ananias. The house of Naaman is also pointed out. Naaman was commander of the Syrian armies, but was a leper. The house said to have been his, is now a hospital for lepers.

Among the most important public structures is the castle in the N. W. part of the city, and above all the great Mosque of the Ommyades, which was originally a heathen temple, and afterwards the church of *St. John the Baptist.* It occupies a quadrangle of 489 feet by 324; is of various styles of architecture, divided into naves and aisles by Corinthian pillars; has a floor of tesselated marble, and three minarets. Besides this there are 80 smaller mosques, the domes and minarets of which are among the chief architectural ornaments of the city.

The Gates of the city are the Gate of the Camels, leading to the Arabs' rendezvous; the Paradise Gate, a large gate with a gloomy archway leading into a bustling bazar, near the centre of the south wall, and "Bab Tooma" or Gate of Thomas, so called in memory of the brave Christian champion who so nobly withstood the Saracen besiegers.

The bazars of Damascus present varied and striking scenes; and the traveler is bewildered amid the gay colors of the various articles exposed for sale, and the groups of people that are seen passing and repassing in all the different and singular costumes of the East. Here may be seen Agas moving with slow and stately tread, dressed in white turbans and scarlet silk cloaks edged with costly fur, with diamond-hilted kandjars and yataghans gleaming in their girdles. They are followed each by five or six obsequious retainers, and a black slave carries their pipes and scarlet tobacco-bags. Swarthy and grim-visaged Arabs and Bedouins from the great desert, with their coarse cloaks hanging upon them like the drapery of an ancient statue, congregate round the tobacco-shops, the armorers, and saddlers. Frequently the crowd is compelled to make way for a procession of great men on horseback—or culprits led about the streets preceded by an officer shouting their crimes, and calling upon all to take warning. The bazars are graced with the presence of women, who make all the purchases for the household; and the gallantry displayed by the shopmen in dealing with their fair customers seems to invite them to linger over their purchases, very much as their more civilized sisters do in London and New York.

In the day-time the narrow streets swarm with men, women, and children. But at night there is but little travel, as the streets are not lighted, and those who do go out carry lanterns as in ancient times. The present population of Damascus is 150,000, of which 130,000 are Moslems, 15,000 Christians, and 5,000 Jews.

The Moslems are very fanatical and vindictive against Christians and all who are not Mohammedans; and in July, 1860, they massacred 6,000 of the Christian population, and burned their quarter of the city. Their thirst for the blood of Christians extended to the mountains of Hermon and Anti-Lebanon, and in a short time 25,000 more were slaughtered and their possessions laid waste.

Among the Christian population were members of the ancient Order of Masons, and this fearful uprising and massacre was checked by one of their number—Abdel-Kadir—a Mohammedan himself, but of large and noble nature. This man saved many thousands of lives by his prompt and resolute action, at the time when Moslem fanaticism threatened the destruction of every Christian in Damascus, and indeed in all Syria. This may well be regarded as one of the most brilliant and chivalric acts of fraternal devotion that has been exhibited in modern times.

SHECHEM,

NOW NABULUS—JACOB'S WELL—THE TOMB OF JOSEPH.

This ancient city is 29 miles north of Jerusalem, between mounts Gerizim and Ebal. It is first mentioned in the history of Abraham, who here erected his first altar in Canaan, and took possession of the country in the name of Jehovah. When Jacob arrived here from Mesopotamia, Shechem was a Hivite city, of which Hamor, the father of Shechem, was the head man. At this time the patriarch purchased from that chieftain "the parcel of the field," which he subsequently bequeathed to his son Joseph.

ABD-EL-KADER.

The value of this field was greater on account of the well which Jacob had dug here, so as not to be dependent on his neighbors for water. The defilement of Dinah—Jacob's daughter—the capture of Shechem, and the massacre of the male inhabitants by Simeon and Levi, are events of this period. Joshua assembled the people here shortly before his death, and delivered to them his last counsel. After the conquest of Canaan, Shechem became a Levitical city, a city of refuge in Ephraim and a gathering-place of the tribes. After the ruin of Samaria by Shalmaneser, Shechem became the capital of the Samaritans; and at the present day it is the seat of a small remnant of that people. The enmity between the Samaritans and Jews is still as great as in the time of Christ.

The present population is about 10,000, consisting of 150 Samaritans, and between 500 and 600 Christians, 100 Jews, and the rest Arabs and Mohammedans. The main street runs E. and W., and contains a well-stocked bazar. Most of the other streets cross the main street, and in the cross streets are the small shops and work-stands of the artisans. Many of the streets are narrow and dark, as the houses hang over them on arches, very much the same as in the closest parts of Cairo. There are no public buildings of any note except the Keniseh, or Synagogue of the Samaritans, and five mosques. The synagogue is a small edifice about four centuries old, containing nothing remarkable except an alcove screened by a curtain, in which their sacred writings are kept.

The houses are high, built of stone with flat roofs,

and surmounted by small domes. There are many springs and natural fountains in and about the city, and some of the many beautiful gardens are watered from the fountains, while others have a soil sufficiently moist. Figs, almonds, walnuts, oranges, grapes, and pomegranates are abundant. But the olive now, as in ancient times, is the principal tree.

This city being, as it were, the gateway between Jaffa and Beirut, on the coast and the interior, is the seat of an active commerce and of a comparative luxury to be found in but few Oriental cities. Here are manufactured many of the coarse woolen fabrics; cloth of camel's hair, and delicate silk goods.

The most remarkable antiquity here is Jacob's well. It is covered by an arched stone chamber, entered by a narrow hole in the roof. The mouth of the well is covered by a large flat stone with a circular aperture, and its depth is 105 feet. This well is on the road from Jerusalem, and is visited by many pilgrims every year. It bears every mark of great antiquity, and is so clearly marked by the Evangelist, that if no tradition existed for its identity, the place could not be mistaken. Wearied with his journey, the Saviour sat near this well and taught the Samaritan woman, saying—"God is a spirit, and they that worship him must worship him in spirit and in truth." Upon the return of the woman to the city she reported her remarkable interview with Jesus to the people, upon which they flocked out to hear him. In addressing them, Christ pointed his disciples to the waving fields of grain in the plain around, exclaiming, "Say not ye there

Shechem.

are yet four months, and then cometh the harvest? Behold, I say unto you, lift up your eyes and look on the fields; for they are white already to harvest." The tomb of Joseph is about a quarter of a mile north of the well. It is a small square enclosure of high walls surrounding a tomb of the ordinary kind. An altar black with the traces of fire is at the head, and another at the foot of the tomb. In the walls are two slabs with Hebrew inscriptions, and the interior is almost covered with the names of pilgrims in Hebrew, Arabic, and Samaritan. The base of Mt. Ebal, opposite the city, is full of ancient excavated tombs, and on Mt. Gerizim are the ruins of a strong fortress.

GAZA

is in the s. w. corner of Palestine, 45 miles s. w. of Jerusalem. It is first mentioned in Genesis as a border town of the Canaanites (B. C. 1920). It was one of the chief cities of the Philistines, and is remarkable for its continuous existence for over 3,800 years. Gaza is situated on the main road between Syria and the valley of the Nile. Its commanding position and strong fortifications rendered it important in a military as well as commercial sense. Its name (=the strong) was well elucidated in its siege by Alexander the Great, which lasted five months, and in which he was wounded. In the conquest of Joshua the territory of Gaza is mentioned as one he was not able to subdue. Samson carried away its gates, but afterwards perished under the ruins of its vast temple. At subsequent periods Gaza was occupied by Chaldeans, Persians, and Egyptians. The Jewish king, Alexander Jannæus, captured it about 96 B. C. In A. D. 634 it came under Moslem rule.

The modern town stands partly on an oblong hill and partly on the low ground, and contains a population of about 15,000 inhabitants. The climate of this place is nearly tropical, but it has deep wells of excellent water.

The ruins of the old city cover a large hill, which is about three miles from the sea. Among the ruins are those of the fortress that so long withstood Alexander the Great.

BEERSHEBA.

Beersheba (the Well of the Oath) is 28 miles southwest of Hebron—at the southern extremity of the Holy Land; Dan lay at the northern extremity; so that the phrase, from Dan to Beersheba, meant from the northern to the southern end of Palestine. Abraham dug a well here, and gave the name Beersheba, because here he and Abimelech, King of the Philistines, "sware" both of them, but the compact was ratified by the setting apart of "seven ewe lambs," and from the Hebrew word, Sheba,—seven, the name of the place.

The town that rose here was first assigned to Judah, and then to Simeon. It was a seat of idolatry in the time of Uzziah. After the captivity it was repeopled by the Jews, and continued a large village many centuries after the coming of Christ. There are at present on the spot two large wells and five smaller ones. The large wells are 100 yards apart, and are visible from a considerable distance. The larger of the two is 12½ feet in diameter, and 44 feet to the surface of the water, which is excellent.

These wells are surrounded by drinking-troughs of stone, for camels and flocks—such as they doubtless have been from patriarchal times.

The curb-stones round the mouth of these wells, like those of a few other ancient wells in Palestine, have deep grooves worn in them by the action of the ropes used in drawing up the water during so many centuries. North of the wells, on some low hills, are the ruins of a town of considerable size, the name of which is unknown.

Beersheba is interesting from its associations, rather than from its intrinsic importance as an inhabited place.

Here Abraham planted a grove, and worshipped Jehovah, the ever-living God. From here he set out to offer up Isaac as a sacrifice on Mount Moriah—the place where Isaac resided when he was bowed down under the infirmities of age—where Jacob stole the blessing from him, the blessing that was meant for Esau—the place where the two brothers met to convey the remains of their aged father to the cave of Machpelah.

BETHEL,

NOW BEITIN,

is 10 miles north of Jerusalem, on the right of the ancient road to Shechem. It occupies the spot near where Jacob slept and had his remarkable dream, in which he saw the ladder reaching from earth to heaven, and the angels of God ascending and descending upon it.

Abraham first pitched his tent in Palestine on the high ground eastward of this spot, still one of the best tracts of pasturage in the whole land.

After the destruction of the Baal worship by Jehu, Bethel comes more prominently into view, and in the time of Jeroboam II. it was a royal residence, with a "king's house," and altars. Another mention of the altar of Jeroboam, with its last loathsome fire of "dead men's bones" burning upon it, is found in the account of Josiah's iconoclasm (xxiii.). The men of Bethel and Ai returned with Zerubbabel from Babylon.

The ruins of the ancient city are found on the south side of a hill, and cover nearly four acres of ground. They consist of many foundations, and crumbling walls of houses and public buildings. On the highest part of the hill, towards the N. N. W., are the remains of a square tower, and near the southern point are the walls of a church, standing within the foundations of a larger and much more ancient structure. The ruins of other churches are also found in this vicinity. Near by are the remains of one of the largest reservoirs in Palestine, measuring 314 feet in length by 217 feet in width. The walls were built of massive stones, and the southern wall is still entire. The bottom of this reservoir is now a grass-plot, having in it two living springs of good water. Whether they are natural springs, or whether they are fed by a buried aqueduct, has not yet been discovered.

BETHLEHEM.

BIRTH-PLACE OF DAVID, AND OF JESUS CHRIST.

Bethlehem is south of Jerusalem, about 4 miles distant, but by the route through Joppa gate and the valley of Rephaim the distance is greater. The road from Jerusalem to Bethlehem is through a wild, uncultivated tract, but beautiful and full of interest. On each side are well-known hills and monuments. On the plain near Bethlehem is the tomb of Rachel, in a solitary spot, without palm, cypress, or any tree to spread its shade.

Bethlehem is situated on the brow of a high hill, and commands an extensive view of the surrounding country. In the time of Christ the hills around it were terraced and clothed with vines, fig and almond trees, and the valleys bore rich crops of grain.

This city is rendered memorable and holy as the birth-place of David, and of Jesus Christ. Over that spot the guiding star hovered; there the eastern sages worshipped the infant Redeemer; and there, where David watched his flocks and praised God, were heard the songs of an angelic host at the Saviour's birth.

The modern town is on a hill facing the east. The village is triangular, and walled in, having one principal street. The roofs of the houses are flat, and upon the house-tops are dovecotes constructed of a series of earthen pots. The sides of the hill, and the slopes without the town, abound in figs, almonds, olives, and aromatic plants.

The plain to the eastward is that on which tradition says the angels appeared to the shepherds, and is called the Shepherds' Field. As the plains were cultivated, it is probable that the shepherds would have been found on the hill, where they now may be found with their flocks.

A church, containing the monuments of the three shepherds, is mentioned by Arculfus as standing in the midst of the fields and terraced gardens. Jerome lived here in a cell, which is now pointed out, where he wrote his Commentaries, and compiled the Latin Vulgate—the best ancient version of the Scriptures.

The present population is about 3,000, nearly all Christians, who manufacture and supply pilgrims with crucifixes, beads, and models of holy places.

A little beyond the northern extremity of the town is the magnificent Church of the Nativity, said to have been built by the Emperor Justinian. The roof of this church is supported by numerous Corinthian columns. The lofty roof of the nave is formed of cedar-wood of most admirable finish, and is still in good preservation. Between the columns lamps are hung, and a chandelier is also suspended from the roof. Two spiral staircases, of 15 steps each, lead down to the grotto of the Nativity, which is some twenty feet below the level of the church. This crypt, which is 39 feet long, 11 feet wide, and 9 feet high, is hewn out of the rock, and the sides and floor are lined with various kinds of marble. A rich altar, where lamps continually burn, stands over the place where the Saviour is said to have been born—the spot being marked by a silver star inlaid with gold, and studded with gems, bearing the inscription—*Hic de Virgine Maria Jesus Christus est.*

In a small recess in one side of the crypt, a little below the level of the floor, is a block of white marble, hollowed out in the form of a manger.

The Prophet Micah thus foretold the birth of Christ —"But thou Bethlehem Ephratah, though thou be little* among the thousands of Judah, yet out of thee shall he come forth unto me *that* is to be Ruler in Israel; whose goings forth *have been* from of old, from everlasting."

SIDON,

NOW SAIDA.

Sidon is on the coast 20 miles N. of Tyre and 145 miles N. of Jerusalem.

This is another of the first settlements of the human family, as it was founded by Zidon, the oldest son of Canaan. In the time of Homer the Zidonians were eminent for their trade and commerce, their wealth and prosperity, and their skill in navigation, astronomy, and the manufactures of glass and metals. Upon the division of Canaan among the tribes by Joshua, Great Zidon fell to the lot of Asher—but that tribe never succeeded in gaining possession of it. The Zidonians continued long under their own government and kings, though sometimes tributary to the kings of Tyre. But they were at length successively subdued by the Babylonians, the Egyptians, and the Seleucidæ. Sidon was the station of the navy of An-

* In point of numbers compared with the other cities in Judea.

tiochus on the eve of a battle with the Rhodian fleet. At the close of the war with Antiochus it passed into the hands of the Romans—who deprived the inhabitants of their freedom.

Jesus thus alludes to Tyre and Sidon, when preaching to the Jews: "Woe unto thee, Chorazin! Woe unto thee, Bethsaida! for if the mighty works which have been done in you, had been done in Tyre and Sidon, they would have repented long ago in sackcloth and ashes. But I say unto you, it shall be more tolerable for Tyre and Sidon at the day of judgment than for you" (Matt. xi. 21, 22).

Saida is situated on a peninsula, running from N. E. to S. W. On the high ground stands the citadel,—an old square tower. A wall protects the city on the land side, running across the peninsula from shore to shore. The ancient harbor was formed by a long, low ledge of rocks lying parallel to the shore, and affording space enough to accommodate quite a fleet of small vessels; but the chief, Fakr-ed-Din, to protect himself against the Turks, caused the harbor to be partially filled up, since which time vessels have to lie outside to the N. of the ledge. On a rock here is an old castle, which is connected with the shore by a stone causeway.

The streets of Saida are narrow and crooked, but the houses are built of stone, and many of them are of good size, and well built. A curious feature of the city is that some of the houses are built on the wall, and constitute a part of it. Within the city are six khans for the use of travelers and merchants. The environs of Saida are watered by a stream from Leb-

SIDON—ITS RUINS.

anon, and are famous for their beautiful gardens of fruit-trees of every kind. The present population is about 5000.

The most notable ruins here are those of an immense theatre. This theatre was one of the largest in Asia Minor—capable of containing 15,000 spectators. The lower half of it was excavated in the solid rock, and the seats were of white marble, beautifully wrought; many of them remain, and are in a good state of preservation. There are also ruins of buildings in and around the town, and of a wall that extended into the sea. The place of sepulture of the ancient Sidonians was on the adjacent mountain—which is honey-combed with cells cut in the rock, and connecting with one another by arched doors. These cells are all rectangular, from 10 to 15 feet square, and contain three niches, one in each wall; the niche opposite the door usually exhibits sculptures in white marble surmounting a sarcophagus. Many of these cells have their walls covered with Phœnician inscriptions in bright colors. These cells are very similar to the Egyptian Catacombs, especially those of Sakara. In one of these sepulchral caves there was discovered in 1855 a singular Phœnician antiquity. It is a sarcophagus of black cyanite, with a lid carved in human form—bandaged like a mummy, the face being bare. On the lid and on the head are inscriptions in which the king of Sidon is mentioned. It evidently belongs to the 11th century B. C. This relic is now in the Louvre, Paris.

The Maronites have a small chapel in a garden at the gates of the town; and the tradition runs that here stood the house in which Mary, the sister of Lazarus, died.

JERICHO,

THE VALLEY OF MURDER.

This was a city of great antiquity and considerable importance—13 miles E. N. E. of Jerusalem, and 7 miles from the Jordan. Jericho was situated at the mouth of Wady Kelt, and where the road from Jerusalem comes into the plain. The Jericho destroyed by Joshua was nearer to the fountain of Elisha—the present Ain Sultan. On the west and north of Jericho rise high limestone hills; one of which, the dreary Quarantina, rises 1,500 feet above the plain. The walls of Jericho were so wide that houses were built on them. The entrance to the city was through several gates, which were closed at dark, the same as is the practice in the East at the present day.

Jericho is first mentioned as the city to which the spies were sent by Joshua; they lodged in the house of Rahab, upon the wall, and departed after promising to save her and all that were found in her house from destruction. In the annihilation that ensued, this promise was religiously kept. This was the first city taken by the Israelites west of the Jordan. Its walls are said to have supernaturally fallen down before the Jews, after being compassed about seven days; it was then burnt with fire—afterwards it was rebuilt, and gradually rose into importance again.

Over against Jericho, beyond the Jordan, "Elijah went up by a whirlwind into heaven." In its plains

THE VALLEY OF MURDER, NEAR JERICHO.

Zedekiah was overtaken and captured by the Chaldeans. In the return under Zerubbabel, the children of Jericho, 345 in number, were included.

Jericho was fortified by Bacchides, and afterwards adorned with palaces, castles, and theatres by Herod the Great. He also founded a new town higher up the plain, and called it Phasælis.

Christ visited Jericho, and between Jerusalem and Jericho was laid the scene of the parable of the good Samaritan. All that is left to represent ancient Jericho is the village of Riha, containing about 60 huts and an old square tower, occupied by a small garrison. The houses are built of stones from the ancient ruins, and are merely four walls with a flat roof. Each house has a garden around it enclosed by a hedge of the thorny boughs of the Nubk, a species of thorn-tree. A strong hedge of the same kind surrounds the whole village. The plain on which the village stands is rich and capable of easy tillage, with a climate to produce anything; but it now lies neglected, and the palm-trees, balsam, and honey for which it was famous, have long since disappeared.

The inhabitants now, as in the earliest time, are noted for their lewdness. In consequence of this the Arabs, when approaching the place, frequently provide themselves with a written paper or charm, as a protection against the wiles of its women.

The ruins about here are quite extensive, but so dilapidated that none of them can be recognized as belonging to any known structure. The most singular relic here is a block of sienite red granite, the fragment of a large circular stone laying partly buried in the earth. The diameter of this stone, when whole, could not have been less than 8 or 10 feet. Its circular edge is full of small round holes. Near by are the remains of a circular foundation, on which it once probably lay. This stone has every appearance of being Egyptian sienite.

About two miles from Jericho is the fountain Ain Sultan. This fountain bursts forth at the east side of a group of mounds. It appears to have been once surrounded by a reservoir of hewn stones, but this is now mostly broken away and gone. These mounds are covered with substructions of unhewn stone.

The route from Jericho to Jerusalem ascends through narrow rocky passes and deep ravines, and is a difficult and dangerous one, robberies being more frequent in it now than in the time of Christ; and the dusky robbers who lie in wait here for travelers are believed to be the veritable descendants of the ancient inhabitants of this district. A short distance up this road, is a deep dell called the Valley of Murder—the traditional scene of the event related in the parable of the good Samaritan. Near this are fonnd some massive ruins, in which is a deep arched vault or chamber, the entrance to which is nearly closed by débris.

SHUSHAN,

NOW SUSA.—CITY OF QUEEN ESTHER, MORDECAI, AND HAMAN.

This ancient and royal city was 800 miles E. of Jerusalem and 120 N. of the Persian Gulf, in what is called Elam on the map of the ancient world.

It was situated between the rivers Eulæus and Shapur—where vast mounds of ruins have been found.

Shushan was originally the capital of the country called Elam (first mentioned in Gen. xv). The first distinct mention of the city is in Dan. vii. 2. In the inscriptions of Asshur-bani-pal, the son and successor of Esarhaddon—he states that he took the place, and exhibits a ground plan of the city upon his sculptures. It was next in the possession of the Babylonians. After the conquest of Babylon by Cyrus it was transferred to the Persian dominions; this transfer was probably the work of Darius Hystaspes. Shortly afterwards the Achæmenian* princes made it the capital of their whole empire, and the chief place of their residence.

Shushan accordingly became the capital of Persia. The city retained its pre-eminence from this time until the period of the Macedonian conquest. When taken by Alexander he found there sixty millions of dollars and all the regalia of the great king.

Alexander's preference for Babylon caused the neglect of Susa by his successors, until it at length fell into the hands of Antigonus, B. C. 315. The town, but not the citadel, was taken by Milo in his rebellion against Antiochus the Great, B. C. 221. At the Arabian conquest of Persia, A. D. 640, it was bravely defended by Hormuzan.

This city was the scene of the remarkable events

* Median.

narrated in the Book of Esther; here Haman conspired against Mordecai and his people, the Jews, and procured an edict for their extermination, but was defeated by Mordecai and Queen Esther. Daniel had the vision of the ram and he-goat at Shushan the palace. Nehemiah was at Shushan when he obtained from Artaxerxes permission to return into Judea and repair the walls of Jerusalem.

The extent and character of the ruins found here indicate the great size and splendor of the city. They cover an area of over 7 miles in circumference, and consist principally of four great artificial mounds or platforms. Of these the western, although the smallest in extent, is much the highest—being 119 feet above the level of the river Shapur. It was constructed of sunburnt bricks, earth, and gravel. In the centre of the top of this mound is a deep circular depression, doubtless a large court, surrounded by elevated piles of buildings, the fall of which has given the present configuration to the surface.

This mound appears to have been the citadel or fortress. To the west of the citadel is the great central platform, covering upwards of 60 acres, 70 feet high, and very steep. The heavy rains of winter have worn deep ravines down the sides of this mound in many places; thus disclosing much of the work of its ancient builders. The northern platform is a square mass, about 1,000 feet each way, and from 50 to 60 feet high. East of the others is another very extensive platform, but lower than the rest. Beyond these a number of smaller mounds are found, extending nearly to the Dizful river.

COLUMN AT SHUSHAN.

RUINS OF THE PALACE AT SHUSHAN.

The most important discoveries made here were in the western mound.

This was the platform on which the king's palace stood. Here were discovered the bases of several of the columns, and the position of the whole of the seventy-two columns which supported the edifice. On the bases of four of these were found inscriptions, according to which this palace was built by Darius Hystaspes, and repaired by Artaxerxes Longimanus. It consisted of a central hall, about 200 feet square, and three great porches on the exterior of this, and separated from it by walls 18 feet thick. These were doubtless the great audience halls of the palace. The great central hall was probably used for all great ceremonies, such as the coronation of the kings, returning thanks, and making offerings to the gods for victories. The "king's gate," where Mordecai sat, was doubtless a hall measuring about 100 feet square, with its roof supported by four pillars, and standing 150 feet from the northern front of the portico. The inner court, where Queen Esther appeared to implore the king's favor, was probably the space between the "king's gate" and the northern terrace wall. The "royal house and the house of the women," it is supposed, were situated behind this great hall, and were connected with it by a covered bridge over the ravine.

As the hight of this splendid palace was 120 feet, and stood on a platform over 60 feet high, surrounded by subordinate palace buildings adorned with trees and shrubs, the whole reflected in the river at its base, the effect must have been truly grand and imposing.

Large blocks of marble covered with hieroglyphics are still found by Arabs when digging for hidden treasure; and at the foot of one of the mounds stands the tomb of Daniel, erected on the spot where the relics of that prophet are believed to rest.

The site of this once beautiful capital is now desolate, its only inhabitants being lions, wolves, lynxes, and jackals.

CHAPTER X.

SHILOH.

This was a famous city of Ephraim—about 18 miles north by east of Jerusalem, and 10 south of Shechem. The Ark of the Covenant remained here from B. C. 1444 to 1116 B. C. In honor of the presence of the Ark, there was a feast of the Lord in Shiloh yearly, in one of which the daughters of Shiloh were seized by a remnant of the Benjamites.

The ruins found here consist of fragments of columns, and large stones of various shapes. An immense oak, evidently of great age, stands among the ruins. Just beyond the precincts of Shiloh stands a dilapidated edifice, called by the natives the mosk of Seilun. At a short distance from the ruins is an ancient fountain, which first flows into a pool, and thence into a large stone reservoir—from which flocks and herds are watered—presenting a scene the same as might have been witnessed here 2000 years ago.

RABBAH.

This was a very strong place east of the Jordan,

RUINS OF RABBAH.

and as far back as the fourth century it was esteemed one of the most remarkable cities in Cœle—Syria. When first mentioned this was the chief city of the Ammonites, and was said to contain the bed, or sarcophagus, of the giant Og.

The site of Rabbah is 35 miles E. N. E. of Jerusalem, and 23 miles E. of the Jordan. It was situated near the southern source of the Jabbok, and on the road between Heshbon and Bostra, and was the last place at which a stock of water could be obtained for the journey across the desert. Its position was such as to render it an important garrison station for repelling the incursions of the wild tribes of the desert.

At the commencement of David's first campaign against the Ammonites, a part of the army under Abishai was sent as far as Rabbah to keep the Ammonites in check, but the main force under Joab remained at Medeba.

After the defeat of the Syrians at Helam the Ammonite war was resumed, and this time Rabbah was the main point of attack. Joab took the command, and laid siege to the city. The siege lasted nearly two years, as the inhabitants made a determined resistance, which was characterized by frequent fierce sallies. After Joab had taken the lower town, he sent for David, as he desired that *he* should have the honor of taking the citadel or stronghold of the place. David shortly after arrived, when the citadel was taken, and its inmates, with great booty, including the idol of Moloch, fell into his hands.

It was during the time of this siege by Joab that

Uriah, by order of David, was placed in the forefront of the battle, where he was slain (Sam. xi. 15, 16, 17).

In the time of Amos, two and a half centuries later, it again had a wall and palaces, and was still the sanctuary of Moloch. At this period it is frequently mentioned in such terms as imply that it was of equal importance with Jerusalem. From Ptolemy Philadelphus (B.C. 285) it received the name of Philadelphia, but afterwards resumed its ancient name. B.C. 30 it was taken from the Arabs by Herod the Great. When the Moslems conquered Syria they found this city in ruins—ruins remarkable for their extent and desolation. The principal ruins are those of a theatre and a fortress. The theatre was very large, and its walls are quite well preserved. The ruins of the fortress show that it was built of large square stones, put together without cement. The remains of private houses are also quite extensive.

SARDIS

is about 100 miles E. of Smyrna, and was formerly the capital of Crœsus, king of Lydia, proverbial for the immensity of his wealth.

Sardis, now Sart, is situated at the foot of Mount Tmolus. The route of Xerxes to Greece lay by Sardis. From its convenient position, and the fertile region surrounding this city, it was a commercial mart of considerable importance in the very earliest times. It was also a slave mart.

The art of dyeing wool is said to have been invented here, and it was the entrepôt of the dyed woolen manufactures. This was also the place where the metal electrum was procured, and here the Spartans sent, in the sixth century B.C., to purchase gold for gilding the face of the Apollo at Amyclæ. This gold was probably furnished from the auriferous sand of the Pactolus, a brook which ran through the forum by the side of the great temple of Cybele. This city changed hands several times during the contests after the death of Alexander. It was taken and sacked by the army of Antiochus the Great in 214 B.C. In the time of the Emperor Tiberius, Sardis was desolated by an earthquake, and a pestilence followed. It was taken and nearly destroyed by Tamerlane, A.D. 1400.

It is now a small village, but contains a large khan for the accommodation of travelers, it being on the road for the caravans coming out of Persia to Smyrna with silk.

The ruins of the ancient city are to the southward of the town, chief among which are those of the massive temple of Cybele, a theatre and a stadium. Two columns of the temple are still standing, and are 6 feet 4½ inches in diameter, at about 35 feet below the capital. One stone in their architrave was calculated to weigh 25 tons. The present soil is more than 25 feet above the pavement. The ruins of the theatre and stadium are on the north side of the Acropolis, overlooking the valley of the Hermus. The diameter of the theatre was 400 feet, and that of the stadium 1,000. The hight on which the citadel was built is badly shattered by an earthquake. The ruins and the countless sepulchral mounds in the vicinity indicate what Sardis was before earthquakes and the sword had laid it waste.

The Turks, in their hatred of all images, have sawn to pieces and burnt into lime nearly all of the beautiful sculptures which adorned the Temple and other public buildings, of which there were thousands of figures of men and animals in the best style of Greek art.

TARSUS

is 385 miles from Jerusalem *via* Joppa and the Mediterranean. It is situated in a fertile plain, on the banks of the river Cydnus, 12 miles from its mouth. This city was at one time the metropolis of Cilicia, and a place of considerable importance. It was distinguished for the culture of Greek literature and philosophy. In the number of its schools and learned men it rivaled Athens and Alexandria. It was also illustrious as the birth-place of the Apostle Paul (Saul).

It is now called Tarsous, and though much decayed and full of ruins, it still contains a population of 7,000 inhabitants in the summer, and 30,000 in the winter, mostly Turks. The excessive heat of summer drives a large part of the people to the highlands of the interior.

As the ancient city contained no public edifices of any considerable size, none of the many ruins can be identified.

TIBERIAS

was a city of Galilee, rebuilt by Herod Antipas, and named by him in honor of the Emperor Tiberias. It is 68 miles N. by E. of Jerusalem, and is situated on the western shore of Lake Gennesareth, not far from where the Jordan issues from the lake. On the shore, about a mile south of the town, are the celebrated warm baths which the Roman naturalist recorded among the greatest known curiosities in the world.

Tiberias was the capital of Galilee from the Roman conquest until the reign of Herod Agrippa II. Many of the inhabitants were Greeks and Romans, and foreign customs prevailed to such an extent as to give offence to the stricter Jews. Herod Antipas built here a palace, and established a race-course. In the Jewish war, which ended in the destruction of Jerusalem, Tiberias bore a conspicuous part, especially during the command of Josephus, in Galilee, who fortified this city. At that time there was here an immense Jewish *proseucha*—a house of prayer, in which he convened a public meeting of the people.

This city and Tarichæa still belonged to Agrippa, and Vespasian marched against them to subdue them again to his allegiance. On his approach to the city, the principal inhabitants went out and made their submission to him, and the Roman army occupied the town. They afterwards erected a fortified camp at Emmaus, which continued to be the headquarters during the siege of Tarichæa. That city was at length taken by troops under the command of Titus; great numbers of the inhabitants having escaped by water in boats, Vespasian had boats built, pursued and overtook them, when a battle was fought, in which the Jews were totally overthrown. In this battle, and in the capture of the city, the slain amounted to 7,700, of whom 1,200, being too old or too young to labor or bear arms, were put to death in cold blood in the stadium of Tiberias.

Celebrated schools of Jewish learning flourished here through a succession of several centuries, and the Mishna was compiled here by the great Rabbi, Judah Hakkodesh (A.D. 190).

During the reign of Constantine this city passed into the possession of the Christians; and during the Crusades it was lost and won repeatedly by the different combatants. Since that time it has been possessed successively by Persians, Arabs, and Turks, and is now under the rule of the latter. During its occupation by the Crusaders they erected a church—in which the Arabs have since housed their cattle.

The modern town, Tŭbarîyeh, stands on a part of the site of the ancient city; and was half destroyed by an earthquake in 1837. It has now a population of only 2,500 inhabitants, one-fourth of whom are Jews, and the rest Mohammedans and Christians. The inhabitants now, as of old, draw a considerable part of their subsistence from the lake, fish being quite plenty in it.

The walls of the town are little better than heaps of ruins, the castle is much shattered, and the whole place has an aspect of extreme wretchedness. South of the town are numerous ruins of a still more ancient city, probably Chinneroth, extending for a mile and a half nearly to the hot springs. The waters of these springs are salt, and too hot for immediate use, but they are still much resorted to by invalids.

CESAREA.

STRATO'S TOWER.

Cesarea was situated on the coast, 28 miles north of Joppa, and 66 from Jerusalem *via* Joppa.

In Strabo's time there was on this part of the coast merely a town, called "Strato's tower," with a landing-place. Afterwards Herod the Great built a city here, on which the utmost care and expense were lavished; a vast breakwater protected its harbor. Here the Herodian kings resided, also Festus Felix, and other Roman Procurators of Judea. Here were the headquarters of the military forces of the province. The population consisted chiefly of Jews, Greeks, and Romans. Constant feuds took place between the Jews and Greeks. At the Jewish synagogue the Old Testament was read in Greek.

At Cesarea, Vespasian was declared Emperor of Rome. This city was a place of considerable importance even as late as the time of the Crusades; but it is now utterly desolate, and its ruins have long been a quarry from which materials for building other towns have been drawn.

SOURCES OF THE JORDAN.

PANEAS, NOW BANIAS—SOURCES OF THE RIVER JORDAN.

Paneas is 120 miles N. N. E. of Jerusalem, at the base of Mount Hermon.

The annals of this city run back from Herod's time into the age of heathenism. It was the Panium of Josephus, and the Paneas of the Greeks and Romans, and the inscriptions are not yet obliterated which show that the god Pan had a sanctuary there. Titus exhibited gladiatorial shows in this city, in which he made the captive Jews fight and kill each other. The modern village is called Banias, the Arabic form of Paneas. It is small and poor, containing only 150 houses. Just north of the village is a well-built stone bridge.

The ruins of the ancient city are extensive, and consist of heaps of stone and architectural fragments. The vast castle above the site of the city is still the most remarkable fortress in Palestine.

At the base of the mountain, at the N. E. side of the village of Banias, is a spacious cavern, from which issues the eastern source of the Jordan. Niches have been cut in the face of the rocks directly above the cavern, and in other places, apparently to receive statues. When these niches were cut they had each an inscription, but they are now so obliterated that only a part of one can be made out. The second source of the Jordan is at a place called Tell el-Kady, three miles W. N. W. of Banias. Here is a small elevation, having a flat space on its top, in which are two springs, one of which is very large. The united waters of these springs form a considerable stream, which unites with that from Banias, 5 miles below. The third source is about 3 miles W. by N. from Hasbeiya. Here is a fountain, the waters of which are confined by a dam, forming a large basin; just below the dam

SOURCE OF THE RIVER JORDAN—PANEAS.

is a bridge. At a short distance west of this fountain are the remarkable pits or mines of solid asphaltum.

The locations of the sources of the Jordan are as follows—viz., the main eastern source, at Banias, is in Lat. 33° 17′, and 35° 40′ east Lon. from Greenwich; and the western source—Hasbeiya—is in Lat. 33° 30′, and Lon. 35° 41′.

Banias is 120 miles N. N. E. of Jerusalem, and Hasbeiya is 135. . . . . . .

CAPERNAUM.

The site of Capernaum is near the N. W. shore of the Sea of Galilee—78 miles N. by E. from Jerusalem. It was on the frequented route from Damascus to the Mediterranean. This was a chief city of Galilee in the time of Christ. It had a synagogue; also a customs station where dues were collected both by stationary and itinerant officers.

Capernaum was the residence of Christ during a considerable part of his ministry, and the scene of many of his wonderful works. It was here he worked the miracle on the Centurion's servant, on Simon's wife's mother, the paralytic, and on the men afflicted with an unclean spirit. The brothers Simon Peter and Andrew belonged at Capernaum. In consequence of the unbelief of the people of this and other cities of the plain, the Lord pronounced their doom: "And thou, Capernaum, which art exalted unto heaven, shalt be brought down to hell: for if the mighty works which have been done in thee had been done in Sodom, it would have remained until this day."

The ruins said to be those of Capernaum consist of walls and foundations covering a space of one-half a mile in length by one-fourth of a mile in width.

ANTIOCH.

DAPHNE—THE FAMOUS GROVE OF APOLLO.

Antioch is 300 miles N. by W. from Jerusalem, and 30 miles east of the Mediterranean Sea. Antioch was founded 301 B. C., by Seleucus Nicator, who named it after his father, Antiochus. It is situated on the left bank of the Orontes, in the midst of a fertile and beautiful plain, nearly surrounded by high hills. The neighborhood of these hills and the Mediterranean impart a freshness and salubrity to the climate of Antioch to be found in but few places in Syria. Its commercial advantages also were great; for the Orontes was navigable for small vessels to the sea, thus bringing it in easy communication with the traffic of the Mediterranean; while on the other side it was conveniently situated for a large caravan trade with the countries in the interior, especially Damascus.

Although Seleucus founded Antioch, the part built in his time was only what ultimately formed about one-fourth of the city; the other three parts were successively added—the last by Antiochus Epiphanes, to whom some of its chief embellishments were due; in particular a magnificent street of about four miles in length, with double colonnades, and crossed at right angles by other streets. Subsequent monarchs added public buildings, among which was a splendid museum built by Antiochus Philopater.

The city grew under the Seleucid (Greek) kings, until it became a metropolis of great extent and remarkable beauty. In its most flourishing period its population is estimated to have been over 300,000. From the first the Jews formed a considerable portion of the population, and enjoyed equal privileges with the Greeks.

At the commencement of the Christian era, Antioch had lost but little of its greatness and refinement—being then a place of high culture, and renowned for the cultivation of the arts and sciences. It was no less noted, however, for its luxurious living, effeminate manners, jocular humor, gross superstition, and licentious idolatry. Not only did the city itself contain unusual incitements to false worship, with their accompanying pollutions, but adjoining the city, and forming a kind of a suburb, was Daphne, with the famous temple and grove of Apollo. This suburb was deeply bosomed in a dense grove of laurels and cypresses, which was ten miles in circumference, and formed a cool and impenetrable shade. Many streams of the purest water, issuing from the hills, preserved the rich verdure of the earth, and temperature of the air; the senses were gratified with harmonious sounds, and aromatic odors. This peaceful grove was consecrated to health, luxury, and love. The vigorous youth pursued like Apollo the object of his desires; and the blushing maid was warned by the fate of Daphne to shun the folly of unreasonable coyness. The philosopher and soldier wisely avoided the temptation of this sensual paradise, where pleasure, assuming the character of religion, imperceptibly dissolved the firmness of manly virtue.

Notwithstanding the city was so corrupt and destructive to public decency, it not only enjoyed a large stated revenue from public pleasures, but was continually receiving fresh gifts from emperors and nobles, to increase the splendor of its edifices and the attractions of its peculiar suburb. Yet in the face of these corrupting agencies, and the powerful support they were receiving, Christianity found in Antioch one of its firmest strongholds; and in the course of time completely turned the tide against the long continued and richly endowed idolatry of the place. So that when the Emperor Julian went, on the occasion of the annual festival, after great preparations and apparent enthusiasm, to prove his devotions to the Daphnian Apollo, no offering was presented along with his, except a single goose, which was provided at the expense of a priest, who was the pale and solitary inhabitant of the decayed temple.

Antioch, the Queen of the East, from the beauty of its situation and the splendor of its buildings, might well deserve the dedication to Apollo which it obtained from Seleucus. But to the Christian it has a higher interest, as being the greatest Archiepiscopal see, filled by St. Peter himself; and the place where the disciples of Christ were first emboldened to adopt the name of the Divine Master. From its own importance as the finest and largest city in that part of Asia Minor, also from its commanding position, it can readily be understood how the first heralds of the Gospel should have sought to carry the tidings of salvation, and lay there the foundation of a Christian church. The efforts of the Apostles were crowned with such success, that this city became distinguished for the variety of its gifts, the liberality of its spirit, and its forwardness in the cause of Christianity.

Ignatius, who suffered martyrdom under Trajan at Rome, was bishop of Antioch forty years; Chrysostom, the eloquent preacher, was born here.

Antioch has suffered greatly by earthquakes, and has had its share in all the vicissitudes that passed over the district in which it is situated: conquered by the Saracens, retaken by the Greeks, again in the hands of the Moslems; during the wars of the Crusaders the scene of terrible battles, sieges, and brilliant exploits; again taken from the Moslems, and finally retaken by them.

In 1822 Antioch contained a population of 20,000, but in that year an earthquake destroyed one-fourth of its inhabitants. It is now an Arab village with a population of about 6000, and occupies only about one-fourth of the area inclosed within the ancient wall; the houses have sloping roofs, are covered with tiles, and are very slightly built,—the heavy snows that often fall in this part of the country, and the frequency of earthquakes, have taught the inhabitants to adopt this style of building. The Orontes is here headed back for the purpose of turning an enormous wheel to raise water, which is conducted by troughs to the farthest extremity of the town, — which, dripping in its passage over the streets, renders many of them impassable except under the cover of an umbrella.

The few Christians remaining in Antioch have no church; and the only external mark that has survived its ancient Christianity is the name borne by its principal gate—St. Paul. Many broken and scattered remains of its greatness are still to be seen among the ruins; and on the s. w. side of the town there is a steep mountain ridge, upon which a considerable portion of the old Roman wall is still standing, of great hight and thickness. At short intervals are high towers, containing a staircase and two or three chambers—probably guard-rooms. There were 400 of these towers. The wall runs in a direct line up the steepest part of the mountain to its top. The intervals between the towers were formed into stairs, by which the soldiers marched to and from their stations and the citadel above. The wall runs along two distinct hill-tops, separated from each other by a deep ravine, across which it was continued upon an arch for the water to pass, called the "Iron Port." But time and repeated earthquakes have nearly demolished this part of it.

After heavy rains antique marble pavements are visible in many parts of the town, and gems, cornelians, and rings are frequently found.

During the present year—1872—a terrible earthquake overthrew a part of the city, and destroyed several hundred of the people.

EPHESUS.

THE RENOWNED TEMPLE OF DIANA.

The site of this ancient city is about 40 miles S. E. of Smyrna, and 600 N. W. of Jerusalem. It was situated near the mouth of the river Cayster, and stood partly on the level ground, and partly on the hills Mt. Prion and Coressus. Its harbor at the mouth of the Cayster was admirably constructed, and was at one time capable of accommodating a large fleet of the shipping of the day. In the Roman times two great roads led eastward from Ephesus; one through the passes of Tmolus to Sardis and Galatia, and the other round the extremity of Pactyas to Magnesia, and up the valley of the Meander to Iconium, from whence the communication was direct to Syrian Antioch and the Euphrates. Corresponding with these roads, there appear to have been, on the E. side of Ephesus, Sardian and Magnesian gates. There were also coast roads leading northward to Smyrna, and southward to Miletus. By the latter the Ephesian elders traveled to meet Paul at the latter city. St. Paul's first visit to Ephesus was about A. D. 54, and on his return from the second missionary circuit. On his second visit he remained over two years, during which time he labored in the synagogue, schools, and in private houses. Here also the Apostle John spent the latter part of his life.

At the head of the harbor stood the great Temple of Diana, the tutelary divinity of the city. In consequence of the swampy nature of the ground, immense substructions were built, on which the temple was erected. The first temple was burnt—this happened the night that Alexander the Great was born (B. C. 356). But by the enthusiastic co-operation of all the inhabitants in this part of Asia, another temple was erected, which in many respects surpassed the first. The dimensions of the second temple were 425 feet long by 220 feet broad. It was built of white marble, cedar, and cypress, and was profusely ornamented with gold. It had 127 columns, each 60 feet high. The magnificence of this edifice was proverbial throughout the world, and the devotion to the goddess Diana was such that criminals were exempted from arrest at the temple, or even within an eighth of a mile of it. Another consequence of the worship of Diana at Ephesus was, that a large manufactory of portable shrines grew up there. These shrines were eagerly purchased by devotees, who set them up in their houses or carried them with them on their journeys.

The next remarkable structure at Ephesus was its theatre—the largest of its kind ever built.—It was 660 feet in diameter, and could accommodate 50,000 spectators.

Asia at this time was a proconsular province, but Ephesus was a free city, and had its own assemblies and magistrates. Conspicuous mention is made of the most important municipal officer of Ephesus—the *Town Clerk, or keeper of records*, who was a person of great responsibility and influence.

The ruins of the city are of vast extent, and the outlines of the theatre still remain in the solid rock.

Vestiges of the Temple of Diana have been traced only the present year by the Rev. J. T. Wood. Sculptures of great beauty and value have been brought to light, and it is expected that the explorations now going on will uncover many valuable relics of this ancient city.

GAD'A-RA

was a strong city 7 miles S. E. of the Sea of Galilee, and 65 N. N. E. of Jerusalem. It was situated near the river Hieromax, on the level summit of a steep limestone hill.

The first mention in history of Gadara is its capture by Antiochus the Great, B. C. 218. During the Jewish civil wars it was destroyed—and rebuilt by Pompey B. C. 63, and afterwards made the capital of a district by Gabinius. On the first outbreak of the war with the Jews, Gadara was captured by Vespasian, its inhabitants massacred, and the city with its surrounding villages burnt.

The ruins are extensive, and comprise the remains of two theatres, a city gate, part of the wall of the city, a straight main street, with its pavement nearly perfect, and prostrate columns on both sides of the street. But the most curious and interesting ruins here are the ancient tombs. They are very numerous in the cliffs around the city, and are cut in the solid rock—chambers from 10 to 20 feet square, with doors of stone turning on stone hinges. In the sides of these rooms are recesses in which the bodies were placed. Many of these sepulchral chambers have changed their character of tombs of the dead for habitations of the living, as the present inhabitants of the place use them for dwellings.

LYDDA

is nine miles from Joppa, on the road to Jerusalem. In the time of Josephus, Lydda was a place of considerable size and inportance. B. C. 45, this city, with the neighboring places, became the prey of the insatiate Cassius, by whom the inhabitants were sold into slavery to raise the exorbitant taxes imposed; but Antony soon restored them to their city and liberty. St. George was a native of Lydda, and after his martyrdom his remains were buried there, over which a church was built and dedicated to his honor. The English Crusaders adopted him as the Patron Saint of England, and many fabulous legends are told of his exploits.

The modern town is small, but for a Mohammedan place is prosperous.

The ruins of the stately Church of St. George present a remarkable appearance.

NAZARETH.

This place is 67 miles north of Jerusalem, 6 miles W. N. W. of Mount Tabor, and nearly half way from the Jordan to the Mediterranean. Nazareth is situated on the side of a hill overlooking a fertile and beautiful valley surrounded by hills, with a narrow outlet towards the south. The surrounding hills vary

RUINS OF GADARA.

in hight from 100 to 500 feet above the level of the valley. The soil is rich and well cultivated, producing a great variety of fruit, grain, vegetables, and flowers, which ripen early and in rare perfection.

From the summit of the hill on which Nazareth stands is a magnificent prospect. Towards the north are seen the many hills of Galilee, and the eye reposes on the majestic and snow-crowned Hermon. On the east, the Jordan valley may be traced; and beyond it the dim hights of ancient Bashan. Towards the south spreads the broad and beautiful plain of Esdrælon, with the bold outline of Mount Tabor, with parts of Little Hermon and Gilboa visible on its eastern border, and the hills of Samaria on the south, while Carmel rises on the west of the plain, and dips his feet in the blue waters of the Mediterranean.

Nazareth derives its celebrity from its connection with the history of Christ. At Nazareth Joseph and Mary lived; here the angel announced to the Virgin the Messiah's birth; to Nazareth the Holy Family returned after their flight into Egypt; here Jesus lived from infancy to manhood; here He taught in the synagogue, and was twice rejected by his townsmen, who attempted on the last occasion to cast him down from "the brow of the hill on which the city was built." The title on the cross designated him as "Jesus of Nazareth." At the Fountain of the Virgin, at the north-eastern extremity of the town, according to tradition, the mother of Jesus received the angel's salutation. A remarkable precipice, nearly perpendicular and 50 feet high, near the Maronite church, is said to be the identical one over which his infuriated townsmen attempted to hurl Jesus.

The modern Nazareth belongs to the better class of Eastern villages. Most of the houses are well built of stone, and appear neat and comfortable; but the streets are narrow and crooked, and after a rain are so full of mud as to be nearly impassable. Its population is between three and four thousand. A few are Mohammedans, the rest Latin and Greek.

The country around is the best cultivated in Palestine; and in the season of rains is fresh and green everywhere, carpeted with flowers, and shady with orchards and groves.

THE KNIGHTS TEMPLARS.

ORIGIN OF THE ORDER—THE BATTLE-FIELD OF HATTIN—MASSACRE OF THE KNIGHTS.

After the conquest of Jerusalem by the Crusaders, pilgrims and other travelers from all parts of Europe visited the Holy Land in great numbers; many of whom, when traveling from one place to another, especially when going from the coast to Jerusalem, were robbed, and subjected to various outrages and indignities by the Mohammedans, who regarded them as interlopers and Christian dogs, and treated them as such whenever an opportunity presented itself. From this state of things arose the necessity of an organization for the protection of pilgrims and others, while traveling in the Holy Land. Hence, in 1118, a society was formed, called the "Poor Soldiers of Jesus," whose duty it was to act as escort and guard for the Christian travelers; especially those visiting Jerusalem. This humble society soon became so popular, that to belong to it was esteemed an honor; and its accessions in numbers and wealth were such as to eventually render it the most powerful and wealthy organization the world has ever seen.

KNIGHTS TEMPLARS.

The buildings allotted to the "Poor Soldiers of Jesus" were in the Temple enclosure, and some of them on the site of Solomon's Temple, from which circumstance they received the name, Knights Templars. In time this order embraced in its ranks many of the best architects of the day; and the ruins of castles, fortresses, and fortified towns, built by them, are monuments of the skill and energy of this warlike and mechanical order.

CAUSES WHICH LED TO THEIR DESTRUCTION.

At this period, Palestine was covered with castles and fortified towns, which were occupied and commanded by petty barons, Knights of St. John, and Knights Templars; but all subject to the king at Jerusalem. Yet the commanders of these fortresses declared war and made peace at their own will and pleasure—not only against the common enemy but against one another; and what renders this state of anarchy more surprising is, that the Christian occupants of Palestine were nearly surrounded by a warlike and watchful enemy, ready to improve the first opportunity for their destruction. Yet at this time, under the leadership of a man of even ordinary capacity, order might have been restored, and the Christian rule perpetuated in the Holy Land. But this opportunity for consolidating their power was soon lost; for, in 1186, the throne was usurped by Guy of Lusignan, who had many enemies, and at least one powerful rival. Among the petty rulers at this time were Count Raymond of Tripolis, and Raynald of Chatillon, Lord of Kerak and other castles, and who had associated with him a large number of Knights Templars. Raymond was a bitter enemy and rival of the king, and had even entered into negotiations with Saladin, and received aid from him. Notwithstanding the situation among the Franks* was such as to invite attack, a truce had been concluded with the Sultan, which might have been followed by a period of repose. But this peace was soon terminated, and that too by the Christians; for the reckless Raynald of Kerak, disregarding the compact with the Sultan, fell upon and plundered a large caravan of merchants passing from Damascus to Arabia, imprisoning the women and children, and massacreing many of the men. Enraged at this, Saladin swore a solemn oath to put Raynald to death with his own hands, should he ever get him into his power; and immediately commenced making immense preparations for avenging this breach of faith on the part of the Franks; and in response to his call hosts of the swarthy and fierce warriors of

* A general name applied to the Europeans by the Turks.

MT. HATTIN—THE BATTLE-GROUND.

the Crescent were soon assembled at Damascus from all parts of the empire.

BATTLE OF HATTIN—MASSACRE OF THE KNIGHTS TEMPLARS.

Mount Hattin, on the slopes of which the great battle was fought, is sixty-five miles north-by-east from Jerusalem, and twenty-four miles east-south-east of Acre; and is nearly on a line between Tabor and Hermon.

The dire intelligence of the preparations of Saladin for war, soon reached the Christian princes, and induced them to cease their strife, and unite at once for mutual defence. They established their rendezvous at the fountain of Sefûrieh, fifteen miles south-east of Acre, where were soon assembled the most chivalric host which had ever fought against the Saracens in the Holy Land. The Hospitalers and Templars came with many troops from their castles; Raymond, with his forces from Tiberias and Tripolis; Raynald, with a train of knights from Kerak and Shŏbek; other barons from Sidon, Antioch, and Cesarea, and the king from Jerusalem, with a host of knights and hired troops, altogether making an army of over 50,000 men.

The position chosen by the Christians was a good one, and had water and other resources in abundance. They were also inspired by the presence of the Holy Cross, which had been brought from Jerusalem by the Bishops of Ptolemaïs and Lydda. Thus prepared, the army waited the approach of the Saracens for over a month, when suddenly the hosts of Saladin appeared on the west side of the Jordan, swooped around the northern end of Lake Tiberias, and thence, southerly, down its west side to the heights north of the village of Tiberias; where they encamped, in the hope of drawing the Franks from their position. Light detachments had preceded the main army; these penetrated to the neighborhood of Nazareth—to Jezreel, and Mount Gilboa, laying waste the land with fire and sword. Upon finding that the Franks did not advance, Saladin sent a detachment of light troops and took possession of Tiberias, the residence of Count Raymond, whose wife, with her children, retired to the castle. On the 3d of July, intelligence of the capture of Tiberias reached the Christian camp. The king immediately called a council of war, to decide upon the measures to be pursued. At first a large majority were for marching at once for the deliverance of Tiberias; but Raymond, although of all others personally the most interested, advised to remain where they were, fortify their camp, and act on the defensive; as experience had taught him that the Fabian policy was the most successful against Saladin. Here, in their fortified position, with abundance of resources of all kinds, they had every reason to hope for complete success against the attacks of the undisciplined hordes of the Sultan; but if they marched on Tiberias, they would expose themselves to constant attacks of myriads of Saracenic cavalry, in a region without water, under the burning heat of summer, where, harassed and exhausted, their retreat might be cut off. This advice was unanimously approved by the king, barons, and all, with but one exception—the Grand Master of the Templars; who, listening only to the dictates of chivalry, went to the tent of the king, after the council had broken up, and conjured him not to let such a stain of cowardice rest upon the Christian name, and fame of the knights, of which the army was so largely composed, but to march at once to the attack of the Mohammedan hosts. To this the king at length yielded, and gave the order to arm, and march at once upon Tiberias.* Upon receiving this unexpected order, the barons repaired to the quarters of the king, to endeavor to dissuade him from this step; but he would not even give them an audience, and his order to advance was immediately carried out. Saladin had great confidence of victory, could he but draw the Franks from their position, and bring on a general engagement; consequently their advance fell in completely with his wishes and plans. He immediately despatched his light troops to harass the Christian army on its march, and posted his main army along the high ground between Tiberias and Tell Hattin. This was on Friday. In the afternoon the Christian army reached the open ground around el Lûbieh, when immediately a sharp engagement between the light troops of the two armies took place, but with no results of importance, as the King's soldiers were so exhausted by their long march under the scorching sun, and suffering so much from thirst, that they made no headway against the fierce Saracens. Pre-

* But few of the military terms in use now were known at the period in which this battle took place.

vious to making the advance, the Christians were filled with confidence in their superior prowess and tactics, consequently the result of the first onset not only astonished them, but filled them with fear and dismay; and instead of pressing on at once, and attacking the army of Saladin, and at least breaking through to the lake, where a supply of water might be obtained, the king gave orders to encamp on the rocky plain, where there was no water, and thus deferred a general engagement until the next day. This was a fatal step, and was said to have been counselled by Raymond, from treachery; and, from the manner of his escape at the termination of the battle, it would appear as though there was some collusion between him and Saladin. The night was a dreadful one for the Christians: suffering from thirst, and not a drop of water within their reach, and in such fear of a night attack that sleep was out of the question. Added to this, the Saracen scouts succeeded in approaching very near their camp and setting fire to the dry shrubs round about it, the heat and smoke of which increased still more their distresses. In this situation the night was passed; and at early dawn they found themselves closely surrounded by the hosts of Saladin, flushed with confidence, and eager for the conflict—which commenced by their attacking the more exposed parts of the Christian army, which brought on a general engagement; and whenever the Franks pressed forward in solid masses, or made a well-directed charge, the Saracens gave way at once, but would again return to the conflict; and, by hovering around and making constant charges against vulnerable points, they succeeded in exhausting and demoralizing the Franks so that the foot-soldiers broke their ranks. Some threw down their arms and surrendered; others fled, and were pursued and cut to pieces; while the great body retreated in confusion to the summit of Mount Hattin, from which the king attempted to rally them to support the knights in protecting the Holy Cross, but without avail. An attempt was then made to encamp around the Cross; but the Saracens now pressed upon them, and discharged a shower of arrows, by one of which the bearer of the Cross was slain. In this extremity the king gave orders to renew the fight; but it was too late, as they were now so exhausted and disheartened that they were but little better than a confused mob; and, in this extremity, Raymond and his followers, when ordered to advance, put their horses to full speed over the dead bodies of their fallen comrades, and rushed through the ranks of the enemy, *which opened to let them pass*, and thus escaped, by a shameful flight, in the direction of Tyre. The king then withdrew to the height of Tell Hattin, with a few knights and other brave followers, where, for a time, they maintained their position against the fearful odds against them, but were at length obliged to yield, when some were driven headlong over the steep precipice on the northern side of the hill, and others were taken prisoners. Among the latter were the King, Raynald of Chatillon, Honroy of Toron, the Bishop of Lydda, and the Grand Master of the Templars. The latter, although his advice to advance might have been injudicious, yet by his conduct throughout this bloody conflict added new lustre to the reputation of the Knights Templars for chivalric courage and fortitude.

Immediately after the battle, the captive princes were led before Saladin, who received them in the antechamber of his pavilion, and with the respect due to their positions--except Raynald, on whom his eye fell fiercely, for he remembered him as the bitter enemy of his people, and as the immediate cause of this conflict, in which so many of his best warriors had lost their lives. At the order of Saladin, cool sherbet was presented to the king; but when the latter passed it to Raynald, Saladin said to him, "Thou givest him drink, not I," in accordance with an Arab custom, that whoever gives drink or food to another, is bound to protect him at all hazards. After the other prisoners had received refreshments, Saladin addressed Raynald, upbraiding him for his cruelty and insolence against the Mohammedans and their religion, and for breaking the truce; and ended by inviting him to embrace Mohammedanism. Raynald replied that he had lived, and would die, only in the Christian faith; upon which, Saladin rose from his seat, drew his scimitar, and at a blow cleft through Raynald's shoulder; when the attendants rushed upon and despatched him. Saladin then assured the king and princes that their lives were safe—that the massacre of Raynald was only the punishment due his atrocities; but, smarting under the remembrance of the many chastisements his people had received at the hands of the Knights Templars, and also that on that day scores

WAR HORSES AFTER THE BATTLE.

of his warriors had been laid low by the strong arms of these same knights, he ordered them to be put to death; when the captive knights were all beheaded without mercy; but the king and princes were sent to Damascus. Thus ended this great battle, and disaster to the Christian army, and, as a consequence, the Christian sway in the Holy Land. For in preparing for this struggle with Saladin, the fortresses throughout the country had been weakened by drawing off the principal part of their garrisons, so that they fell an easy prey to the Sultan, and surrendered, one after another, until the third of October, when the Holy City itself capitulated.

Among the results of this battle were the loss of the Holy Land to the Christians, and its return to semi-barbarism; and the almost total annihilation of the Knights Templars—rendering it, in its effects on civilization and its tragic termination, one of the most important and remarkable battles ever fought in this quarter of the globe.

ATHLEET.

The ruins of this singular ancient city are a short distance south of Mt. Carmel, on the shore of the Mediterranean. The traveler approaching them from the north first sees a vast column, which seems to spring from the waves, but on a nearer approach it is found to be a part of a mass of magnificent ruins. First of all is found an immense wall, perfectly similar, in its form and the finish of its stones, to the Coliseum at Rome; behind it is seen the beautiful fretted remains of a monument, a mosk, and the ruins of divers ancient buildings—parts of some of them standing and in a good state of preservation. About half a mile from this the shore rises abruptly, and changes from sand to soft rock. In this rock many curious apartments are found cut. This might have been a primitive town, which was cut in the rock before mankind had learned the art of raising stones from the ground, and erecting their dwellings on its surface; and is doubtless one of those subterranean towns of which the earliest historians speak. Many of these artificial caverns are of great extent, with elevated entrances, approached by broad steps; and are lighted by openings pierced through the rock, and the entrances and windows open upon streets deeply cut in the bowels of the hill. Several of these streets, deep and wide, can be plainly traced, and the marks of chariot wheels are still visible. In some places canals had been dug to the sea, through which glimpses are obtained of the gulf behind the town. The only inhabitants now are vultures and starlings, multitudes of which start up at the approach of the explorer. Passing through these wonderful labyrinths, an opening through the ancient wall of the city is found; passing through this, the traveler is equally astonished at the wonderful relics of the past, and the fierce tribe of Arabs which now inhabit the place. In every direction are seen ruins of public edifices, towers, monuments, and private dwellings; and among these, in every conceivable kind of shelter, are the families of the wild tribe which make this their citadel and place of abode;—some living in a room that was once a part of a splendid dwelling, some under an immense block of stone, one end of which rests on another, while others have tents, made by stretching skins of the black goat from the base of one column to another.

On an elevation at the entrance to the town are the ruins of a Roman temple, several of the columns of which have fallen together in such a way as to form a large cave, which is occupied by the Sheik and his family. Swarthy, ferocious men, women, horses, and black goats may be seen, in groups and singly, in all directions; the scene is novel and striking. The dwellings of this tribe are mingled and confounded with the ruins of theaters, churches, and ancient dwellings. Women are seen milking she-goats on the steps of a theater. In another direction a flock of sheep may be seen, jumping one by one through the deep windows of a palace or a church, and Arabs, seated cross-legged, are smoking their pipes under the carved arch of a Roman gateway.

At the end of the town, near the edge of the sea, are the ruins of an immense temple,—which the Arabs hold in great reverence. The traveler approaching this spot is met with fierce threats from the men, and floods of abuse from the women and children. This edifice appears to have served in turn as a heathen temple, Christian church, and Mohammedan mosk; but time, which sports with the productions of men, is fast changing these ruins to dust; and the knee of the camel now bends on flags on which many generations in religion have in turn bent before different gods; and climbing vines hang in leafy and flowery tufts from the tops of broken arches and columns.

PERGAMOS:

ITS FORMER MAGNIFICENCE AND GRAND ARCHITECTURAL REMAINS.

Pergamos stood on the river Caicus, and about 64 miles north of Smyrna. This city was the capital of ancient Mysia, and was long the centre of a considerable empire. It was a city of high antiquity and great magnificence. Six successive kings reigned in it from 283 to 133 B.C. It then fell under the power of the Romans; a usurper subsequently re-erected its throne, but it was again brought under subjection by the Romans, who destroyed many of its inhabitants by poisoning the public waters. A famous library of 200,000 volumes was collected at Pergamos by its kings, and was afterwards carried away by Cleopatra and added to the library at Alexandria. Parchment was invented and first used at Pergamos. It was also remarkable as being the birthplace of Galen the physician, and Apollodorus the mythologist, and as the chief scene of the worship of Æsculapius.

The ruins of this ancient city are many and grand; and the situation indicates the people who selected it. It embraces in its view the plain of Pergamos, with its chain of mountains, and is lit by the rising sun. There is in the middle of the city a group of ruins of great extent, and appear to be the remains of a palace. The river was spanned by five bridges, one of which was of splendid masonry, and so wide that it forms a tunnel a furlong in length, upon which a portion of the great palace stood. Many vaults and several mosks and khans occupy the buildings of the ancients. The walls of the Turkish houses, being built of the ancient ruins, are full of relics of marble, with ornaments of the richest Grecian art.

All the works standing are magnificent. The amphitheater southwest of the castle, though in ruins, is a wonderful building; a river runs through it, and the arches under ground are beautiful specimens of masonry. The arches above ground were equally fine, but although they now stand tier above tier, all the joints have been chipped as in the Coliseum at Rome, and not a seat remains; but the stupendous works under ground will defy the efforts of the Turks to remove them. Triumphal arches and houses in ruins are to be seen in the modern town, among which are the huts of the Turks, bearing about the same proportion to them as the nests of the storks to the ruined palaces in which they alone now reign. Many fine relics are found in the Turkish cemeteries; and one of these cemeteries in the vicinity of the ancient theatre has for ages been supplied with marble embellishments from the ruins of that great structure. Columns and ornamented stones are used by the Turks for building material and a great variety of other purposes. Many beautiful marbles and other relics have been carried away for the museums of Europe. The ancient Acropolis crowns a hill, and, including the citadel and a heathen temple, covers an area of over eight acres and commands the city, also a grand and picturesque view of the surrounding country.

Burgamo, the modern town, has a population of only 15,000 inhabitants, of whom 13,000 are Turks, 1,500 Greeks, and the rest Armenians and Jews. The only representative of the immense ancient library is a collection of about 50 volumes—and a dirty Italian quack is the chief physician in the city of Galen and Æsculapius.

GERGESHA.

This splendid ancient city was situated on the river Jabbok, about 23 miles east of the Jordan, and 38 miles south-east of Lake Tiberias. It was one of the ten cities of the Roman colony of Decapolis. In the wars of the Jews with the Romans it was stormed, taken, and pillaged by Alexander, chiefly on account of its wealth; and was afterwards fired and destroyed by the enraged Jews, in revenge of the massacre of a number of their nation at Cesarea. Afterwards it was attacked, nearly demolished, and a large number of its inhabitants slain, by a detachment of the Roman army during the preparation for the siege of Jerusalem. Subsequently it was restored and served as a frontier fortress of the Lower Empire, along the side of the Syrian provinces. But it finally received its death-blow from the Saracens, and sank into profound oblivion, and only within a few years past has it again been known to the civilized world. Its site and ruins were first discovered by Dr. Séetzen; and has since been visited by several eminent travelers.

The size and magnificence of this ancient city are attested by its ruins, which are unrivalled even by those of Baalbek and Tadmor. Fallen as the ruins are now, enough is left to prove that the banks of a stream of that oft-derided land were once so enriched and adorned, and that too by a people given up to idolatry, as to challenge in their magnificence, though in ruins, any spot in Europe. The streets of Gergesha were lined with colonnades from end to end, and opened a way to public edifices which yet lost not their distinction, while statelier or fairer columns were doubled or multiplied around them.

The ruins are found on both sides of a stream which divided the city nearly in the middle. The walls, where not almost entire, form a distinct lineal mound of hewn stones of a considerable height, and enclose an immense space, almost entirely covered with ruins. The principal street extends nearly from one end of the ruins to the other, and was lined on both sides with splendid columns, many of which are now fallen, many fractured and shortened, and not a few are still standing unbroken—some 30 feet high, others 25, and the lowest about 20. On one side of the street, in less than a third of its length 34 columns are yet standing. Behind the columns there are in some places vaulted apartments which appear to have been shops. Cross streets diverging from the long central street, had also their colonnades and were adorned with public edifices or bridges, while the more distant spaces on each side are covered with indiscriminate ruins of the habitations of the lower class of people. The remains of pavement found in many of the streets would put to shame that in use in the capital of France. One of the bridges was built very high, so as to render the acclivity less dangerous; and transverse lines were found cut in the pavement, in places where the grade was steep, to prevent the horses from slipping. Not far from the centre of the ruins is a copious fountain of the clearest water, and near this are the ruins of a large building, with massive walls, consisting of arched chambers similar to Roman baths, and which was doubtless a public bath. Opposite to the large bath, in a straight line across the city, is an arched gateway facing the principal street, which leads to the splendid remains of a magnificent temple, such as few countries have ever shown. The fallen roof now covers the base of this edifice; three of the walls are still standing, and in the sides of which the niches for images are seen. The front of the temple was adorned with a noble portico, having three rows of grand Corinthian columns 40 feet in height, the capitals of which are beautifully ornamented with *acanthus leaves.* The spacious area in which it stood was surrounded in like manner by a double row of columns, the total number of which could not have been less than 200. This temple was built in the form of an oblong square, and is about 140 feet in length by 70 in width. Its front is open to the south-east, and there is here a noble portico of 12 columns disposed in three rows. All of the columns of the great portico are still standing, and these, being nearly 6 feet in diameter and 50 feet in height, have an air of great grandeur, and present a happy combination of strength and beauty.

Triumphal Arch, Gerash.

Colonnade—Gerash.

Near the great temple stands a theatre which has 16 rows of benches, with a tier of 6 boxes, between every two of which is a niche, forming a very elegant ornament, and as befitting a place for idols as the walls of a church. But the transformation this theatre has undergone is such, that in 1839 a fine crop of tobacco was raised in the arena, which is about 50 paces in diameter.

On an eminence at one end of the city, opposite to the termination of the grand street are another temple and theatre. The hill on which they stood was connected with the princely street by a magnificent semicircle of Ionic columns, 57 of which are still standing. Their height was varied with the rising ground, to give a uniform level to the whole entablature. This immense theatre, larger than that of Bacchus at Athens, and capable of containing 8,000 spectators, was partly cut in the rock and partly built. The proscenium is very perfect, and embellished within by five richly decorated niches, which are connected together by a line of columns, of which there is another parallel range within. The remains of a beautiful temple stood near this theatre; it was ornamented with pilasters surrounded by Corinthian capitals; without it was surrounded by a peristyle of grand columns of the same order supporting an entablature; and facing the city there was a noble portico of two rows of columns, to which a grand flight of stairs led from below.

The view from this spot is still wonderful; but in the days of Gergesha's glory, it must have been a spectacle of unequalled magnificence. The whole town, including a vast area and surrounded by an immense wall, is embraced in the view. Immediately below is the noble Ionic crescent, from the centre of which the main street extends. Of the lines of columns on each side, eighty-three are now standing with their entablatures, and portions and pedestals of the remainder are plainly visible. Around them on every side are confused heaps of ruins, which have only fallen from the violence of ruthless barbarism. These columns, raising their slender forms among the general wreck, and stretching in long lines amidst the remains of former magnificence, produce an effect hardly surpassed by anything found in Egypt, Greece, or Italy. A traveler thus describes the general effect: "The circular colonnade, the avenues of Corinthian pillars forming the grand street, the southern gate of entrance, the naumachia, and the triumphal arch beyond it, the theatres, temples, aqueducts, and all the assemblage of noble buildings which presented their vestiges to view, seemed to indicate a city built only for luxury, splendor, and pleasure." It would be vain to attempt a picture of the impressions produced by such a sight.

THE HAURAN.

Land of Mystery—Its Ruins of Ancient Cities—Its many Deserted Villages.

Hauran is the general name of an extensive plain which begins about thirty miles east of the river Jordan. It is sometimes level, sometimes undulating, with occasionally a low round hill.

Part of the principal street, Gerash.

Gerash. Great Temple from the Colonnade.

This district is covered in every direction with the ruins of ancient cities, and deserted towns of a more recent date—the later being of Roman origin. Most of the remains of ancient cities are mere heaps of ruins and rubbish, while many of the buildings in the Roman towns are nearly as perfect as when left centuries ago by their original occupants. Owing to a want of timber, the buildings were almost entirely constructed of stone, mostly black basalt. The doors are thick slabs of stone, fixed into their sockets when the houses were built, and many of the roofs rest on arches. The present inhabitants, Arabs, occupy the same houses and enter by the same doors as did the old Romans. The best of these houses are found at Zarava—modern Ezra. This town is of great extent, and the buildings are in a good state of preservation, even whole streets being still in good repair. At Nedjraun is a mansion of unusual size, being large enough to accommodate half a dozen families. It was doubtless built by a wealthy Roman, perhaps the principal man of the place. The courts of this building are large and nearly square. The front door was very large, and above it is a square window; it had also a window on each side. The upper rooms are small, very numerous, and now occupied by several families of Arabs, whose appearance would doubtless astonish the original occupants. The upper story recedes the width of the hall, leaving a small terrace on which the doors of the several apartments open. The wings are also full of rooms; the ground floor of that to the right is in part occupied by a beautiful stable, seven paces long by nine deep, and spanned by an arch. This stable, which ages ago sheltered Roman steeds, is now filled with the horses of the Arabs. This whole mansion is extremely well built of hewn stones, and nearly all the rooms are entire. Most of the large towns in the Hauran exhibit traces of architectural magnificence, which Rome so freely lavished on her remotest colonies; but what is still more striking here is the consideration evidenced and pains taken to promote the welfare and comfort of her people. There is scarcely a village without its stone tank, for holding rain-water, and stone bridge—structures so solidly built that many of them are still as good as new.

A striking peculiarity in the manners and customs of the inhabitants of the Hauran is, that the richest live like the poorest, the only difference being that the former makes a display of his wealth on the arrival of strangers, while the hospitality of the latter is unattended with any display.

The ancient buildings afford spacious and convenient dwellings for a large portion of the modern inhabitants, and those who occupy them may have three and four rooms for each family; but in newly built villages the whole family, with its furniture, horses, saddles, guns, and yataghans, are all huddled together in one apartment. Here also they keep their wheat and barley in a reservoir (formed from a clay called *kawara*), which is about five feet deep by two in diameter. The chief articles of furniture are a hand-mill, some copper kettles, and mats. In the richer houses some coarse woollen stuffs used principally for carpets and horse-cloths are met with; real

RUINS OF AN ANCIENT CITY IN THE HAURAN.

carpets are seldom seen, except on the arrival of strangers of consequence. Each family has a large, singular shaped earthen jar, which is filled every morning by the females at the birket, or spring, for the day's use. In every house of any considerable size is a room set apart for the use of strangers, and has in the midst of it a fire-place for boiling coffee—hospitality being a characteristic of the people of the Hauran. A traveler may alight at any house he pleases, a mat will be spread for him, coffee made, and breakfast or dinner set before him. It often happens on entering a village that several persons will present themselves to the traveler, each begging that he will lodge at his house, and the same care is taken of the horse or camel as of the rider.

Wealth is estimated by these people by the number of horses, camels, and oxen a man has. If it is asked if such a one has property, the answer is, "A great deal," he drives six oxen, or he has camels, horses, and oxen, a great many. The Fellahs often cultivate one another's fields in company, but the Turkish and Christian proprietors cultivate their lands by hired laborers, or let their fields for a share of the produce. A laborer who has a pair of oxen usually receives one gharara of corn at planting-time, and at harvest takes one-third of the crop. The master pays the tax, called the miri, to the government, and the laborer pays 10 piasters annually. A considerable portion of the agricultural population of the Hauran consists of day-laborers, and they generally earn their living very hardly. A young man was once met with here who had served seven years for his food and clothing, but at the expiration of that period obtained in marriage the daughter of his master, for whom he would otherwise have had to pay from seven to eight hundred piasters. Daughters are paid for according to the respectability and wealth of the father, from seven to fifteen hundred piasters.

The Druses are the most superior race in this country; their Sheiks and elderly men are always well and often handsomely dressed, while their women are neatness itself; and they never go out without veiling their faces, as the stern morality of this people forbids the slightest indication of boldness or levity. A fearful instance of the uncompromising severity with which the Druses visit female frailty is related by a recent traveler, to whom the deputy of a local governor told the tale as follows:—"I was asleep in bed, when in the middle of the night I heard a knock at the door of my room. 'Who is there?' I said. A voice answered, 'Nas-reddin.' I opened the door and in came a Druse with a sack on his back. 'What brings you here at this untimely hour?' I said. 'My sister has had an intrigue, and I have killed her; there are her horn and other ornaments in the sack, and I am afraid the governor will do something to me: I want your intercession.' 'Why, there are two horns in the sack,' said I. 'I killed her mother too; she knew of the intrigue.' 'There is no power but in God Almighty: if your sister was impure, was that a reason for killing your mother? but lie down and sleep.' In the morning I said to him, 'I suppose you were too uneasy to sleep?' 'By Allah! so unhappy has dishonor made me, that

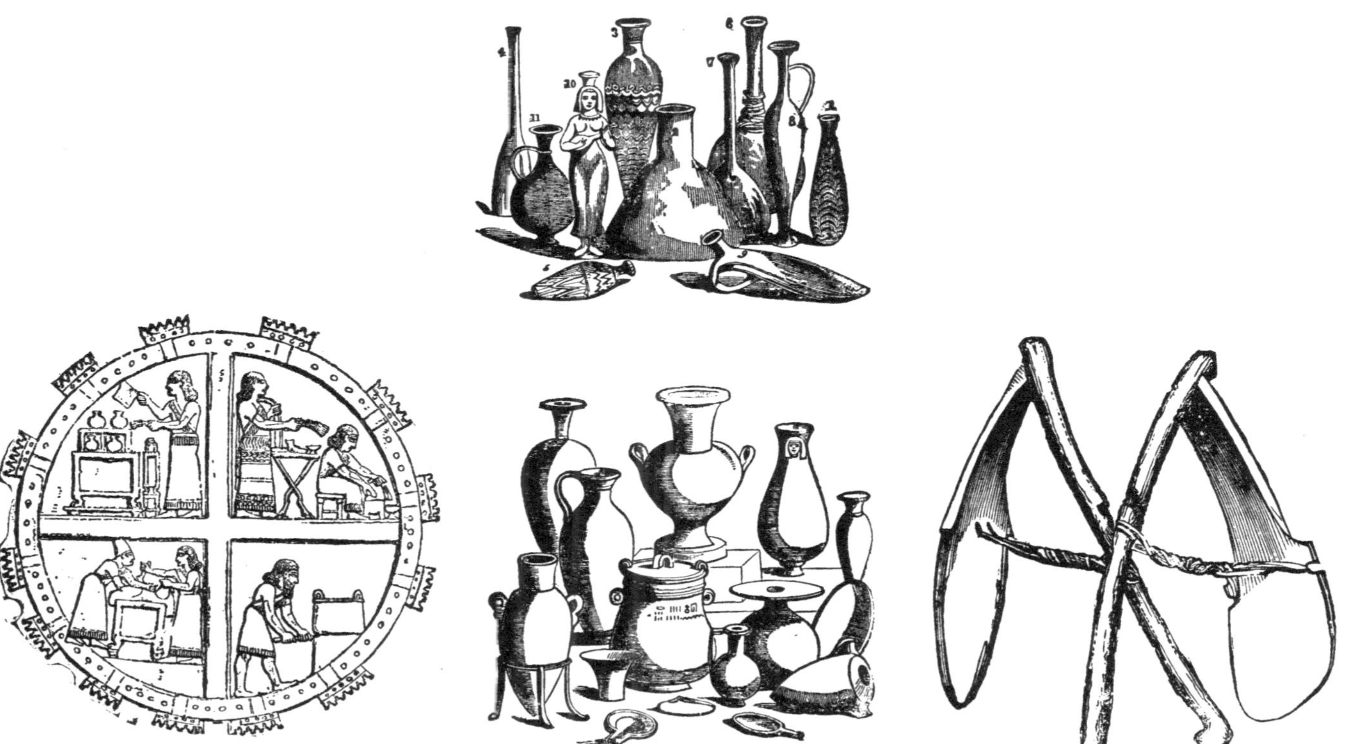

ANCIENT KITCHEN AND UTENSILS.—ANCIENT HOES.

for a year I have not slept soundly till last night. I then went with him to the governor, and said, 'Will you give Nas-reddin the handkerchief of amnesty?' The governor said to Nas-reddin, 'Speak without fear;' upon which he recounted his story, when the governor said, 'La bas' (no harm), on which he kissed the governor's hand and went away."

The whole of this region was once thickly studded over with towns and cities, and appears to have been one of the most fertile and densely populated countries on the face of the earth; but, in consequence of bad government, the population is rapidly decreasing, and many once flourishing villages and cities now contain only empty dwellings and desolate ruins. The present population is estimated to be only about 50,000.

The view over the Hauran is at all times most striking, and from many points extremely beautiful. Gebel Sheik, or Hermon, the last mountain of the chain of Anti-Lebanon, is always visible to the N.W. Gebel Hauran—a range of hills—limits the view to the E., but to the S.E. it is boundless. The soil is naturally excellent; numerous corn-fields surround every village, while in many places the pasturage is good, and is grazed by the flocks of the Bedouins, who visit the Hauran in swarms every spring.

E.N.E. of the Hauran is a very singular region called the Szaffa; it is a stony district, much resembling the Ledja, except that the rocks with which it is covered are larger. Its circumference is equal to two or three days' travel, and it is a place of refuge for the Arabs who fly from the Pasha's troops, or from their enemies in the desert. The Szaffa has no springs, the only supply being rain-water collected in cisterns. There is but one entrance into this region, and that is through a narrow pass called Bab-el Szaffa—a cleft between high perpendicular rocks, not more than two yards wide—which none dare to enter as enemies. Many sanguinary encounters between pursued and pursuers have taken place at this pass, as is attested by numerous skeletons and human bones met with here.

CHAPTER XI.

PLACES CONNECTED WITH THE CRUCIFIXION.

David's Tomb, The Last Supper—The Garden of Gethsemane, Christ's Agony—Hill of Evil Counsel—Church of the Holy Sepulchre—Place of Crucifixion—Holy Sepulchre—Place of Ascension.

DAVID'S TOMB, OR RESTING-PLACE, THE LAST SUPPER.

THIS place is on the southern slope of Mount Zion, a short distance from its summit, and is covered by a pile of buildings, in one of the most ancient of which, it is believed, was the room where Jesus held his last supper with his disciples. "He will show you," said the Saviour, "a large upper room." This room is about fifty feet long and thirty wide. The great antiquity of this building none can question. Epiphanius, towards the close of the fourth century, states that this building, with a few others near it, escaped destruction when Titus overthrew the city.

No. 61. —THE GARDEN OF GETHSEMANE, CHRIST'S AGONY.

Just east of the Kidron, at the foot of the Mount of Olives, is the Garden of Gethsemane. A part of it is enclosed by a strong stone wall about ten feet high. This enclosure is shaded by eight venerable old olive trees, and planted with beds of flowers and various kinds of shrubbery. Its close proximity to the city, and the nature of the grounds, would point it out as a suitable place for a public garden. The place is so plainly indicated in the Scripture narrative, as to leave no room to doubt but that this enclosure is a part of the ancient Garden of Gethsemane. And he said, "Abba, Father, all things are possible unto thee; take away this cup from me: nevertheless, not what I will, but what thou wilt." (St. Mark xiv. 36.)

HILL OF EVIL COUNSEL.

This hill takes its name from a tradition that the residence of Caiaphas was located upon its summit, and that here the chief priests and scribes assembled together to take counsel against Jesus. It rises to a height of nearly five hundred feet above the pool of Siloam, and is situated near the lower part of the valley.

THE PLACE OF CRUCIFIXION.

The question as to *where* the Crucifixion did take place has been carried on until recently without any reasonable determination.

It has been supposed that the Holy Sepulchre Church included the place of the Crucifixion, but the course of the ancient walls, which have now been

The Garden of Gethsemane.

very accurately traced out, has settled that point against the claim that this church covered the true site, although there is undoubted historical evidence that it was originally built in the fourth century, and on a site which was traditionally said to have been the Calvary of the Gospel narrative. But two or three hundred years must have impaired the tradition, for it can be safely said that the name and skull-shaped hill over the Jeremiah Grotto should have pointed out the right place to all observing eyes. We know from a comparison of the plans of the city in the time of Arculf, A.D. 700, of the Crusaders, 1190, and also in Sandys, 1610, that the location of St. Stephen's Gate had been changed from the *north* side of the city, now called *Damascus Gate*, to the east side, where it is now, and which was known as the Little Gate, A.D. 700, and Jehoshaphat Gate in the Crusades.

Attention was called to the probability of the true site being north of the city 20 years ago by Thenius, whose views were adopted by other scholars such as Fisher, Robinson, Howe (Oriental Scenes, 1854); A. L. Rawson (Map of Palestine, 1856); Robert Morris (Youthful Explorers in the Holy Land, 1870).

The requirements of the Scripture narrative as to the place will be seen from the following.

And he bearing his cross *went forth* into a place called the place of a *skull*, which is called in the Hebrew, *Golgotha*.

And Pilate wrote a title, and put it on the cross. And the writing was, JESUS OF NAZARETH THE KING OF THE JEWS.

This title then read many of the Jews: for the place where Jesus was crucified was *nigh to the city:* and it was written in Hebrew, and Greek, and Latin.

Now in the place where he was crucified there was a *garden;* and in the garden a new sepulchre, wherein was never man yet laid. St. John, xix. 17, 19, 20, 41.

And they bring him unto the place *Golgotha*, which is, being interpreted, the place of a *skull* (St. Mark, xv. 22).

And as they *came out* they found a man of Cyrene, Simon by name: him they compelled to bear his cross.

And when they were come unto a place called *Golgotha*, that is to say a place of the *skull* (Mathew, xxvii. 32, 33).

Wherefore Jesus also that he might sanctify the people with his own blood suffered *without* the gate (Hebrews, xiii. 12).

MEETING THE REQUIREMENTS.

GOLGOTHA.

This name is derived from the Hebrew for skull, and being translated into Greek is Kranium, and into Latin is Calvaria, which also means skull. All of these terms apply to a skull-shaped hill which has been known as the Grotto of Jeremiah, though without any connection with that prophet historical or traditional. This hill is very distinctly skull-shaped as may be seen in the engraving, and it also answers most, if not all, of the requirements of the text.

1. The place is said in the Gospel account to have been out of the city; this place is so now, and there

Golgotha.

is little doubt that it was at that time outside of the walls. The city may have been extended beyond this place *after* the Crucifixion, but it certainly did not include the high plain around Golgotha *before* that event.

2. It is described in the text as being "*nigh* unto the city," and it is about 500 feet from the wall near the Damascus Gate (formerly St. Stephen's Gate).

3. The Gospel account mentions a garden, and this place is now, and doubtless was then, capable of cultivation.

4. It is near one of the most traveled roads both at that time and at present, being the one leading from the Damascus Gate north towards Shechem, and to Joppa by Beth-horon.

5. As there is no other site or place that meets the foregoing requirements of the Scripture narrative, the conclusion is very evident that this is the spot which was hallowed by the blood of the Saviour.

CHURCH OF THE HOLY SEPULCHRE.—No. 9.

This church is in the Christian quarter of the city, at the termination of Dolorosa. (See plan.) Tradition, and some of the earliest written records, point to the area occupied by this structure as the place of the burial, if not the crucifixion of Christ. Yet because of its being so far within the walls of the city it has been claimed by many that it could not be the place.

This place was originally the side of a slight elevation or hill, but its summit and sides have been graded down to accomodate the surface to the immense structure that now occupies it. The origin of this church is credited to Constantine, who completed and dedicated it A.D. 335; in A.D. 614 it was destroyed by the Persians; rebuilt, it was again destroyed, and completely demolished by the Kaliph Hakim in 1048; rebuilt again, it stood until 1808, when it was destroyed by an accidental fire. It was again rebuilt and dedicated in 1810.

The present Church of the Holy Sepulchre is a collection of buildings under one roof, without regard to order or style of architecture; 350 feet long by 280 wide, including many sacred places, presided over by different sects in separate chapels.

Like its predecessors, this church was erected to cover and enshrine the Holy Sepulchre and the place of crucifixion.

The extent and number of interesting objects included within this building can best be indicated on a plan, and it may not be without interest to remark that this plan is nearly identical with one engraved in the work of Sandys, 1610, so few have been the changes in the last two centuries.

No. 1. Entrance from Via Dolorosa.

2. Chapel of the Angel.

3. The Holy Sepulchre.

4. The centre (or navel) of the world—according to the Greek interpretation of Ezekiel v. 5.

5. The Latin Church.

6. 49 steps cut in the solid rock leading down to the Chapel of the finding of the Cross.

7. Calvary—which is reached by finely cut marble steps from near No. 1.

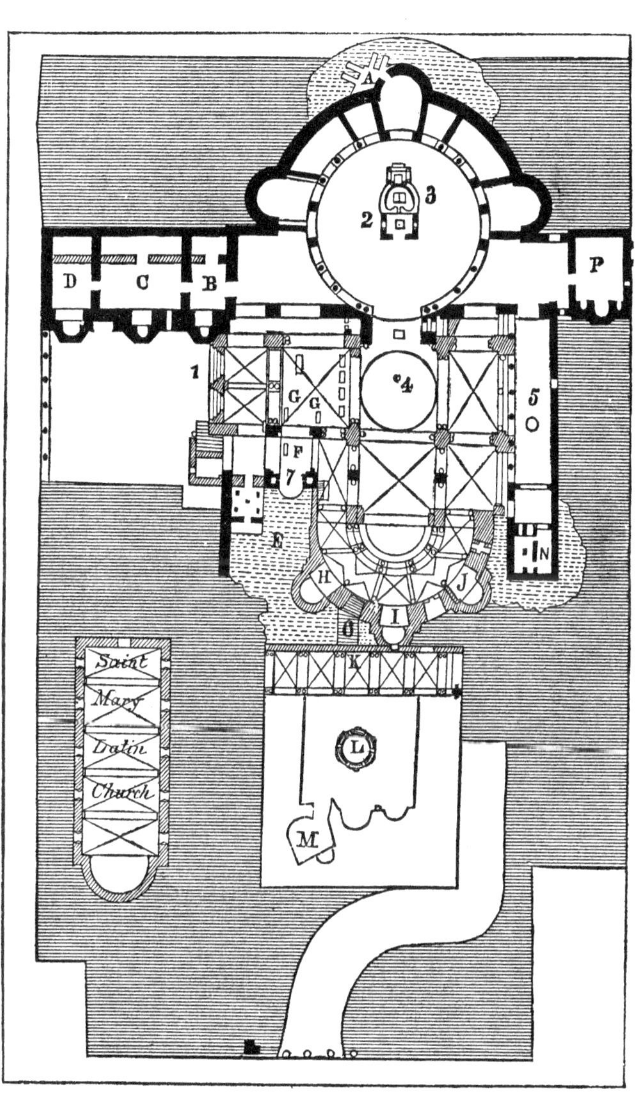

Plan of the Church of the Holy Sepulchre.

In addition to these the following are pointed out as veritable antiquities, miraculously preserved.

The spot where the Saviour was nailed to the Cross.

The Chapel of the Sacrifice of Isaac.

Chapel of the Altar of Melchizedec.

The spot where the garments of Jesus were divided by the soldiers.

Where the Lord was confined in prison.

The stone of unction, on which Jesus was prepared for the tomb; tomb of Melchizedec; tomb of Adam, and of John the Baptist; the place where the Virgin Mary stood at the Crucifixion; Chapel marking the spot on which the Angel stood who appeared to Mary Magdalene; tombs of Joseph and Nicodemus; and the pillar of flagellation—to which Jesus was bound to be whipped.

THE CHAPEL OF THE CRUCIFIXION.

In this chapel, at the eastern end, is a platform ten feet long, six feet wide, and elevated about eighteen inches above the floor. On this platform is a richly decorated altar; under it, in the middle of the marble floor, are three round holes, cased with silver; beneath these holes is the spot on which it is claimed the crosses stood. The one on which Christ was crucified in the centre, and those of the two malefactors on the right and left.

THE HOLY SEPULCHRE.

The Sepulchre was originally a grotto, cut in the rock like other Jewish tombs, but is now detached from the hillside, and is all above ground, and elevated a little above the level of the floor. It stands in the centre of the great rotunda, and directly under the dome of the church. The Sepulchre is covered by a small structure of yellow and white marble, twenty-six feet long, and eighteen feet broad; a small dome in the form of a crown surmounts the top. The house of the Sepulchre is profusely ornamented. The whole exterior is nearly covered with pictures, crucifixes, and images, and hung round with gold and silver lamps. There are also standing by its sides several wax candles, nearly as large as a man's body, and about ten feet high. A low, narrow opening in the wall, only large enough to admit one person at a time, leads to a chamber about twelve feet square. This is the outer room or vestibule of the tomb, and is called "The Chapel of the Angel." At the western side of this room is a low, narrow opening, barely large enough to admit a medium-sized person, and such only can effect an entrance by bending very low and crawling through. The Sepulchre is a room six feet one way by seven the other, and is covered by a dome roof, which is supported by marble pillars. Forty-two lamps of gold and silver, richly wrought, are suspended around the sides of this grotto, and kept continually burning. A small platform of stone, about two feet high, stands on the right side of the entrance; on which is a plain marble slab, bearing evidence of great antiquity. Such slabs were used for the reception of the dead, and on this, it is believed, the Saviour was laid.

Among the few *genuine* antiquities found in this

Bethany.

church are the tombs of Godfrey de Bouillon, and Baldwin his brother, who were buried near the cross for which they fought so valiantly; and in the Latin sacristy the sword and spurs of Godfrey are preserved. The Superior of the Franciscans, called the Reverendissimo, uses the sword in conferring the order of Knight of the Holy Sepulchre, an order instituted by Godfrey himself.

BETHANY—THE PLACE OF ASCENSION.

This place is called by the Arabs LAAZRIYEH, and is situated on the eastern slope of the Mount of Olives, and near its base. It is now a small Arab village, containing about twenty houses, all of which have the appearance of being ancient and time-worn.

This is the place where Mary and Martha, with their brother Lazarus, had their home, and to which Jesus was wont to return at night from Jerusalem for refreshment and rest. This is also the place of the Ascension. "And he led them out as far as to Bethany; and he lifted up his hands, and blessed them. And it came to pass, while he blessed them, he was parted from them, and carried up into heaven." (St. Luke xxiv. 50, 51.)

CHAPTER XII.

SCRIPTURE ACCOUNT OF BUILDING KING SOLOMON'S TEMPLE.

Mt. Moriah—David's preparation for building the Temple and Charge to Solomon.—Solomon builds the Temple—Its Dedication.—Destruction.

AND God sent an angel unto Jerusalem to destroy it: and as he was destroying, the Lord beheld, and he repented him of the evil, and said to the angel that destroyed it, It is enough, stay now thine hand. And the angel of the Lord stood by the threshing-floor of Ornan the Jebusite.*

And David lifted up his eyes, and saw the angel of the Lord stand between the earth and the heaven, having a drawn sword in his hand stretched out over Jerusalem. Then David and the elders *of Israel, who were* clothed in sackcloth, fell upon their faces.

And David said unto God, *Is it* not I *that* commanded the people to be numbered? even I it is that have sinned and done evil indeed; but *as for* these sheep, what have they done? let thine hand, I pray

* On Mount Moriah.

thee, O Lord my God, be on me, and on my father's house; but not on thy people, that they should be plagued.

Then the angel of the Lord commanded Gad to say to David, that David should go up, and set up an altar unto the Lord in the threshing-floor of Ornan the Jebusite.

And David went up at the saying of Gad, which he spake in the name of the Lord.

And Ornan turned back, and saw the angel; and his four sons with him hid themselves. Now Ornan was threshing wheat.

And as David came to Ornan, Ornan looked and saw David, and went out of the threshing-floor, and bowed himself to David with *his* face to the ground.

Then David said to Ornan, Grant me the place of *this* threshing-floor, that I may build an altar therein unto the Lord: thou shalt grant it me for the full price: that the plague may be stayed from the people.

And Ornan said unto David, Take *it* to thee, and let my lord the king do *that which is* good in his eyes: lo, I give *thee* the oxen *also* for burnt-offerings, and the threshing instruments for wood, and the wheat for the meat-offering; I give it all.

And king David said to Ornan, Nay; but I will verily buy it for the full price: for I will not take *that* which *is* thine for the Lord, nor offer burnt-offerings without cost.

So David gave to Ornan for the place six hundred shekels of gold by weight.

And David built there an altar unto the Lord, and offered burnt-offerings and peace-offerings, and called

Ancient Drinking Cups.

upon the Lord; and he answered him from heaven by fire upon the altar of burnt-offering.

And the Lord commanded the angel; and he put up his sword again into the sheath thereof.

At that time when David saw that the Lord had answered him in the threshing-floor of Ornan the Jebusite, then he sacrificed there.

For the tabernacle of the Lord, which Moses made in the wilderness, and the altar of the burnt-offering, *were* at that season in the high place at Gibeon.

But David could not go before it to inquire of God: for he was afraid because of the sword of the angel of the Lord. (1 Chron. xxi. 15 to 30.)

DAVID'S PREPARATION FOR BUILDING THE TEMPLE, AND CHARGE TO SOLOMON.

And David commanded to gather together the strangers that *were* in the land of Israel; and he set masons to hew wrought stones to build the house of God.

And David prepared iron in abundance for the nails for the doors of the gates, and for the joinings; and brass in abundance without weight;

Also cedar-trees in abundance: for the Zidonians and they of Tyre brought much cedar-wood to David.

And David said, Solomon my son *is* young and tender, and the house *that is* to be builded for the Lord *must be* exceeding magnifical, of fame and of glory throughout all countries: I will *therefore* now make preparation for it. So David prepared abundantly before his death.

Then he called for Solomon his son, and charged him to build a house for the Lord God of Israel.

And David said to Solomon, My son, as for me, it was in my mind to build a house unto the name of the Lord my God:

But the word of the Lord came to me, saying, Thou hast shed blood abundantly, and hast made great wars: thou shalt not build an house unto my name, because thou hast shed much blood upon the earth in my sight.

Behold, a son shall be born to thee, who shall be a man of rest; and I will give him rest from all his enemies round about: for his name shall be Solomon, and I will give peace and quietness unto Israel in his days.

He shall build a house for my name; and he shall be my son, and I *will be* his father; and I will establish the throne of his kingdom over Israel for ever.

Now, my son, the Lord be with thee; and prosper thou, and build the house of the Lord thy God, as he hath said of thee.

Only the Lord give thee wisdom and understanding, and give thee charge concerning Israel, that thou mayest keep the law of the Lord thy God.

Then shalt thou prosper, if thou takest heed to fulfil the statutes and judgments which the Lord charged Moses with concerning Israel: be strong, and of good courage; dread not, nor be dismayed.

Now, behold, in my trouble I have prepared for the house of the Lord a hundred thousand talents of gold, and a thousand thousand talents of silver; and of brass and iron without weight; for it is in abundance timber also and stone have I prepared; and thou mayest add thereto.

Moreover, *there are* workmen with thee in abundance, hewers and workers of stone and timber, and all manner of cunning men for every manner of work.

Of the gold, the silver, and the brass, and the iron, *there is* no number. Arise *therefore*, and be doing, and the Lord be with thee.

David also commanded all the princes of Israel to help Solomon his son, *saying*,

Is not the Lord your God with you? and hath he *not* given you rest on every side? for he hath given the inhabitants of the land into mine hand; and the land is subdued before the Lord, and before his people.

Now set your heart and your soul to seek the Lord your God; arise therefore, and build ye the sanctuary of the Lord God; to bring the ark of the covenant of the Lord, and the holy vessels of God, into the house that is to be built to the name of the Lord. (1 Chron. xxii. 2 to 19.)

Then David gave to Solomon his son the pattern of the porch, and of the houses thereof, and of the treasuries thereof, and of the upper chambers thereof, and of the inner parlors thereof, and of the place of the mercy-seat,

And the pattern of all that he had by the Spirit, of the courts of the house of the Lord, and of all the chambers round about, of the treasuries of the house of God, and of the treasuries of the dedicated things:

Also for the courses of the priests and the Levites, and for all the work of the service of the house of the Lord, and for all the vessels of service in the house of the Lord.

He gave of gold by weight for *things* of gold, for all instruments of all manner of service; *silver also* for all instruments of silver by weight, for all instruments of every kind of service:

Even the weight for the candlesticks of gold, and for their lamps of gold, by weight for every candlestick, and for the lamps thereof: and for the candlesticks of silver by weight, *both* for the candlestick, and *also* for the lamps thereof, according to the use of every candlestick.

And by weight *he gave* gold for the tables of shewbread, for every table; and *likewise* silver for the tables of silver:

Also pure gold for the flesh-hooks, and the bowls, and the cups: and for the golden basins *he gave gold* by weight for every basin; and *likewise silver* by weight for every basin of silver:

And for the altar of incense refined gold by weight; and gold for the pattern of the chariot of the cherubim, that spread out *their wings*, and covered the ark of the covenant of the Lord.

All *this, said David,* the Lord made me understand in writing by *his* hand upon me, *even* all the works of this pattern.

And David said to Solomon his son, Be strong and of good courage, and do *it:* fear not, nor be dismayed, for the Lord God, *even* my God, *will be* with thee; he will not fail thee, nor forsake thee, until thou hast finished all the work for the service of the house of the Lord.

And, behold, the courses of the priests and the Levites, *even they shall be with thee* for all the service of the house of God: and *there shall be* with thee for all manner of workmanship every willing skilful man, for any manner of service: also the princes and all the people *will be* wholly at thy commandment. (1 Chron. xxviii. 11 to 21.)

Furthermore David the king said unto all the congregation, Solomon my son, whom alone God hath chosen, *is yet* young and tender, and the work *is* great: for the palace *is* not for man, *but for the Lord God.*

Now I have prepared with all my might for the house of my God the gold for *things to be made* of gold, and the silver for *things* of silver, and the brass for *things* of brass, the iron for *things* of iron, and wood for *things* of wood; onyx stones, and *stones* to be set, glistering stones, and of divers colors, and all manner of precious stones, and marble stones in abundance.

Moreover, because I have set my affection to the house of my God, I have of mine own proper good, of gold and silver, *which* I have given to the house of my God, over and above all that I have prepared for the holy house,

Even three thousand talents of gold, of the gold of Ophir, and seven thousand talents of refined silver, to overlay the walls of the houses *withal:*

The gold for *things* of gold, and the silver for *things* of silver, and for all manner of work *to be made* by the hands of artificers. And who *then* is willing to consecrate his service this day unto the Lord?

Then the chief of the fathers and princes of the tribes of Israel, and the captains of thousands and of hundreds, with the rulers of the king's work, offered willingly,

And gave, for the service of the house of God, of gold five thousand talents and ten thousand drams, and of silver ten thousand talents, and of brass eighteen thousand talents, and one hundred thousand talents of iron.

And they with whom *precious* stones were found gave *them* to the treasure of the house of the Lord, by the hand of Jehiel the Gershonite.

Then the people rejoiced, for that they offered willingly, because with perfect heart they offered willingly to the Lord: and David the king also rejoiced with great joy.

Wherefore David blessed the Lord before all the congregation: and David said, Blessed *be* thou, Lord God of Israel our father, for ever and ever. (1 Chron. xxix. 1 to 10—26, 27, 28.)

Thus David the son of Jesse reigned over all Israel.

And the time that he reigned over Israel *was* forty years; seven years reigned he in Hebron, and thirty and three *years* reigned he in Jerusalem.

And he died in a good old age, full of days, riches, and honor: and Solomon his son reigned in his stead.

Then Solomon sat on the throne of the Lord as king instead of David his father, and prospered; and all Israel obeyed him.

And all the princes, and the mighty men, and all the

ANCIENT MUSICAL INSTRUMENTS.

sons likewise of king David, submitted themselves unto Solomon the king.

And the Lord magnified Solomon exceedingly in the sight of all Israel, and bestowed upon him such royal majesty as had not been on any king before him in Israel. (1 Chron. xxix. 23, 24, 25.)

Then Solomon spake unto all Israel, to the captains of thousands and of hundreds, and to the judges, and to every governor in all Israel, the chief of the fathers.

So Solomon, and all the congregation with him, went to the high place that *was* at Gibeon ; for there was the tabernacle of the congregation of God, which Moses the servant of the Lord had made in the wilderness.

But the ark of God had David brought up from Kirjath-jearim to *the place which* David had prepared for it : for he had pitched a tent for it at Jerusalem.

Moreover the brazen altar, that Bezaleel the son of Uri, the son of Hur, had made, he put before the tabernacle of the Lord : and Solomon and the congregation sought unto it.

And Solomon went up thither to the brazen altar before the Lord, which *was* at the tabernacle of the congregation, and offered a thousand burnt-offerings upon it.

In that night did God appear unto Solomon, and said unto him, Ask what I shall give thee.

And Solomon said unto God, Thou hast shewed great mercy unto David my father, and hast made me to reign in his stead.

Now, O Lord God, let thy promise unto David my father be established: for thou hast made me king over a people like the dust of the earth in multitude.

Give me now wisdom and knowledge; that I may go out and come in before this people: for who can judge this thy people, *that is so* great?

And God said to Solomon, Because this was in thine heart, and thou hast not asked riches, wealth, or honor, nor the life of thine enemies, neither yet hast asked long life; but hast asked wisdom and knowledge for thyself, that thou mayest judge my people, over whom I have made thee king:

Wisdom and knowledge *is* granted unto thee; and I will give thee riches, and wealth, and honor, such as none of the kings have had that *have been* before thee, neither shall there any after thee have the like. (II Chron. i. 2 to 12.)

And Solomon's wisdom excelled the wisdom of all the children of the east country, and all the wisdom of Egypt.

For he was wiser than all men; than Ethan the Ezrahite, and Heman, and Chalcol, and Darda, the sons of Mahol: and his fame was in all nations round about.

And he spake three thousand proverbs: and his songs were a thousand and five.

And he spake of trees, from the cedar-tree that *is* in Lebanon even unto the hyssop that springeth out of the wall: he spake also of beasts, and of fowl, and of creeping things, and of fishes.

And there came of all people to hear the wisdom

PORCH OF THE TEMPLE

of Solomon, from all kings of the earth, which had heard of his wisdom.

And Hiram king of Tyre sent his servants unto Solomon; for he had heard that they had anointed him king in the room of his father: for Hiram was ever a lover of David.

And Solomon sent to Hiram, saying,

Thou knowest how that David my father could not build a house unto the name of the Lord his God, for the wars which were about him on every side, until the Lord put them under the soles of his feet.

But now the Lord my God hath given me rest on every side, *so that there is* neither adversary nor evil occurrent.

And behold, I purpose to build a house unto the name of the Lord my God, as the Lord spake unto David my father, saying, Thy son, whom I will set upon thy throne in thy room, he shall build a house unto my name.

Now therefore command thou that they hew me cedar-trees out of Lebanon; and my servants shall be with thy servants: and unto thee will I give hire for thy servants according to all that thou shalt appoint: for thou knowest that *there is* not among us any that can skill to hew timber like unto the Sidonians.

And it came to pass, when Hiram heard the words of Solomon, that he rejoiced greatly, and said, Blessed *be* the Lord this day, which hath given unto David a wise son over this great people.

And Hiram sent to Solomon, saying, I have considered the things which thou sentest to me for: *and*

I will do all thy desire concerning timber of cedar, and concerning timber of fir.

My servants shall bring *them* down from Lebanon unto the sea; and I will convey them by sea in floats unto the place that thou shalt appoint me, and will cause them to be discharged there, and thou shalt receive *them:* and thou shalt accomplish my desire, in giving food for my household.

So Hiram gave Solomon cedar-trees and fir-trees *according to* all his desire.

And Solomon gave Hiram twenty thousand measures of wheat *for* food to his household, and twenty measures of pure oil: thus gave Solomon to Hiram year by year.

And the Lord gave Solomon wisdom, as he promised him: and there was peace between Hiram and Solomon; and they two made a league together.

And king Solomon raised a levy out of all Israel; and the levy was thirty thousand men.

And he sent them to Lebanon, ten thousand a month by courses: a month they were in Lebanon, *and* two months at home: and Adoniram *was* over the levy.

And Solomon had threescore and ten thousand that bare burdens, and fourscore thousand hewers in the mountains;

Besides the chief of Solomon's officers which *were* over the work, three thousand and three hundred, which ruled over the people that wrought in the work.

And the king commanded, and they brought great stones, costly stones, *and* hewed stones, to lay the foundation of the house.

CEDARS OF LEBANON.

And Solomon's builders and Hiram's builders did hew *them*, and the stone-squarers: so they prepared timber and stones to build the house. (1 Kings iv. 30 to 34; also v.)

SOLOMON BUILDS THE TEMPLE.

And it came to pass in the four hundred and eightieth year after the children of Israel were come out of the land of Egypt, in the fourth year of Solomon's reign over Israel, in the month Zif, which *is* the second month, that he began to build the house of the Lord.

And the house which king Solomon built for the Lord, the length thereof *was* threescore cubits, and the breadth thereof twenty *cubits*, and the height thereof thirty cubits.*

And the porch before the temple of the house, twenty cubits *was* the length thereof, according to the breadth of the house; *and* ten cubits *was* the breadth thereof before the house.

And for the house he made windows of narrow lights.

And against the wall of the house he built chambers round about, *against* the walls of the house round about, *both* of the temple and of the oracle: and he made chambers round about.

The nethermost chamber *was* five cubits broad, and the middle *was* six cubits broad, and the third *was* seven cubits broad: for without *in the wall* of the house he made narrowed rests round about, that *the beams* should not be fastened in the walls of the house.

And the house, when it was in building, was built

Cubit—18 inches.

of stone made ready before it was brought thither: so that there was neither hammer nor axe *nor* any tool of iron heard in the house, while it was in building.

The door for the middle chamber *was* in the right side of the house: and they went up with winding stairs into the middle *chamber*, and out of the middle into the third.

And *then* he built chambers against all the house, five cubits high: and they rested on the house with timber of cedar.

And the word of the Lord came to Solomon, saying,

Concerning this house which thou art in building, if thou wilt walk in my statutes, and execute my judgments, and keep all my commandments to walk in them; then will I perform my word with thee, which I spake unto David thy father:

And I will dwell among the children of Israel, and will not forsake my people Israel.

And he built the walls of the house within with boards of cedar, both the floor of the house, and the walls of the ceiling: *and* he covered *them* on the inside with wood, and covered the floor of the house with planks of fir.

And he built twenty cubits on the sides of the house, both the floor and the walls with boards of cedar: he even built *them* for it within, *even* for the oracle, *even* for the most holy *place.*

And the house, that *is*, the temple before it, was forty cubits *long.*

And the cedar of the house within *was* carved with knops and open flowers: all *was* cedar; there was no stone seen.

And the oracle he prepared in the house within, to set there the ark of the covenant of the Lord.

And the oracle in the forepart *was* twenty cubits in length, and twenty cubits in breadth, and twenty cubits in the height thereof: and he overlaid it with pure gold; and *so* covered the altar *which was of* cedar.

So Solomon overlaid the house within with pure gold: and he made a partition by the chains of gold before the oracle; and he overlaid it with gold.

And the whole house he overlaid with gold, until he had finished all the house: also the whole altar that *was* by the oracle he overlaid with gold.

And within the oracle he made two cherubim *of* olive-tree, *each* ten cubits high.

And five cubits *was* the one wing of the cherub, and five cubits the other wing of the cherub: from the uttermost part of the one wing unto the uttermost part of the other *were* ten cubits.

And the other cherub *was* ten cubits: both the cherubim *were* of one measure and one size.

The height of the one cherub *was* ten cubits, and so *was it* of the other cherub.

And he set the cherubim within the inner house: and they stretched forth the wings of the cherubim, so that the wing of the one touched the *one* wall, and the wing of the other cherub touched the other wall; and their wings touched one another in the midst of the house.

And he overlaid the cherubim with gold.

And he carved all the walls of the house round about with carved figures of cherubim and palm-trees and open flowers, within and without.

And the floor of the house he overlaid with gold, within and without.

And for the entering of the oracle he made doors *of* olive-tree: the lintel *and* side posts *were* a fifth part *of the wall.*

The two doors also *were of* olive-tree; and he carved upon them carvings of cherubim and palm-trees and open flowers, and overlaid *them* with gold, and spread gold upon the cherubim, and upon the palm-trees.

So also made he for the door of the temple posts *of* olive-tree, a fourth part *of the wall.*

And the two doors *were of* fir-tree: the two leaves of the one door *were* folding, and the two leaves of the other door *were* folding.

And he carved *thereon* cherubim and palm-trees and open flowers: and covered *them* with gold fitted upon the carved work.

And he built the inner court with three rows of hewed stone, and a row of cedar beams.

And king Solomon sent and fetched Hiram out of Tyre.

He *was* a widow's son of the tribe of Naphtali, and his father *was* a man of Tyre, a worker in brass: and he was filled with wisdom, and understanding, and cunning to work all works in brass. And he came to king Solomon, and wrought all his work.

For he cast two pillars of brass, of eighteen cubits high apiece: and a line of twelve cubits did compass either of them about.

And he made two chapiters *of* molten brass, to set upon the tops of the pillars: the height of the one

EAST GATE, OF THE TEMPLE ENCLOSURE.

chapiter *was* five cubits, and the height of the other chapiter *was* five cubits:

And nets of checker work, and wreaths of chain work, for the chapiters which *were* upon the top of the pillars; seven for the one chapiter, and seven for the other chapiter.

And he made the pillars, and two rows round about upon the one network, to cover the chapiters that *were* upon the top, with pomegranates: and so did he for the other chapiter.

And the chapiters that *were* upon the top of the pillars *were* of lily work in the porch, four cubits.

And the chapiters upon the two pillars *had pomegranates* also above, over against the belly which *was* by the network: and the pomegranates *were* two hundred in rows round about upon the other chapiter.

And he set up the pillars in the porch of the temple: and he set up the right pillar, and called the name thereof Jachin: and he set up the left pillar, and called the name thereof Boaz.

And upon the top of the pillars *was* lily work: so was the work of the pillars finished.

And he made a molten sea, ten cubits from the one brim to the other: *it was* round all about, and his height *was* five cubits: and a line of thirty cubits did compass it round about.

And under the brim of it round about *there were* knops compassing it, ten in a cubit, compassing the sea round about: the knops *were* cast in two rows, when it was cast.

It stood upon twelve oxen, three looking toward the north, and three looking toward the west, and three looking toward the south, and three looking toward the east: and the sea *was set* above upon them, and all their hinder parts *were* inward.

And it *was* a handbreadth thick, and the brim thereof was wrought like the brim of a cup, with flowers of lilies: it contained two thousand baths.

And he made ten bases of brass, four cubits *was* the length of one base, and four cubits the breadth thereof, and three cubits the height of it.

And the work of the bases *was* on this *manner:* they had borders, and the borders *were* between the ledges:

And on the borders that *were* between the ledges *were* lions, oxen, and cherubim: and upon the ledges *there was* a base above: and beneath the lions and oxen *were* certain additions made of thin work.

And every base had four brazen wheels, and plates of brass: and the four corners thereof had undersetters: under the laver *were* undersetters molten, at the side of every addition.

And the mouth of it within the chapiter and above *was* a cubit: but the mouth thereof *was* round *after* the work of the base, a cubit and a half: and also upon the mouth of it *were* gravings with their borders, foursquare, not round.

And under the borders *were* four wheels; and the axletrees of the wheels *were joined* to the base: and the height of a wheel *was* a cubit and half a cubit.

And the work of the wheels *was* like the work of a chariot wheel: their axletrees, and their naves, and their felloes, and their spokes, *were* all molten.

And *there were* four undersetters to the four corners

of one base: *and* the undersetters *were* of the very base itself.

And in the top of the base *was there* a round compass of half a cubit high: and on the top of the base the ledges thereof and the borders thereof *were* of the same.

For on the plates of the ledges thereof, and on the borders thereof, he graved cherubim, lions, and palm-trees, according to the proportion of every one, and additions round about.

After this *manner* he made the ten bases: all of them had one casting, one measure, *and* one size.

Then made he ten lavers of brass: one laver contained forty baths: *and* every laver was four cubits: *and* upon every one of the ten bases one laver.

And he put five bases on the right side of the house, and five on the left side of the house: and he set the sea on the right side of the house eastward, over against the south.

And Hiram made the lavers, and the shovels, and the basins. So Hiram made an end of doing all the work that he made king Solomon for the house of the Lord:

The two pillars, and the *two* bowls of the chapiters that *were* on the top of the two pillars; and the two net-works, to cover the two bowls of the chapiters which *were* upon the top of the pillars;

And four hundred pomegranates for the two net-works, *even* two rows of promegranates for one net-work, to cover the two bowls of the chapiters that *were* upon the pillars;

And the ten bases, and ten lavers on the bases;

And one sea, and twelve oxen under the sea;

And the pots, and the shovels, and the basins: and all these vessels, which Hiram made to king Solomon for the house of the Lord, *were of* bright brass.

In the plain of Jordan did the king cast them, in the clay ground between Succoth and Zarthan.

And Solomon left all the vessels *unweighed*, because they were exceeding many: neither was the weight of the brass found out.

And Solomon made all the vessels that *pertained* unto the house of the Lord: the altar of gold, and the table of gold, whereupon the shew-bread *was*,

And the candlesticks of pure gold, five on the right *side*, and five on the left, before the oracle, with the flowers, and the lamps, and the tongs *of* gold,

And the bowls, and the snuffers, and the basins, and the spoons, and the censers *of* pure gold; and the hinges *of* gold, *both* for the doors of the inner house, the most holy *place, and* for the doors of the house, *to wit*, of the temple.

So was ended all the work that king Solomon made for the house of the Lord. And Solomon brought in the things which David his father had dedicated; *even* the silver, and the gold, and the vessels, did he put among the treasures of the house of the Lord. (1 Kings vii. 13 to 51.)

In the fourth year was the foundation of the house of the Lord laid, in the month Zif:

And in the eleventh year, in the month Bul, which *is* the eighth month, was the house finished throughout all the parts thereof, and according to all the fashion of it. So was he seven years in building it. (1 Kings vi. 37, 38.)

Interior View of the Temple.

DEDICATION OF THE TEMPLE.

Then Solomon assembled the elders of Israel, and all the heads of the tribes, the chief of the fathers of the children of Israel, unto king Solomon in Jerusalem, that they might bring up the ark of the covenant of the Lord out of the city of David, which *is* Zion.

And all the men of Israel assembled themselves unto king Solomon at the feast in the month Ethanim, which *is* the seventh month.

And all the elders of Israel came, and the priests took up the ark.

And they brought up the ark of the Lord, and the tabernacle of the congregation, and all the holy vessels that *were* in the tabernacle, even those did the priests and the Levites bring up.

And king Solomon, and all the congregation of Israel, that were assembled unto him, *were* with him before the ark, sacrificing sheep and oxen, that could not be told nor numbered for multitude.

And the priests brought in the ark of the covenant of the Lord unto his place, into the oracle of the house, to the most holy *place, even* under the wings of the cherubim.

For the cherubim spread forth *their* two wings over the place of the ark, and the cherubim covered the ark and the staves thereof above.

And they drew out the staves, that the ends of the staves were seen out in the holy *place* before the oracle, and they were not seen without: and there they are unto this day.

There was nothing in the ark save the two tables of stone, which Moses put there at Horeb, when the Lord made *a covenant* with the children of Israel, when they came out of the land of Egypt.

And it came to pass, when the priests were come out of the holy *place*, that the cloud filled the house of the Lord,

So that the priests could not stand to minister because of the cloud: for the glory of the Lord had filled the house of the Lord.

Then spake Solomon, The Lord said that he would dwell in the thick darkness.

I have surely built thee a house to dwell in, a settled place for thee to abide in for ever.

And the king turned his face about, and blessed all the congregation of Israel: and all the congregation of Israel stood;

And Solomon stood before the altar of the Lord in the presence of all the congregation of Israel, and spread forth his hands towards heaven:

And he said, Lord God of Israel, *there is* no God like thee, in heaven above, or on earth beneath, who keepest covenant and mercy with thy servants that walk before thee with all their heart:

Who hast kept with thy servant David my father that thou promisedst him: thou spakest also with thy mouth, and hast fulfilled *it* with thine hand, as *it is* this day.

Therefore now, Lord God of Israel, keep with thy servant David my father that thou promisedst him, saying, There shall not fail thee a man in my sight to sit on the throne of Israel; so that thy children take heed to their way, that they walk before me as thou hast walked before me.

And now, O God of Israel, let thy word, I pray thee, be verified, which thou spakest unto thy servant David my father.

But will God indeed dwell on the earth? behold, the heaven and heaven of heavens cannot contain thee; how much less this house that I have builded?

And it was *so*, that when Solomon had made an end of praying all this prayer and supplication unto the Lord, he arose from before the altar of the Lord, from kneeling on his knees with his hands spread up to heaven.

And he stood, and blessed all the congregation of Israel with a loud voice, saying,

Blessed *be* the Lord, that hath given rest unto his people Israel, according to all that he promised: there hath not failed one word of all his good promise, which he promised by the hand of Moses his servant.

The Lord our God be with us, as he was with our fathers: let him not leave us, nor forsake us:

That he may incline our hearts unto him, to walk in all his ways, and to keep his commandments, and his statutes, and his judgments, which he commanded our fathers.

And let these my words, wherewith I have made supplication before the Lord, be nigh unto the Lord our God day and night, that he maintain the cause of his servant, and the cause of his people Israel at all times, as the matter shall require:

That all the people of the earth may know that the Lord *is* God, *and that there is* none else.

Let your heart therefore be perfect with the Lord our God, to walk in his statutes, and to keep his commandments, as at this day.

And the king, and all Israel with him, offered sacrifice before the Lord.

And Solomon offered a sacrifice of peace-offerings, which he offered unto the Lord, two and twenty thousand oxen, and a hundred and twenty thousand sheep. So the king and all the children of Israel dedicated the house of the Lord.

And it came to pass, when Solomon had finished the building of the house of the Lord, and the king's house, and all Solomon's desire which he was pleased to do,

That the Lord appeared to Solomon the second time, as he had appeared unto him at Gibeon.

And the Lord said unto him, I have heard thy prayer and thy supplication, that thou hast made before me: I have hallowed this house, which thou hast built, to put my name there for ever; and mine eyes and mine heart shall be there perpetually.

And if thou wilt walk before me, as David thy father walked, in integrity of heart, and in uprightness, to do according to all that I have commanded thee, *and* wilt keep my statutes and my judgments;

Then I will establish the throne of thy kingdom upon Israel for ever, as I promised to David thy father, saying, There shall not fail thee a man upon the throne of Israel.

But if ye shall at all turn from following me, ye or your children, and will not keep my commandments *and* my statutes which I have set before you, but go and serve other gods, and worship them;

Presentation in the Temple.

Then will I cut off Israel out of the land which I have given them; and this house, which I have hallowed for my name, will I cast out of my sight; and Israel shall be a proverb and a by-word among all people:

And at this house, *which* is high, every one that passeth by it shall be astonished, and shall hiss; and they shall say, why hath the Lord done thus unto this land, and to this house?

And they shall answer, because they forsook the Lord their God, who brought forth their fathers out of the land of Egypt, and have taken hold upon other gods, and have worshiped them, and served them: therefore hath the Lord brought upon them all this evil.

And it came to pass at the end of twenty years, when Solomon had built the two houses, the house of the Lord, and the king's house,

(*Now* Hiram the king of Tyre had furnished Solomon with cedar-trees and fir-trees, and with gold, according to all his desire,) that then king Solomon gave Hiram twenty cities in the land of Galilee.

And Hiram came out from Tyre to see the cities which Solomon had given him; and they pleased him not.

And he said, What cities *are* these which thou hast given me, my brother? And he called them the land of Cabul unto this day. (1 Kings viii. 1 to 14.—22 to 27.—54 to 64.—Also ix. 1 to 13.)

THE DESTRUCTION OF THE TEMPLE AND BABYLONISH CAPTIVITY.

And it came to pass in the ninth year of his reign,

in the tenth month, in the tenth *day* of the month, *that* Nebuchadnezzar king of Babylon came, he, and all his host, against Jerusalem, and pitched against it; and they built forts against it round about.

And the city was besieged unto the eleventh year of king Zedekiah.

And on the ninth *day* of the *fourth* month the famine prevailed in the city, and there was no bread for the people of the land.

And the city was broken up, and all the men of war *fled* by night by the way of the gate between two walls, which *is* by the king's garden: (now the Chaldees *were* against the city round about:) and *the king* went the way toward the plain.

And the army of the Chaldees pursued after the king, and overtook him in the plains of Jericho: and all his army were scattered from him.

So they took the king, and brought him up to the king of Babylon to Riblah; and they gave judgment upon him.

And they slew the sons of Zedekiah before his eyes, and put out the eyes of Zedekiah, and bound him with fetters of brass, and carried him to Babylon.

And in the fifth month, on the seventh *day* of the month, which *is* the nineteenth year of king Nebuchadnezzar king of Babylon, came Nebuzar-adan, captain of the guard, a servant of the king of Babylon, unto Jerusalem:

And he burnt the house of the Lord, and the king's house, and all the houses of Jerusalem, and every great *man's* house burnt he with fire.

And all the army of the Chaldees, that *were with*

King Zedekiah and other Captives carried before Nebuchadnezzar at Riblah.

the captain of the guard, brake down the walls of Jerusalem round about.

Now the rest of the people that were left in the city, and the fugitives that fell away to the king of Babylon, with the remnant of the multitude, did Nebuzar-adan the captain of the guard carry away.

But the captain of the guard left of the poor of the land *to be* vine-dressers and husbandmen.

And the pillars of brass that *were* in the house of the Lord, and the bases, and the brazen sea that *was* in the house of the Lord, did the Chaldees break in pieces, and carried the brass of them to Babylon.

And the pots, and the shovels, and the snuffers, and the spoons, and all the vessels of brass wherewith they ministered, took they away.

And the firepans, and the bowls, *and* such things as *were* of gold, *in* gold, and of silver, *in* silver, the captain of the guard took away.

The two pillars, one sea, and the bases which Solomon had made for the house of the Lord; the brass of all these vessels was without weight.

The height of the one pillar *was* eighteen cubits, and the chapiter upon it *was* brass: and the height of the chapiter three cubits; and the wreathen work, and pomegranates upon the chapiter round about, all of brass: and like unto these had the second pillar with wreathen work.

And the captain of the guard took Seraiah the chief priest, and Zephaniah the second priest, and the three keepers of the door:

And out of the city he took an officer that was set over the men of war, and five men of them that were in the king's presence, which were found in the city and the principal scribe of the host, which mustered the people of the land, and threescore men of the people of the land *that were* found in the city:

And Nebuzar-adan captain of the guard took these, and brought them to the king of Babylon to Riblah:

And the king of Babylon smote them, and slew them at Riblah in the land of Hamath. So Judah was carried away out of their land. (II. Kings. xxv 1 to 21.)

RETURN FROM THE CAPTIVITY AND COMMENCEMENT OF BUILDING OF THE TEMPLE OF ZERUBBABEL.

Now in the first year of Cyrus king of Persia, that the word of the Lord by the mouth of Jeremiah might be fulfilled, the Lord stirred up the spirit of Cyrus king of Persia, that he made a proclamation throughout all his kingdom, and *put it* also in writing, saying,

Thus saith Cyrus king of Persia, The Lord God of heaven hath given me all the kingdoms of the earth; and he hath charged me to build him a house at Jerusalem, which *is* in Judah.

Who *is there* among you of all his people? his God be with him, and let him go up to Jerusalem, which *is* in Judah, and build the house of the Lord God of Israel, (he *is* the God,) which *is* in Jerusalem.

Then rose up the chief of the fathers of Judah and Benjamin, and the priests, and the Levites, with all *them* whose spirit God had raised, to go up to build the house of the Lord which *is* in Jerusalem.

And all they that *were* about them strengthened

their hands with vessels of silver, with gold, with goods, and with beasts, and with precious things, besides all *that* was willingly offered.

Also Cyrus the king brought forth the vessels of the house of the Lord, which Nebuchadnezzar had brought forth out of Jerusalem, and had put them in the house of his gods:

Even those did Cyrus king of Persia bring forth by the hand of Mithredath the treasurer, and numbered them unto Sheshbazzar, the prince of Judah.

And this *is* the number of them: thirty chargers of gold, a thousand chargers of silver, nine and twenty knives,

Thirty basins of gold, silver basins of a second *sort* four hundred and ten, *and* other vessels a thousand.

All the vessels of gold and of silver *were* five thousand and four hundred. All *these* did Sheshbazzar bring up with *them of* the captivity that were brought up from Babylon unto Jerusalem.

Now these *are* the children of the province that went up out of the captivity, of those which had been carried away, whom Nebuchadnezzar the king of Babylon had carried away unto Babylon, and came again unto Jerusalem and Judah, every one unto his city;

Which came with Zerubbabel: Jeshua, Nehemiah, Seraiah, Reelaiah, Mordecai, Bilshan, Mizpar, Bigvai, Rehum, Baanah. The number of the men of the people of Israel:

The whole congregation together *was* forty and two thousand three hundred *and* threescore.

And *some* of the chief of the fathers, when they

came to the house of the Lord which *is* at Jerusalem, offered freely for the house of God to set it up in his place:

They gave after their ability unto the treasure of the work threescore and one thousand drams of gold, and five thousand pounds of silver, and one hundred priests' garments.

And when the seventh month was come, and the children of Israel *were* in the cities, the people gathered themselves together as one man to Jerusalem.

Then stood up Jeshua the son of Jozadak, and his brethren the priests, and Zerubbabel the son of Shealtiel, and his brethren, and builded the altar of the God of Israel, to offer burnt offerings thereon, as *it is* written in the law of Moses the man of God.

And they set the altar upon his bases; for fear *was* upon them because of the people of those countries: and they offered burnt-offerings thereon unto the Lord, *even* burnt-offerings morning and evening.

They gave money also unto the masons, and to the carpenters; and meat, and drink, and oil, unto them of Zidon, and to them of Tyre, to bring cedar-trees from Lebanon to the sea of Joppa, according to the grant that they had of Cyrus king of Persia.

Now in the second year of their coming unto the house of God at Jerusalem, in the second month, began Zerubbabel the son of Shealtiel, and Jeshua the son of Jozadak, and the remnant of their brethren the priests and the Levites, and all they that were come out of the captivity unto Jerusalem; and appointed the Levites, from twenty years old and upward, to set forward the work of the house of the Lord.

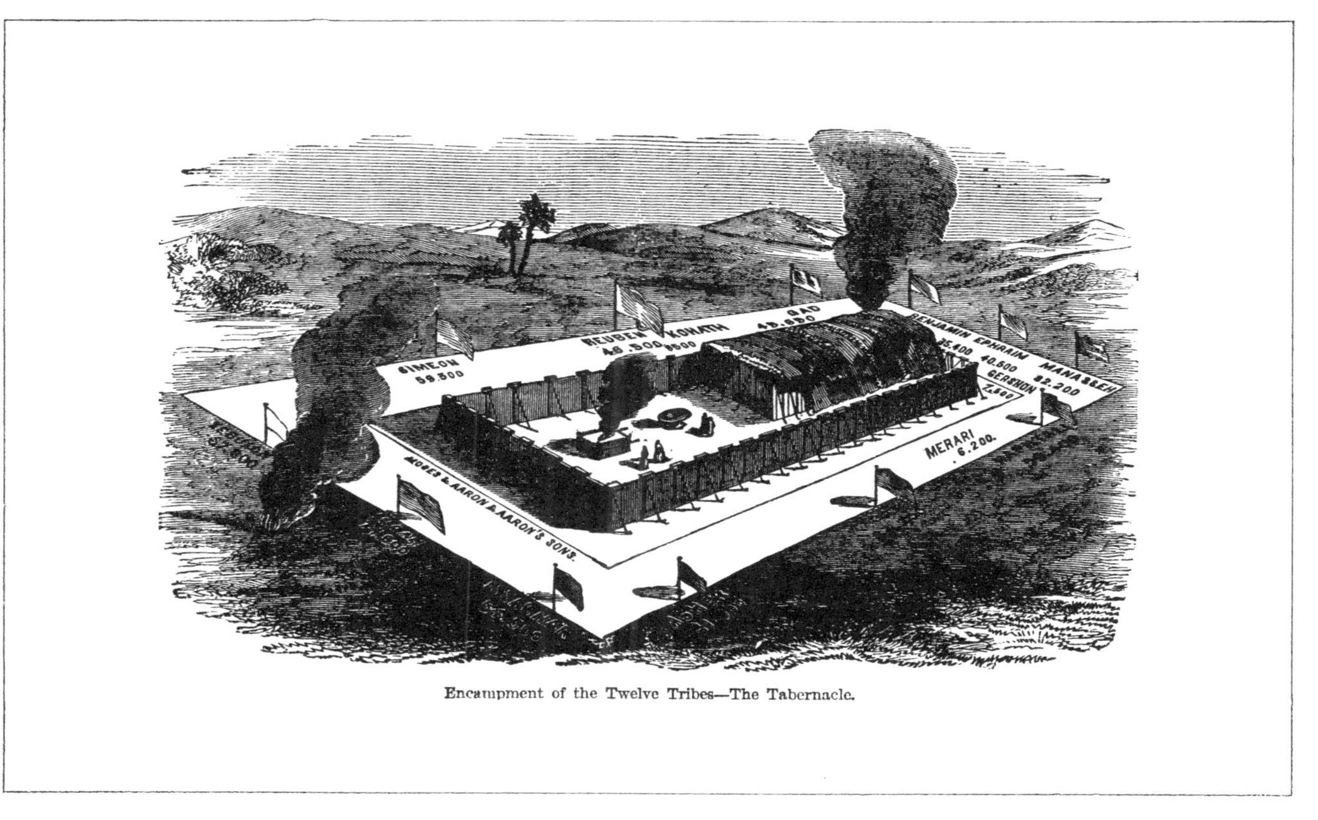

Encampment of the Twelve Tribes—The Tabernacle.

Now when the adversaries of Judah and Benjamin heard that the children of the captivity builded the temple unto the Lord God of Israel;

Rehum the chancellor and Shimshai the scribe wrote a letter against Jerusalem to Artaxerxes the king in this sort:

Then sent the king an answer unto Rehum the chancellor, and *to* Shimshai the scribe, and *to* the rest of their companions that dwell in Samaria, and *unto* the rest beyond the river, Peace, and at such a time.

The letter which ye sent unto us hath been plainly read before me.

Give ye now commandment to cause these men to cease, and that this city be not builded, until *another* commandment shall be given from me.

Now when the copy of king Artaxerxes' letter *was* read before Rehum, and Shimshai the scribe, and their companions, they went up in haste to Jerusalem unto the Jews, and made them to cease by force and power.

Then ceased the work of the house of God which *is* at Jerusalem. So it ceased unto the second year of the reign of Darius king of Persia.

Then the prophets, Haggai the prophet, and Zechariah the son of Iddo, prophesied unto the Jews that *were* in Judah and Jerusalem in the name of the God of Israel, *even* unto them.

Then rose up Zerubbabel the son of Shealtiel, and Jeshua the son of Jozadak, and began to build the house of God which *is* at Jerusalem: and with them *were* the prophets of God helping them.

At the same time came to them Tatnai, governor on

this side the river, and Shethar-boznai, and their companions, and said thus unto them, Who hath commanded you to build this house, and to make up this wall?

Then said we unto them after this manner, What are the names of the men that make this building?

But the eye of their God was upon the elders of the Jews, that they could not cause them to cease, till the matter came to Darius: and then they returned answer by letter concerning this *matter*.

The copy of the letter that Tatnai, governor on this side the river, and Shethar-boznai, and his companions the Apharsachites, which *were* on this side the river, sent unto Darius the king:

They sent a letter unto him, wherein was written thus; Unto Darius the king, all peace.

Be it known unto the king, that we went into the province of Judea, to the house of the great God, which is builded with great stones, and timber is laid in the walls, and this work goeth fast on, and prospereth in their hands.

Then asked we those elders, *and* said unto them thus, Who commanded you to build this house, and to make up these walls?

We asked their names also, to certify thee, that we might write the names of the men that *were* the chief of them.

And thus they returned us answer, saying, We are the servants of the God of heaven and earth, and build the house that was builded these many years ago, which a great king of Israel builded and set up.

But after that our fathers had provoked the God of

heaven unto wrath, he gave them into the hand of Nebuchadnezzar the king of Babylon, the Chaldean, who destroyed this house, and carried the people away into Babylon.

But in the first year of Cyrus the king of Babylon, *the same* king Cyrus made a decree to build this house of God.

And the vessels also of gold and silver of the house of God, which Nebuchadnezzar took out of the temple that *was* in Jerusalem, and brought them into the temple of Babylon, those did Cyrus the king take out of the temple of Babylon, and they were delivered unto *one*, whose name *was* Sheshbazzar, whom he had made governor;

And said unto him, Take these vessels, go, carry them into the temple that *is* in Jerusalem, and let the house of God be builded in his place.

Now therefore, if *it seem* good to the king, let there be search made in the king's treasure house, which *is* there at Babylon, whether it be *so*, that a decree was made of Cyrus the king to build this house of God at Jerusalem, and let the king send his pleasure to us concerning this matter.

Then Darius the king made a decree, and search was made in the house of the rolls, where the treasures were laid up in Babylon.

And there was found at Achmetha, in the palace that *is* in the province of the Medes, a roll, and therein *was* a record thus written:

In the first year of Cyrus the king, *the same* Cyrus the king made a decree *concerning* the house of God at Jerusalem, Let the house be builded, the place where they offered sacrifices, and let the foundations thereof be strongly laid; the height thereof threescore cubits, *and* the breadth thereof threescore cubits;

With three rows of great stones, and a row of new timber: and let the expenses be given out of the king's house:

And also let the golden and silver vessels of the house of God, which Nebuchadnezzar took forth out of the temple which *is* at Jerusalem, and brought unto Babylon, be restored, and brought again unto the temple which *is* at Jerusalem, *every one* to his place, and place *them* in the house of God.

Let the work of this house of God alone; let the governor of the Jews and the elders of the Jews build this house of God in his place. (Ezra i.—ii. 1, 2, 63, 64.—iii. 1, 3, 7, 8.—iv. 1, 8, 17, 18, 21, 23, 24.—v. 1, 15, 17.—vi. 1, 5, 7.

CHRONOLOGY OF

REMARKABLE EVENTS IN THE HISTORY OF JERUSALEM.

FROM THE EARLIEST RECORDS OF THE CITY TO 1844.

1450

1444 B.C. First notice, and first accounts of Jerusalem. Josh. x-xv.-xviii.

1400 First siege. Judges i. 8, 21.

Zion repeatedly besieged from this time till 1049, but without success.

1049 David takes the stronghold of the Jebusites, and makes Jerusalem his capital. 1 Chron. xi.-xii.

1046 David removes the ark from Kirjath-Jearim to the house of Obed Edom; thence to Jerusalem. 1 Chron. xii.-xiv.

1041 Victories over Moab, Philistia, Syria, and Edom. 1 Chron. xviii.

1038-37 David defeats Ammon and Syria. 1 Chron. xix.

1036-34 David's adultery; siege of Rabbah; murder of Uriah. 1 Chron. xx.

1033 Birth of Solomon. 2 Sam. xii.

1031 Absalom kills Amnon, and flies. 2 Sam. xiii.

1025 Absalom raises a revolt against David, his father. 2 Sam. xv.

David retreats to Mahanaim.
Joab defeats and slays Absalom.
David returns. 2 Sam. xviii., xix.
1021 The three years' famine. 2 Sam. xxi.
1019 Last wars with the Philistines.
David subdues his enemies. 1 Chron. xx.
1018 David numbers Israel; the plague. 1 Chron. xxi.
1016 David collects materials, and instructs Solomon as to the building of the Temple. 1 Chron. xxii.
Rebellion of Adonijah; Solomon proclaimed David's successor; Adonijah submits. 1 Kings i.
David's final charge to Solomon; directs Joab and Shimei to be put to death. 1 Kings ii.
1016 King Solomon's reign begins.
Adonijah and Joab put to death. 1 Kings ii.
1015 Solomon collects men and materials for building the Temple. 1 Kings v.
1012 Solomon marries Pharaoh's daughter. 1 Kings iii.
Commences building the Temple.
1005 The Temple completed and dedicated. 2 Chron. v.
993 The Queen of Sheba's visit to Solomon. 2 Chron. ix.
977 The wives of Solomon seduce him into idolatry.
976 Death of Solomon. 1 Kings xi.
Rehoboam succeeds his father on the throne. 1 Kings xii.
The revolt; ten tribes, under Jeroboam, form the kingdom of Israel, with their capital at Shechem.
Judah and Benjamin remain with Rehoboam, and form the kingdom of Judah. 1 Kings xii.
974 Rehoboam fortifies his kingdom. 2 Chron. xi.
972 Jerusalem plundered by Shishak. 1 Kings xiv.
958 Death of Rehoboam; he is succeeded by Abijah. 1 Kings xiv.
Abijah defeats Jeroboam in battle. 2 Chron. ii.
Death of Abijah; he is succeeded by Asa.
951 Asa puts away idolatry. 1 Kings xv.
Asa defeats the Ethiopians. 2 Chron. xiv.
Asa bribes Benhadad, king of Syria, to attack Baasha. 1 Kings xv.
914 Death of Asa; succeeded by Jehoshaphat. 1 Kings xv.

906 Disastrous expedition to Ramoth.
Jehoshaphat and Ahab unite in battle against the Syrians. 2 Chron. xviii.
897 Jehoshaphat joins Ahaziah in a commercial expedition, his ships wrecked; refuses to join in another expedition. 1 Kings xxii., 48, 49.
891 Jehoram begins to reign with Jehoshaphat.
889 Death of Jehoshaphat.
Jehoram continues to reign.
886 Ahaziah reigns as viceroy to his father.
885 Death of Jehoram.
Ahaziah joins Joram against Hazael.
882 Ahaziah slain by Jehu.
Athalia usurps the throne, and destroys all the seed royal except Joash, who is concealed by his aunt, Jehosheba. 2 Kings xi.
877 Joash begins to reign; Athalia slain. 2 Kings xi.
840 Joash and the people fall into idolatry; Zachariah reproves them, and is slain in the Temple court. Matt. 23.
838 Joash slain by his servants; Amaziah succeeds him on the throne. 2 Kings xii.
827 Hires an army of Israelites to assist him against the Edomites; but, at the prophet's command, sends them back.
Amaziah then defeats the Edomites and worships their idols.
826 Afterwards provokes the King of Israel to battle, and is taken prisoner by him. 2 Kings xiv.
808 Amaziah slain; succeeded by Azariah. 2 Kings xiv.
787 Increases his army.
765 Struck with leprosy for invading the priest's office.
761 Jotham made regent. 2 Kings xv.
756 Death of Azariah; Jotham king.
742 Syria and Israel begin to afflict Judah; Jotham dies, and is succeeded by Ahaz. 2 Kings xvi.
740 Judah devastated; Jerusalem taken by Syria and Israel; Ahaz, being hard pressed, hires Tiglath Pileser, the king of Assyria, against them. 2 Kings xvi.

726 Death of Ahaz; succeeded by Hezekiah. 2 Kings xviii.

713 Sennacherib comes up against Judah, but is pacified by a tribute and returns. 2 Kings xviii.

711 Sennacherib again invades the kingdom of Judah; his army destroyed near Jerusalem by an angel. Isa. xxxv.-vii.

697 Death of Hezekiah; succeeded by Manasseh.

Jerusalem taken by the King of Assyria; Manasseh carried away captive to Babylon.

642 Death of Manasseh. 2 Chron. xxxiii.

He is succeded by Amon. 2 Kings xxi.

640 Amon slain by his servants; succeeded by Josiah. 2 Chron. xxxiii.

623 Josiah prepares to repair the Temple. 2 Kings xxii.

622 A solemn celebration of the passover by Josiah. 2 Kings xxiii.

609 In attempting to stop the King of Egypt from crossing his territory, Josiah is slain in battle. 2 Chron. xxxv.

Jehoahaz succeeds him; reigns three months, then deposed by Pharaoh Necho, and taken to Egypt; Jehoiakim succeeds him. 2 Kings xxiii.

606 Nebuchadnezzar takes Jerusalem; puts Jehoiakim in fetters; afterwards releasing him, makes him tributary; spoils the Temple. 2 Kings xxiv. 2 Chron. xxxvi.

Orders the master of his eunuchs to select and send to Babylon some of the royal family and nobility to stand in the king's palace.

Daniel, Hananiah, Mishael, Azariah, Shadrach, Meshach, and Abednego are selected, and taken there. Dan. i.

599 Death of Jehoiakim; succeeded by Jehoiachin.

Jerusalem again taken by Nebuchadnezzar; Jehoiachin, with many of his subjects, carried to Babylon; Zedekiah made king. 2 Kings xxiv.; Jer. lii.

593-90 Zedekiah rebels; Nebuchadnezzar lays siege to Jerusalem for the third time. 2 Kings xxv.

589 The Chaldeans raise the siege to march against the approaching Egyptian army. Jer. xxxvii.

The Chaldeans return; Jerusalem taken; the Temple burnt, and the people carried away captive; Gedaliah appointed governor; Ishmael slays Gedaliah. 2 Kings xxv.

536 Decree of Cyrus for the rebuilding the Temple, and restoration of the Jews. 2 Chron. xxxvi.

535 Zerubbabel commences to build the second Temple. Ezra iii.

534 The work on the Temple interrupted by the Samaritans. Ezra iv.

520 Building of the Temple resumed. Hag. i.

516 Dedication of the second Temple. Ez. vi.

445 Nehemiah receives a commission from Artaxerxes tc visit Jerusalem and rebuild the wall; the wall completed and dedicated. Neh. i.-vi.

413 Jehoiada high-priest.

373 Johanan high-priest.

332 Alexander visits Jerusalem; plants Jews in Alexandria.

320 Ptolemy Lagus captures Jerusalem; plants Jews in Alexandria and Cyrene.

300 Simon the Just high-priest.

285 Version of the Seventy commenced, Alexandria.

216 Ptolemy Philopater prevented from entering the Holy of Holies; he attempts to destroy the Jews at Alexandria, but is miraculously prevented.

200 The sect of the Sadducees founded.

199 Scopas, an Egyptian general, recovers Jerusalem to the King of Egypt.

198 Antiochus regains Judea.

176 Heliodorus attempts to plunder the Temple, but is prevented by an angel.

170 Antiochus Epiphanes takes Jerusalem, and slays 40,000 persons; he also profanes the Temple.

165 Judas Maccabæus purifies the Temple, and institutes the feast of dedication.

161 Judas Maccabæus slain; succeeded by his brother Johnathan.

144 Johnathan murdered by Typhon; is succeeded by Simon, his brother, who is made ruler by Demetrius.

135 Simon murdered; succeeded by his son, John Hyrcanus.

130 John Hyrcanus throws off the Syrian yoke, and establishes his independence; he destroys the Temple on Mt. Gerizim.

107 Aristobulus succeeds his father Hyrcanus.

106 Alexander Jannæus succeeds his brother Aristobulus.

79 Jannæus dies; is succeeded by Alexandra, his wife, who makes her son Hyrcanus high-priest.

70 Death of Alexandra; is succeeded by Hyrcanus, who is forced to yield the crown to his younger brother Aristobulus.

65 Pompey the Great reduces Syria to a Roman province; Hyrcanus endeavors to regain the crown.

63 He and his brother appeal to Pompey, who decides for Hyrcanus; Pompey takes Jerusalem.

57 Aristobulus and his son raise disturbances, and are vanquished by Gabinius, the Roman governor of Syria.

54 Crassus plunders the Temple.

47 Julius Cæsar appoints Antipater procurator of Judea; who makes his son Herod governor of Galilee, and Phasael of Jerusalem.

44 Walls of Jerusalem rebuilt.

43 Antipater poisoned; Herod and Phasael revenge his death.

40 Jerusalem taken by the Parthians, who slay Phasael, and place Antigonus upon the throne; Herod flies to Rome, and is appointed King of Judea.

37 Herod takes Jerusalem, beheads Antigonus, and is established King of Judea; he makes Aristobulus, brother of his wife Mariamne, high-priest, but afterwards murders him.

17 Herod begins to rebuild and enlarge the Temple.

AD 1. NATIVITY OF JESUS CHRIST.

12 Jesus visits Jerusalem.

26 Pilate sent from Rome as Governor of Judea.

29 John the Baptist begins his ministry.

30 Jesus baptized by John.

33 The crucifixion.
34 Ananias and Saphphira struck dead.
35 Stephen stoned, and the church persecuted.
42 Herod Agrippa made King of Judea.
44 James beheaded by Herod; liberation of Peter by an angel.
63 Paul sent a prisoner to Rome.
65 The Jewish war begins; siege of Jerusalem by the Romans.
70 Jerusalem besieged and taken by Titus; 1,100,000 Jews perish by the sword, fire, famine, and crucifixion, besides 97,000 who were sold as slaves.
71 Jerusalem razed to its foundations.
95 John banished to the Isle of Patmos by Domitian.
96 John writes the Revelation.
97 John liberated.
100 John, the last surviving Apostle, dies.
132 The Jews revolt, and become masters of Jerusalem.
135 Jerusalem retaken by the Romans.
326 The Empress Helena visits Jerusalem, and builds two churches.
362 The attempt to lay the foundation of another Temple.
453 Jerusalem made an independent patriarchate.
529 The Emperor Justinian founded at Jerusalem a splendid church in honor of the Virgin.
614 The Persian army, under Chosroes, takes Jerusalem.
627 Chosroes defeated by Heraclius; the city recovered by the Greeks.
637 Jerusalem taken by the Khalif Omar; commencement of the reign of Mohammedanism.
868 Jerusalem taken by Ahmed, a Turkish sovereign of Egypt.
1048 Ortok made ruler of the city by Tutush.
1099 The crusaders under Godfrey Bouillon take the city, the conqueror made king; is succeeded by his brother Baldwin.
1118 Baldwin dies.

1187 Saladin, Sultan of the East, captured the city.
1242 Jerusalem restored to the Latin princes.
1291 It is taken from them by the Sultans of Egypt.
1517 Selim, the Turkish Sultan, takes the city.
1542 The present walls built.
1832 Mohammed Ali, Pasha of Egypt, takes Jerusalem.
1834 Taken possession of by the Fellahin (tillers of the soil).
1840 Restored to the Sultan of Turkey.

COURSE AND DISTANCE

FROM THE CENTRE

OF THE CITY OF JERUSALEM

TO THE FOLLOWING PLACES.

TO	COURSE.	DISTANCE, VERY NEAR.* GEO. MILES.	
Askelon	W.S.W.	34	
Acre	N.N.W.	80	
Antioch	N. by W.	300	
Bethany	E.S.E.	2	
Bethlehem	S.	4	
Beeroth	N.	7	
Bethel	N.	10	
Beersheba	S.S.W.	40	
Bethsaida	N. by E.	85	
Baalbek	N.N.E.	195	
Babylon	E.N.E.	530	Air-line.
Chorazin	N. by E.	80	
Capernaum	N. by E.	78	
Cæsarea	N.N.W.	66	Via Joppa.
Dead Sea	S.E	12	
Damascus	N.N.E.	150	
Ephesus	N.W.	600	Via Joppa, and Mediterranean.
Gaza	S.W.	45	
Gadara	N.N.E.	65	
Gebal	N. by E.	186	Via Joppa.
Hebron	S. by W.	17	
Hamath	N.N.E.	250	

* As but few of these roads or routes have ever been surveyed, the exact distances cannot be given.

TO	COURSE.	DISTANCE, GEO. MILES.	
Jericho	E.N.E.	13	
Joppa	N.W.	35	
Kirjath-Jearim	N.W.	9	
Lydda	N.W.	25	
Nazareth	N.	67	
Nineveh	N.E.	550	Air-line
Palmyra	N.E.	245	
Rabbath	E.N.E.	42	
Shiloh	N. by E.	18	
Shechem	N.	29	
Succoth	N.E.	40	Air-line.
Samaria	N. by W.	40	
Sidon	N.	145	
Sardis	N. by W.	600	Via Joppa and Med.
Shushan	E.	800	Air-line.
Tiberias	N. by E.	68	
Tarsus	N.	385	Via Joppa and Med.

SOURCES OF THE JORDAN.

Paneas	N.N.E.	120	
Hasbeiya	N.N.E.	135	

MOUNTAINS.

Ararat	N.E.	775	
Lebanon Summit	N. by E.	195	
Harbor from which the cedar timber was floated to Joppa	N. by W.	165	Via Joppa
Carmel	N.W.	68	Air-line.
Gilboa	N. by E.	50	
Gerizim	N.E.	35	
Hermon	N.N.E.	118	
Pisgah	E.	25	
Ramoth Gilead	N.E.	36	
Tabor	N. by E.	60	
Hor	S. by E.	100	
Horeb	S. by W.	225	

List of Interesting and Valuable Works on the Holy Land.

CATALOGUE.

REDDING & CO.,

PUBLISHERS OF

Standard Masonic Works,

Temple Building, 544 Broadway, New York.

Practical Monitor and Compend of Masonic Law and Jurisprudence.* Containing the Monitorial instructions pertaining to the first three degrees, unincumbered with matter not practised with the Work, everything not used in connection with the Work and Lectures being excluded, while the Monitorial that is practised is arranged in the exact order in which it occurs in the Ritual. Followed by a practical Compend of Masonic Law and Jurisprudence, with the decisions of the different Grand Lodges in this country on all important points and questions. To officers and members who desire a Manual in which the information is *readily accessible,* this work will commend itself. By M. WOLCOTT REDDING. Embellished with a beautiful chromo lithograph—"Pass of the Jordan."

Cloth...$0 65
Morocco Tuck, full gilt 1 00

Webb's Freemasons' Monitor. Miniature edition.
Cloth...$0 75

A Manual of the Lodge; or, Monitorial Instructions in the First Three Degrees. Including the Ceremonies of Installations, Dedications, Laying of Corner-Stones, &c. By ALBERT G. MACKEY. In one 8vo volume, handsomely bound....$2 00

Cross's Masonic Text-Book. Containing Monitorial Instructions in the Degrees, from Entered Apprentice to Knights Templar, inclusive. Illustrated with 100 engravings. 32mo, full gilt $1 50

Moore's Pocket Trestle Board. 32mo $0 75

Mackey's Masonic Ritualist; or, Monitorial Instructions from Entered Apprenticeship to Select Master. 32mo, tuck. Price.....................................$1 60

History of Masonic Persecutions. By GEORGE OLIVER, D.D. One vol. 12mo, cloth.................$2 00

Origin and Early History of Freemasonry. By G. W. STEENBRENNER. Price...................$1 00

History of the Ancient and Accepted Scottish Rite. By FOLGER. Cloth $5 50

---

* A new work.

Findell's History of Freemasonry. 1 vol. 8vo. Cloth. $6 00

Chase's Digest of Masonic Law. A complete Code of Regulations and Decisions upon questions of Masonic Jurisprudence. Containing a compend or digest of forty Grand Constitutions and Regulations,—including every Grand Lodge in America, and those of England, Ireland, and Scotland,—and comprising over four thousand decisions, &c.
12mo, 464 pages, cloth.............................$2 00

Lockwood's Masonic Law and Practice...$1 00

Text-Book of Masonic Jurisprudence. By ALBERT G. MACKEY, M.D. Newly revised. Cloth.............$2 75

Mackey's Lexicon of Freemasonry. Revised edition, with Portrait of the Author. One vol. 12mo, cloth gilt. Price...$3 00

Book of Marks. For Royal Arch Chapters. 8vo, half Turkey morocco.
100 Marks...$3 50
150 Marks... 4 00
200 Marks... 4 50

Guide to the Chapter; containing the degrees of Mark Master, Past Master, Most Excellent Master, and Royal Arch; together with the Order of High-Priesthood, etc. 12mo. Cloth...$1 50

N. Y. Royal Arch Companion, containing Monitorial Instructions in the Degrees of Mark Master, Past Master, Most Excellent Master, Royal Arch and Order of High-Priesthood; together with the Ceremonies of Constituting and Dedicating Chapters, etc. Cloth..............................$1 00

Masonic Code of the State of New York, containing Constitutions and General Regulations of the Grand Lodge of New York, and the resolutions and Decisions now in force; also a standard form of By-Laws for Subordinate Lodges; with the Forms and Course of Procedure on Masonic Trials, etc. Cloth.. 50

www.ingramcontent.com/pod-product-compliance
Lightning Source LLC
LaVergne TN
LVHW011148110826
845150LV00006B/1182

* 9 7 8 1 4 2 5 5 4 7 8 0 6 *